D1561606

CHALLENGES IN
JEWISH-CHRISTIAN RELATIONS

Studies in Judaism and Christianity

Exploration of Issues in the Contemporary Dialogue between Christians and Jews

Editor in Chief for
Stimulus Books
Helga Croner

Editors
Lawrence Boadt, CSP
Helga Croner
Rabbi Leon Klenicki
Kevin A. Lynch, CSP
Dennis McManus
Dr. Ann Riggs
Rabbi Leonard Schoolman

 A STIMULUS BOOK

CHALLENGES IN JEWISH-CHRISTIAN RELATIONS

Edited by
James K. Aitken and Edward Kessler

BM
535
C43
2006

A STIMULUS BOOK

PAULIST PRESS ◆ NEW YORK ◆ MAHWAH, N.J.

Extracts from the Documents of the Second Vatican Council are the Author's translation and from Walter Abbot's edition of *The Documents of Vatican II* © 1966 by America Press used by kind permission of America Press. Visit: www. americamagazine.org.

Cover Art: Pope Benedict XVI is welcomed to Cologne synagogue. Photo copyright ©2006 by Oliver Bert/Pool/Reuters/Corbis

Cover design by Sharyn Banks

Copyright © 2006 by the Stimulus Foundation

All rights reserved. No part of this book may be reproduced or transmitted in any form or by any means, electronic or mechanical, including photocopying, recording, or by any information storage and retrieval system without permission in writing from the Publisher.

Library of Congress Cataloging-in-Publication Data

Challenges in Jewish-Christian relations / edited by James K. Aitken and Edward Kessler.
    p. cm. — (Studies in Judaism and Christianity)
    Some of the chapters were originally presented as papers at a conference in September 1999 to mark the first year of the Centre for the Study of Jewish-Christian Relations in Cambridge.
    Includes bibliographical references and index.
    ISBN 0-8091-4392-5 (alk. paper)
    1. Judaism—Relations—Christianity—1945- 2. Christianity and other religions—Judaism—1945- I. Aitken, J. K. (James Keltie), 1968- II. Kessler, Edward, Dr. III. Series.
BM535.C43 2006
261.2′6—dc22

                                       2006002752

Published by Paulist Press
997 Macarthur Boulevard
Mahwah, New Jersey 07430

www.paulistpress.com

Printed and bound in the
United States of America

Contents

Acknowledgments

Some of the chapters included here started life as papers at a conference in September 1999 to mark the first year of the Centre for the Study of Jewish-Christian Relations in Cambridge. A selection from that conference has been supplemented by chapters that explore further issues in the contemporary challenges facing Jewish-Christian relations. We are grateful to the Spalding Trust and to Jesus College, Cambridge, for the grants they awarded in support of that conference. Particular thanks are due to Deborah Patterson Jones for taking on the burden of organizing the conference and to all the staff of the Centre for their work that has enabled the completion of this book. Finally, we would like to thank Lawrence Boadt, editor at Paulist Press, for accepting the book for publication, and all his staff for their assistance.

J. K. Aitken
E. D. Kessler

1
Introduction

James K. Aitken and Edward Kessler

THE DEVELOPMENT OF CONTEMPORARY
JEWISH-CHRISTIAN RELATIONS

Jewish-Christian relations as a subject of study could be described as a child of the twentieth century. As a scholarly discipline and a mode of dialogue between religious communities it is a discourse that is still in its infancy compared to the traditions of the academy and the classical subjects that have been studied both in universities and in religious circles. And it is in sharp contrast to the long history of relations between Jews and Christians in earlier centuries, marked often by social exclusion, hostility, or a scholastic dialogue that often had little to do with the equality or intellectual honesty expected today. Given this radical change in the relations between the two faith communities, the process both of learning the language of dialogue and of understanding how to express the encounter is slow and sometimes thwart. The events of the past century have brought questions to bear on the nature of God, the very role of religion in society, and the responsibility of one community to another not only in what it does but also in what it says and teaches. A discipline that arose so rapidly without precedents to guide it, and yet at the same time had to face such important questions, inevitably would arouse points of disagreement and calls for reconsideration of certain issues. Nothing less is to be expected when faced with one of the most major crises of faith in modern times.

Subjects develop, new paradigms are formed while others are rejected, and new areas of study are brought into play. The items on the agenda of Jewish-Christian relations from the start (e.g., the significance of the Shoah, antisemitism within the church, the role of Israel) are still influential and require repeated consideration. The issues were primarily theological and historical. The roles of the New Testament and the church fathers were considered in works by Krister Stendhal, Rosemary Radford Ruether, and Robert Wilken.[1] This continues to be an important question to this day, demonstrated by the recent collection of essays edited by W. R. Farmer.[2] The theological problems associated with the Shoah have been expressed by R. L. Rubenstein in a book now in its second revised edition, but the question has also been applied in recent years to wider issues, such as the role of the Bible.[3] The language with which we speak of events has, however, changed as the language of theology and intellectual discussion has itself changed. Although there remain many unresolved aspects regarding these original questions, new topics have come to the fore, arising from the path broken through by the pioneers of Jewish-Christian relations and also from the challenges of contemporary society.

Many of those pioneers in the relationship were Europeans responding to the situation in their countries. Before the Second World War, British scholars such as James Parkes, Claude Montefiore, and R. Travers Herford wrote a number of influential works, which not only tackled the history of prejudice and misrepresentation but more radically showed an appreciation—and presented—the other in positive terms. Their writings sometimes resulted in controversy. When viewed with hindsight we can see that, for the first time, Jews and Christians were becoming aware of the existence of a new academic discipline, the study of Jewish-Christian relations (even if it was not described as such).

After the war this work was continued by writers and activists such as the Frenchman Jules Isaac and the Englishman William Simpson, each of them intensely aware, as one would expect in the aftermath of the Shoah, of Europe's contribution to the history of antisemitism and prejudice. Yet the European experience of antisemitism over many centuries was not the only explanation for their studies because the positive contributions by each religion to the other also provided strong motivations. However, in recent years it has been in the United States—where Jewish-Christian cooperation was already underway in the early twentieth century and where the effect of immigration from Europe has been most acute—that many developments have taken place. At the present time there now exist approximately twenty centers for Jewish-Christian dialogue in many parts of the country (in contrast to the few in Europe), educational programs have been established, and recommendations from churches and religious institutions have been heeded more acutely.[4] It is perhaps no surprise that a recent Jewish statement on the relationship, *Dabru Emet,* was largely an American enterprise. It is from America, too, that the larger number of books on the topics of the relations and dialogue arise.

However, the modern European contribution, both Jewish and Christian, is not always recognized and for a number of reasons it is essential to integrate it with the work presently being undertaken in the United States. First, there have been many changes within the European context that have had and continue to have a global impact. Many issues of religion and nationalism are still being played out across the continent. For example, the political map has recently changed dramatically with the fall of communism and the breakup of the Soviet Union. The prejudice that remains often has targets other than Jews, although the role of contemporary antisemitism can still be felt in many countries.

Second, the developments within the Roman Catholic Church in the last twenty-five years have been supported, if not initiated, by the personal mission of the late Polish pope John Paul II, whose personal commitment to Jewish-Christian dialogue arose out of his Polish context. He was clearly influenced by the Shoah and by his loss of Jewish school friends who perished, as well as by the struggle for democracy in Poland, which was led by the Roman Catholic Church.

Third, the changing European demography has had, and continues to have, its effect too. The migration of peoples as a result of war, ethnic hostility, or religious prejudice results in new relations between groups, bringing with it new contacts between religions. The expansion of the European Union and increased cooperation among countries facilitates contact and migration, resulting in new possibilities as well as new problems and the resurgence of old prejudices. The outbreak of hostilities in Bosnia, Serbia, and Croatia, for example, has significant implications for the relationship between Jews and Christians, not to mention Muslims.

Therefore, we should not make the mistake of assuming that in the changing situation in Europe the issues of the Jewish-Christian relationship are the same as those of the first half of the twentieth century. In this book, European voices engage with American, each responding to the other's work. The issues that affect Europe today and that generate concerns in an international context are addressed. The collaboration between Jews and Christians in such diverse areas as biblical scholarship and the language of dialogue is shown to have made an enriching contribution to the dialogue. Each side can learn from the other and European and American approaches to the challenges will ensure that Jewish-Christian relations are studied in a truly international context.

THE TASK FOR CONTEMPORARY
JEWISH-CHRISTIAN RELATIONS

It is no surprise that modern Jewish-Christian relations arose in the early decades of the twentieth century when a joint attempt by some Christians and Jews to combat a rise in antisemitism also resulted in a positive expression of beliefs within each faith.[5] The first organization for Jewish-Christian dialogue, the National Conference of Christians and Jews, was founded in the United States in 1928. At the same time we see the appearance of the Christian ecumenical movement, expressing similar principles of dialogue, understanding, and tolerance. The World Missionary Conference, for example, met in Edinburgh, Scotland, in June 1910 and there realized the need for the examination of the causes of division as a first step toward achieving cooperation. The 1920s saw the rise of a number of Student Christian Movements across Europe, and in the cold January of 1927 the first meeting was held of the Fellowship of St. Alban and St. Sergius, where Western and Eastern (notably Russian refugees from the Communist revolution) theologians met to debate theology and to understand each other better.[6] Indeed, it is increasingly being recognized nowadays that the two movements—Jewish-Christian relations and ecumenism—are related issues and should be treated together.[7] They both are a part of the intellectual and social movements of the time, tackling new understandings within the church, drawing on the experiences of encounter through trade and conquest, and responding to the changing political climate and the consequential social constituency of the countries concerned. The same applies today, as Jewish-Christian relations draw on and inform the contemporary intellectual and social movements.

The analysis of Jewish-Christian relations is therefore a complex enterprise, which cannot be reduced to simple theological or historical narratives, as some studies have tended to do. It must take into account politics, sociology, education, language, history, biblical studies, hermeneutics, and, of course, theology. It must also grapple with the traditions in each of these fields, within the religious communities, and within our own intellectual frameworks. In the words of Cambridge theologian David Ford,

> If that dialogue avoids the most difficult issues and the complex discourses...it cannot claim to offer thorough diagnosis or healing....Both Judaism and Christianity have for many centuries been grappling with the most sophisticated available thought and have been coping with huge intellectual as well as other challenges. (p. 158)

It is, therefore, appropriate to ask, "What are those challenges now?"

The complexity is exacerbated by its combination of an intellectual discourse with a practical, even pastoral, need in the field. Accordingly, the choice of authors here has been guided by a selection of those who are able to combine an academic perspective on the subject with real practical experience of Jewish-Christian relations. Some of the contributors will be new to Jewish-Christian relations but are specialists in their particular field. It has been fruitful to invite such specialists from both sides of the Atlantic to apply their knowledge to the specific question of the relations. Others are more familiar to the field but have been asked to think again or to think further. Many of the authors are young or at the height of their careers, forging the language and thought of tomorrow, all of them interpreting the relations in the light of the contemporary world. Some of the issues raised here will be new too, others more familiar. In raising some of the questions that confront us in the modern era, we move away from older emphases and actually find that in some of the chapters these emphases, which at one time were the grounds for the meeting of Jews and Christians, are becoming causes of division. The historical sequential approach, for example, often tinged by historical memory, has hindered the dialogue on a religious basis (as outlined by Saperstein). A call for a greater religious and theological dialogue is made by some contributors, while others apply new approaches to old questions. In every case a new perspective is offered on the issue, and, in many, bold criticism of the current situation is given. In each case a challenge for the future relations is addressed.

ISSUES WITHIN CONTEMPORARY
JEWISH-CHRISTIAN RELATIONS

History is the opening of many a book on Jewish-Christian relations. This one is no exception. History is not an abstract concept, however, but rather forms a part of individual and national conscience. The memory of events is affected by our own understanding and expectations, and memories are shared, as Paul Fussell has portrayed so well in his study of writers on the First World War.[8] It is for this reason that the other topics in this book can only be fully considered with an appreciation of their historical legacy. The aim of the opening chapter is to show the reader that, on the one hand, without an understanding of the past, Jewish-Christian relations cannot flourish for very long, while on the other hand, it points out forcefully that historical memory can be a burden that not only weighs down heavily upon us but even makes the current task of Jewish-Christian relations that much more difficult. Marc Saperstein, from the United States, provides examples from Europe in the medieval period to show that the generally accepted lachrymose memory of the Jew as victim is not necessarily accurate. There is widespread evidence of the existence of positive Christian encounters with Judaism. The author points to examples of Jewish and Christian exegetes clearly influencing each other and incorporating opinions into their own scholarship. Evidence also exists to show that Jews were not solely victims, but on some occasions when they had sufficient power, they could be as brutally cruel as their Christian overlords. He does not deny the frequent persecution of Jews but wishes to set it in proportion, since a popular memory can often distort and produce a picture that is inimical to true dialogue.[9]

As already outlined, the Bible has always had a prominent role in Jewish-Christian relations, but John Sawyer, from the United Kingdom, considers the problems of the negative influence of biblical readings less than the positive contributions that can be made to the relations by drawing on contemporary hermeneutical approaches. He pays some attention to the twentieth-century situation, discussing the impact of the Holocaust and the creation of the State of Israel, as well as to changes in the official attitudes of the churches to the Jews. This section raises issues that will be developed in other chapters devoted to these topics. Special prominence is given to hermeneutical approaches to the Bible in scholarship today. In turning his attention to hermeneutics, Sawyer reflects on the impact on Jewish-Christian relations of biblical texts having more than one meaning. Second, he considers the significance of the reception history *(Wirkungsgeschichte)* of a text, in other words, how the text has been used in different spheres such as politics and literature. Third, Sawyer discusses the ethical implications of biblical exegesis for Jewish-Christian relations in the future.

One of the most pressing contemporary issues in Jewish-Christian relations, and one that reveals the influence of a theological legacy, is relations with the Orthodox churches. Its importance today means that two contributors, one Jewish and one Russian Orthodox, have each provided insights from their perspectives. Cambridge scholar Nicholas de Lange notes how the growth in understanding and trust between Jews and Western Christians throws into sharp relief the slow rate of progress in dialogue between Jews and Orthodox Christians. He traces the history of relations, the historical impediments, and the necessity today for such dialogue. From a Jewish perspective, he also notes the similarities in practice and thought between Jews and Orthodox Christians, which suggest that there is a way forward for the dialogue. The author concludes that improvement in relations between Jews and Orthodox Christians depends not only on rediscovering what they have in common but also in Russian Orthodox Christianity purging itself of the promotion of antisemitism, which all too often is still found festering beneath its domes. Irina Levinskaya, from St. Petersburg, considers the particular situation of the Russian Orthodox Church and explains the present problems within the church in the light of present politics, historical legacies, and theological tradition. She suggests that a way forward might be found in theological reflection, especially on the theme of suffering. It is a topic that is central both to Jewish experience and to recent Russian history, and is a theme in Christian theology itself. Relations with Orthodox Christians is a topic that other contributors will return to, especially with regard to the position of contemporary Europe and to relations between institutions and organizations.

As a practitioner and educator in the field of Jewish-Christian relations, Fr. Remi Hoeckman, secretary of the Pontifical Commission for Religious Relations with the Jews, examines the present difficulties in the relationship. In particular he draws attention to the dominance of a Jewish agenda, propagated by Jewish agencies and institutions with vested interests. This has impeded dialogue, especially when moves by the Vatican have not been recognized or understood by the said Jewish agencies. He calls instead for reciprocity in the relations, a shared discovery of each other's heritage and spiritual values, a discovery that Ochs and Ford put into practice later in this book. Such discovery should lead to common declarations, emphasizing the religious values shared by both, thereby moving away from a political agenda. In this, and in parallel to Saperstein's analysis, Hoeckman calls for us to understand and know history better, to reevaluate historical memory (especially of Jesus the Jew and Christian origins), and for each community to ensure that they are accountable for the future and not only for the past.

Dialogue begins with an encounter between individuals, but the dialogue between institutions is also essential. It is an area that has not been discussed in Jewish-Christian relations, but the problems that it raises have been expressed from the Catholic side by Remi Hoeckman. Friedhelm Pieper, himself general secretary of an interfaith organization (the International Council of Christians and Jews), considers in broader scope the role of institutions and organizations in the dialogue. For changes to be implemented one needs the support of religious institutions, and any theological change can only be achieved if it is seen to be consistent with the theology of the particular religious bodies. At the same time, institutions are often a source of misunderstanding and even hatred and therefore their role must be addressed. While criticism of certain Jewish organizations has already been raised by Hoeckman, churches and international church organizations have not always been as proactive as they should. The Catholic Church has led the way with its document *Nostra Aetate* (1965), but no equivalent statement exists from the World Council of Churches (WCC) or from Protestant churches, although some documents do touch on the issues. The discussion following the recent publication of the Catholic document "We Remember" shows how much we still have to learn of each other.

Institutions are by nature unwilling to admit their own mistakes, and this in part accounts for the lack of any statement from the WCC. As a result of the worldwide issues it faces, Jewish-Christian relations are not a high priority for the WCC, although the participation of Jews at its meetings is becoming commonplace. Given the situation within the community of the Orthodox churches, the WCC should provide an excellent opportunity for Orthodox Christians to meet with Jews. Unfortunately the main agenda there is the relationship of the Orthodox Churches with WCC itself. Therefore, with regard to institutions, two needs are highlighted for the future: One is the need for more forums outside of official institutions in which individuals can meet and discuss issues. The other is for greater theological study in the field of Jewish-Christian relations to enable institutions to prove theologically that insights gained in dialogue are a legitimate interpretation of their faith traditions.

Many of the influences on Jewish-Christian relations are not only theological but political, as seen most keenly in the role of the Russian Orthodox Church. British historian David Weigall, therefore, considers the wider political position of Jewish-Christian relations, and especially its role in contemporary Europe. The term *New Europe* was coined after 1989 to describe the collapse of the central and eastern European communist governments and the reunification of Germany. Much was promised but little was delivered other than history reasserting itself in a traditionally violent way. The resurgence of the extreme right across Europe voiced its anger against minorities, and antisemitic statements have remained commonplace. Even though Jews may not be implicated in the various crises it is noticeable that when extreme nationalism is confronted with pluralistic society it usually returns to traditional antisemitic arguments of the mythological variety. The future of Europe is partly dependent upon how effectively the states of central and eastern Europe manage effectively to become "civic" states, that is, without regard to the ethnicity or religion of the citizens. The churches also have an important role to play. The author examines their role since 1989 and explores the problem that, if being a Pole, Hungarian, Slovak and so on means being a Christian, a significant part of the population is excluded. The author argues that Christians should face up to the ambiguities of the history of Europe and participate in a plural order of things. If there is an emphasis on Christian Europe nationalist tensions will be further aggravated.

Moving beyond the edge of Europe, Israel has always played a leading role in Jewish-Christian relations, notably since its establishment in 1948, both as a unique state in which Jews are in the majority and as a symbol for many Christians of the events of the Holocaust and the need for a Jewish state. Israel is most often presented in terms of the Palestinian, but, Andrew White argues, this has allowed an often-overlooked crisis to arise in Jewish-Christian relations regarding Israel. There is an increasing polarization of opinions between those who are supportive of Israel and those who are extremely antagonistic toward it. This chapter, written by a former canon of Coventry Cathedral in England, considers three main theological positions held by churches. *Remnant theology* sees the Jews and Israel as living proof of the truth of Christianity in the existence of a mere remnant in Israel. *Replacement theology* sees the church as having replaced Israel and therefore has little regard for the modern state. Palestinian liberation theology gains much of its attack on the State of Israel from these two theological stances, and by that means can claim political support from Christians for the Palestinian side. *Recognition theology,* which recognizes the need for Israel both in Jewish theology and in the light of the Holocaust, is to be preferred. All these positions are profoundly influenced by the political situation of the day, and thus cannot be separated from the events that are affecting the daily lives of the people of Israel. Each envisages Israel in a certain light, which in turn imprints associations with the modern state in people's minds. It even has an influence in the choice of travel agents used by churches on pilgrimages to the Holy Land.

The Holocaust has become the most important prism through which the relationship between Jews and Christians has been viewed. Continuing the theme of the opening chapter on historical memory, Stephen Smith, founder of the United Kingdom's first Holocaust Educational Centre, considers how memories of the Holocaust serve not to unite but to divide. The Holocaust reflects the destructive nature of the relationship between Christians and Jews. The author also discusses how Jews and Christians bridge the divided memory of the Holocaust and face the consequences of its disruptive nature. This, in his opinion, is the context within which the Jewish-Christian relationship exists today. Smith argues that Jews and Christians experience the Holocaust in different ways and remember it differently. From a Christian perspective he explores three different categories "memory, justice, and continuity" and argues that, for the most part, Christians have used each one in the defense of Christianity. This is because to profess Christianity is to defend Christianity, whereas, he argues, the reality of the Holocaust should force Christians to question even Christianity itself and be prepared to let it go. Until Christians are prepared to struggle with their own identity, to be confronted by the consequences of justice, and to face the possibility of discontinuity (and, by extension, the demise or reformation of Christianity) there is not, nor can there be, a meaningful relationship between Jews and Christians.

The next chapter is presented as a theological dialogue between two figures, one American and the other British, in contemporary theological discourse, and attempts to express the needs of Jewish-Christian relations in modern times. Ochs and Ford, in dialogue with each other, bring together many of the themes of the book and transfer them into a contemporary theological language. They see ourselves as living in a third epoch following from the Holocaust (Shoah), and diagnose the problem of the Shoah as the problem of modernity and its inadequacies. A need for healing and mending is now upon us, but this should not be by a return to the premodern or a descent into nihilism but by a journey into the postmodern, a creativity that transcends the crisis in religion, manifest in traditionalism or liberalism. All religions are marginalized in late modern (capitalist) culture, and the call is for a dialogue that is theological. To take account of the complexities of real Jews and real Christians, dialogue must be complex, drawing on philosophy (ethics, sociology, theology, economics) and scripture (the Bible, religious tradition, religious culture) together. The approach to the Bible and to tradition is through a pragmatic "productive vagueness." Ochs and Ford illustrate their arguments through an analysis of each other's recent writing, in which Ochs (a Jewish scholar) discusses what he has learned from Ford's work that draws on Jewish thought, and Ford (a Christian scholar) reflects on Ochs's work that draws on Christian thinking.

The changing and challenging role of women in Jewish-Christian relations is examined by Christine Trevett, from Wales. She observes how women in both faith traditions are faced with the reinterpretation of text and tradition, a concern that is also for men. She notes the opposition of some secular feminists to religion, and therefore the bond and common enterprise that has been developing between Christian and Jewish feminists. She examines the changing understanding of women's approaches to the biblical text (as also touched upon by Sawyer), tradition, spiritual need, and public expression in recent decades. From an earlier interest in recovering women's stories, feminists are now considering the sociological background to religion. The challenge for the future is to make these changes known to others, to transmit the information from academic circles to a wider public, and for the experience to be shared by both women and men. The reciprocal nature of the learning, as encouraged by Hoeckman and demonstrated by Ford and Ochs, is an important feature of Jewish and Christian women's studies. The writer draws on personal experience of ecumenical and interfaith activity as well as academic studies.

Whether a new era of Jewish-Christian relations has dawned or not, the publication of *Dabru Emet* and the dissemination of the concept of "Christianity in Jewish terms" have been seen as a welcome move by both communities. Kessler and Aitken examine the significance of the first broad-based Jewish response to Christianity in recent times. Edward Kessler examines the changing attitudes in Jewish-Christian relations over the century that have led to the declaration by Jewish scholars on Christians and Christianity. He examines the tenets made in that declaration, welcoming them as a sign of the true basis of dialogue, namely, respect for the other. It may be possible to say that the future of mankind rests on such a principle. James Aitken responds by considering the question of the "irreconcilable difference" between Jews and Christians, and its consequences for the whole concept of "Christianity in Jewish terms." It has been received very favorably by both communities, but does it misrepresent *both* Judaism *and* Christianity? It is important to begin the dialogue with the contemporary communities and their differences rather than with historical issues, but it is also important to portray Christianity as it really is. That might involve something of its mystery—a mystery inherent to every religion.

The final chapter argues that Jewish-Christian dialogue is of more import than simply to Jews and Christians, and considers the place of Jewish-Christian dialogue in the multifaith context. The author, Martin Forward, who has many years' experience of working in the field of interreligious dialogue, especially in Britain and India, begins by examining the encounter in the context of the Abrahamic faiths—in other words, the issue of including Islam as a partner. He goes further, however, and explores what contribution the specific experience of the

Jewish-Christian relationship offers both to the wider society, and in particular to other religious dialogues. For example, do the lessons of Christian antisemitism shed light on the process of scapegoating and marginalization between other faiths? Hindu attitudes toward Muslims and Christians in India, and Muslim attitudes to Hindus and Christians in Pakistan are examples of this phenomenon. The author explores these and other examples, using the Jewish-Christian example as a paradigm. The encounters that are discussed are presently taking place within a context of rapid globalization that is causing many religious thinkers to reflect as never before on what they share in common.

The one challenge that each of these chapters individually addresses and together demonstrate, is that of holding in view at the same time all the political, social, historical, and theological questions that impinge on Jewish-Christian relations. That is the challenge for Jewish-Christian relations in the contemporary world.

NOTES

1. Krister Stendahl, *Paul among Jews and Gentiles, and Other Essays* (London: SCM Press, 1977); Rosemary Radford Ruether, *Faith and Fratricide: The Theological Roots of Anti-Semitism* (New York: Seabury Press, 1979); Robert L. Wilken, *John Chrysostom and the Jews: Rhetoric and Reality in the Late Fourth Century* (Berkeley: University of California Press, 1983).

2. W. R. Farmer, ed., *Anti-Judaism and the Gospels* (Harrisburg, PA: Trinity Press International, 1999). See also the British CCJ pamphlet by Gareth Lloyd-Jones, *Hard Sayings: Difficult New Testament Texts for Jewish-Christian Dialogue* (London: CCJ, 1993).

3. R. L. Rubenstein, *After Auschwitz: History, Theology, and Contemporary Judaism,* 2nd ed. (Baltimore, MD/London: John Hopkins University Press, 1992). For the role of the Shoah in biblical criticism, see T. Linafelt, ed., *Strange Fire: Reading the Bible after the Holocaust* (Sheffield: Sheffield Academic Press, 2000).

4. In this regard one may note the article by E. J. Fisher, "Theological Education and Christian-Jewish Relations," in *Academic Approaches to Teaching Jewish Studies,* ed. Z. Garber (Lanham, MD/New York/London: University Press of America, 2000), 213–32.

5. On the formation of the British Council of Christians and Jews and some of the motives behind the early pioneers, see M. Braybrooke, *Children of*

One God: A History of the Council of Christians and Jews (London: Vallentine Mitchell, 1991).

6. On the founding of the Fellowship, see N. Zernov, in collaboration with M. Zernov, *The Fellowship of St. Alban and St. Sergius: A Historical Memoir* (Oxford: Fellowship of St. Alban & St. Sergius, 1979).

7. See, e.g., Berard L. Marthaler, ed., *Introducing the Catechism of the Catholic Church: Traditional Themes and Contemporary Issues* (London: SPCK, 1994). Ecumenical concerns are discussed in the chapter by John Borelli, "The Catechism and Interreligious Dialogue: The Jews and World Religions," 72–86.

8. Paul Fussell, *The Great War and Modern Memory* (London: Oxford University Press, 1979).

9. For an earlier period of history, one can now read a similar critique of the lachrymose view of Jewish history by Günter Stemberger, *Jews and Christians in the Holy Land: Palestine in the Fourth Century,* trans. Ruth Tuschling (Edinburgh: T&T Clark, 1999).

2
Jews Facing Christians: The Burdens and Blinders from the Past

Marc Saperstein

As a historian, I am deeply committed to the principle that without knowledge of the past we are like plants without roots, unlikely to flourish for very long. If Jews and Christians are to communicate with each other meaningfully, intelligently, we must bring to this exchange some knowledge of the history of our relationships. We cannot pretend that a new chapter can be opened by simply burning the earlier part of the book.

Yet history can also be a burden, and historical memory can load us down with baggage that makes our current task more difficult.

For example, a group of five hundred American and European Christian pilgrims came to Jerusalem at the end of a three-year walk on the nine-hundredth anniversary of the conquest of that city in the First Crusade to seek forgiveness for the slaughter of innocent Muslims and Jews—and Israel's chief rabbi Lau associated the First Crusade with the Holocaust and said "we have no authorization to forgive."[1] Wheaton College, an evangelical Christian school in Illinois, decided to abandon its seventy-year-old mascot, the Crusader, because of "how offensive the image of the Crusades is to large segments of the world."[2] A Vatican representative (Father David Yager, with a good record on fostering Jewish-Christian understanding) accused Israel of a "blood libel" against Pope Pius XII for citing, in the context of beatification proceedings, his failure to issue an explicit public condemnation of Nazi mass murder of Jews.[3] Even a recent proposal to make Isidore of Seville a patron saint of the

Internet has generated a dispute over his alleged anti-Jewish influence in the seventh-century Visigothic Church. Crusade, blood libel, anti-semitism: these words have powerful resonance from the past. The burden is there whether we like it or not and we had better try to understand the nature of the baggage that each side brings to the conversation when we encounter the other.

Let me start with the Christian side. For centuries, a series of negative historical memories and labels determined the way Jews were understood by most Christians. The most notorious of these labels was, of course, the definition of the Jew as the Christ-killer, guilty of the unforgivable sin of deicide, condemned to suffer throughout history because of the crowd of Jews who, according to one of the most horrible libels in world literature, as recorded in the Gospel of Matthew, "cried out, in unison (!), 'his blood be on us and on our children'" (Matt 27:25).[4]

Second, Christians nurtured historical memories of the Jews having persecuted the early followers of Jesus. The first Christian martyrs were put to death not by the Romans, but by the Jews.[5] It was the Jews—according to this historic memory—who drove the Christians out of the synagogue and cursed the Christians in their daily liturgy. Many Christians in the Middle Ages and early modern period apparently believed that Jews nurtured a deep and abiding hatred for Christians and exploited every realistic opportunity to harm them. This belief undergirds the notorious ritual murder charge and blood libel, first attested in twelfth-century Norwich: that Jews tortured and murdered innocent Christian children as a kind of reenactment of their murder of the Christ.[6]

Consider how Martin Luther expressed his understanding of the historical relationship between Christians and Jews: "[The Jews] have been bloodthirsty bloodhounds and murderers of all Christendom for more than 1400 years in their intentions, and would undoubtedly prefer to be such with their deeds. Thus they have been accused of poisoning water and wells, of kidnapping children, of piercing them through with an awl, of hacking them in pieces, and in that way secretly cooling their wrath with the blood of Christians, for all of which they have often been condemned to death by fire."[7] His historical "memory" is of Jews having continually persecuted Christians—or at least, continuously wanting to do so!

Fortunately, we live in a time when most Christians have abandoned such distorted constructions of the past. New Testament scholarship has illuminated the way in which the Gospels shifted blame for the crucifixion from Romans to the Jews. The Catholic Church and virtu- ally every Protestant denomination have repudiated the tendency to blame all Jews living at the time of Jesus and in subsequent centuries for the passion and death on the cross. The older image of the Jew as the Christ-killer may linger today in some circles, perhaps buttressed by Gospel readings that remain part of the liturgy for Good Friday, but it certainly is not a major factor in Jewish-Christian relations. Similarly, the ritual murder charge and the associated image of the Jew as lurking to harm innocent Christian children — a libel that was consis- tently condemned as false by medieval popes — though used in Nazi propaganda and in Poland even after the war, and popping up in some virulent strains of Arab anti-Jewish discourse,[8] has disappeared in all but the most primitive circles of Christendom — disappeared, at least, outside the realm of rhetoric.[9]

Instead, a very different historical memory has emerged among Christians. Expressed in statements by various Protestant denomina- tions and by the Catholic Church, it recognizes a legacy of Christians persecuting a relatively powerless Jewish minority. The 1998 Vatican statement on the Shoah affirms that, "Sentiments of anti-Judaism in some Christian quarters, and the gap which existed between the Church and the Jewish people, led to a generalized discrimination, which ended at times in expulsions or attempts at forced conversions." Jews welcome this substitution of a new kind of historical memory, much closer to the truth.

But what about the Jewish side? Jews often come to their Christian neighbors burdened by memories of a long and tragic history of persecution against Jews, committed by Christians in the name of their faith from the fourth century to the twenty-first. Ask the average educated Jew about the nature of Jewish life under Christendom in the past and you are likely to hear a litany of horrors: Crusades, forced bap- tism, ritual murder, Inquisition, massacres.

This view of Jewish history is presented rather starkly, for example, in a book by the noted Nazi hunter Simon Wiesenthal, entitled *Every Day Remembrance Day: A Chronicle of Jewish Martyrdom.* Under each day of the year, from January 1 to December 31, there is a list of events in which Jews were persecuted or murdered. We are told in the introduc- tion, "*As the calendar shows,* the story of the persecution of the Jews has always been directed by Christians: first of all by the Roman Catholic Church, then by the Orthodox Church."[10] The impression given by a book like this is that for almost two thousand years, Christians did little other than persecute, and Jews little other than suffer.

A pamphlet published by the American Reform Jewish Movement's Department on Interreligious Affairs in the spring of 1986 contains the following assertion: "Approximately 1,000,000 Jews were killed by marauding Crusaders who were too cowardly to risk the seas and to face a well-armed enemy in the Holy Land, and so they chose to pillage and rape and riot in the ghettos of Europe instead." There is no question that in the wake of the First Crusade, Jews living in communities of the Rhineland were massacred. This had a devastating impact on Jewish life in northern Europe. But the scholarly consensus about the number of Jewish victims of the First Crusade is approximately five thousand.[11] Without minimizing the impact of that tragedy, I think it is fair to say that the leap from five thousand to one million is an error of such magnitude that it changes history into mythos.

To take just one more example, here is a passage from a recent popular book called *1001 Questions and Answers about Judaism*—a kind of catechism for the ignorant Jew of today: "What was the lot of the Jews in Christian Europe...from the 12th to the 14th centuries? Persecutions, massacres, humiliations, and exile hounded the Jewish communities....Were it not for a number of outstanding Jewish leaders, many doubt that they could have survived."[12]

I believe this kind of historical memory is unfortunate, for two reasons. First, it often functions to foster a sense of guilt among Christians, and guilt is not a sound basis for any healthy relationship. When contemporary Jews approach contemporary Christians with the attitude, "Your ancestors persecuted my ancestors," all communication is tainted with smug self-righteousness on the one side, and either an understandable defensiveness or a self-abasing vicarious contriteness on the other.

Second, the litany often entails distortion of the historical record, not only in the exaggeration of numbers we have seen, but in the general picture it suggests. Our mentor, James Parkes, once wrote, "bad history cannot be the foundation of good theology,"[13] and I would add, or of healthy interreligious dialogue. The prevailing presentation is exasperating to many historians because two full generations have passed since S. W. Baron—arguably the preeminent Jewish historian of the twentieth century—launched his critique of what he dubbed "the lachrymose conception of Jewish history."[14] This is the view of Jewish historical experience under Christian rule as a vale of tears, of unrelieved oppression and suffering, a view fostered by the tendency of medieval Jews to write chronicles not during normal times but precisely during times of crisis, in order to memorialize the dead or to communicate a message of hope and encouragement to the survivors.

Historians of the past generation, including Baron, have not avoided investigating the discourse of opprobrium and the lethal anti-Jewish violence that periodically erupted in Christian society. But they have raised other questions as well. If Jews were subjected to such an unrelenting barrage of attacks, how did the Jewish people survive for well more than a thousand years under Christian domination, when Christian rulers certainly had the power to eliminate the Jews completely? Some answers might resort to divine providence, others—as in the example I cited—to the outstanding talents of Jewish leaders or the perseverance and faithfulness of the Jewish masses. But many historians also credit factors in the Christian world.[15]

Such factors certainly include a doctrine, first articulated by St. Augustine and reaffirmed consistently by medieval popes, that Jews are *not* to be killed or attacked or forced to accept baptism, that the continued existence of the Jewish people, observing its own faith, was God's will. Thus, when Jews were indeed attacked in 1348 during the panic of the Black Death, Pope Clement VI, citing ten earlier popes as precedent, issued a papal bull stating, "Let no Christian dare to wound or kill these Jews or to seize their property."[16] This was an *official* doctrine of toleration. Not so noble or exalted by the standards of contemporary political correctness, to be sure. The ground rules of toleration were that Jews had to live a life of dispersion, subjugation, and inferiority that would reflect their reprobate status in God's sight. But it was much more lenient and tolerant than the church's policy toward the pagans of Europe, or toward their own Christian heretics. And in addition to this doctrine, there were the Christian rulers who welcomed Jews to their realms, issued charters that guaranteed specific rights, and tolerated and protected them because the Jews were useful as sources of revenue and spurs to the economy.[17] Again, not our modern conception of the inalienable rights of all human beings. Jews always recognized that the kings had the right to expel them; but these rulers made it possible for Jewish communities to live with a modicum of stability and security and, in many cases, even to flourish.

This leads to a second set of questions, now of a comparative nature. The Middle Ages were a violent and intolerant time not just for Jews but for everyone. Recent work has provided a basis for comparison, a control, by more thoroughly investigating the treatment of other minority groups: Muslims, Christian heretics, lepers, homosexuals, prostitutes, "witches." For example, R. I. Moore, in his little book called *The Formation of a Persecuting Society,* has argued that, for various reasons, Christian society became more intolerant in the twelfth century not just toward Jews but toward everyone deemed deviant.[18] Research on the Muslim communities in Christian Spain by John Boswell, Mark Meyerson, and David Nirenberg has shown that to a striking degree, the Christian treatment of tolerated Muslim communities was quite similar to that of the Jews, indicating that it was not always "anti-Judaism" but often a more rational policy that determined the lives of the minority.[19] Joseph Shatzmiller's study of moneylending in the late Middle Ages reveals archival sources indicating that Christians in need of a loan sometimes preferred a Jewish creditor to a fellow Christian, believing that the Jew was less harsh, more benign, and would offer a better deal.[20] To turn from the economic to the social realm, the many discussions of sexual relations across religious boundaries (some of them involving servant women or prostitutes, but others freely consensual) indicate a level of social interaction at variance with the picture of isolation and contempt—this despite the condemnations by the authorities on both sides.[21] As another recent study concludes, it is "by no means clear that Jews were universally and unvaryingly hated and feared—either in early-thirteenth-century Paris or at almost any other point in the High Middle Ages."[22]

How would the standard of living of the average thirteenth-century French or English or Italian Jew have compared with that of his Christian neighbor in a town? How would the Jew's average life expectancy have compared with that of a noble, burgher, or serf in the countryside? I do not know the answer to these questions; I am not sure that anyone does, although I have a strong suspicion that the Jews would come off fairly well.[23] But until we have solid answers, is it not irresponsible to repeat platitudes about Jewish life under Christendom as a valley of weeping?[24]

A third set of questions applies to Jewish attitudes and behavior. I would argue that an honest dialogue requires that Jews confront the elements of intolerance in our own tradition with more honesty and anguish than is usually apparent. The ancestors of the Jewish people attained a revolutionary insight about the fundamental unity of humankind under the one God, and they envisioned a messianic age in which all nations would learn to live in peaceful harmony. But there are other doctrines in the classical Jewish texts that suggest quite a different picture: biblical and rabbinic descriptions of the messianic age as one of catastrophic blood-letting for the Gentiles or their subjugation to Jewish rule (*Pesikta Rabbati, Piska* 36, end); a Talmudic dictum that a non-Jew who studies Torah is liable to the death penalty (*b.Sanh.* 59a);[25] Kabbalistic teachings that the Gentile nations of the world are to be identified with the cosmic forces of evil, their souls derived from demonic powers (e.g., *Zohar* I: 121a–b, III: 72b–73a).[26] Research and publication by Israeli scholars such as Moshe Idel (on demonic conceptions of Christianity in Kabbalistic texts) and Israel Yuval (on Ashkenazi Jews calling for divine vengeance against their Christian neighbors) has dramatically concretized such discourse.[27]

To put it bluntly, there are sources in the Jewish tradition that can be used to justify the fascist, racist politics of Meir Kahane and his followers, as well as the politics of *Tikkun Magazine* and the other Jewish liberals. Needless to say, this is not to endorse the long tradition of individuals who collected the most intolerant statements in rabbinic literature and presented them as evidence of a religion that itself embodied the "teaching of contempt."[28] It is rather to argue what should be obvious: that Judaism, like every long and complex tradition, can provide in its authoritative texts a basis for narrowly particularistic as well as openly universalistic conclusions. We can say which of these doctrines we prefer, but it does not follow that the more humane, tolerant, liberal teaching is necessarily the more authentic expression of the tradition. It is therefore less than honest when we restrict our presentation of Judaism to a few platitudes about universal tolerance ("The righteous of all nations have a share in the world to come"[29] and the like), dismiss any expression of hostility as a natural response to oppression, and juxtapose this with the most intolerant expressions in Christian literature.[30]

But, it may be argued, these texts remain on the level of theory, of words. Christians not only had terrible things to say about Jews, they translated them into action. But were—are—Jews religiously or temperamentally incapable of resorting to violence? Were Meir Kahane, Baruch Goldstein (the mass murderer of the Hebron mosque), and

Yigal Amir (Rabin's assassin) total anomalies? Both the responsa literature and archival texts provide ample evidence that medieval Jews
were indeed capable of violence against one another; a recent study
based on the archives of the Crown of Aragon finds sixty cases of murder of Jews by Jews between 1257 and 1327![31] The Jewish chronicles
that recorded the events of 1096 in the Rhineland suggest that as many
Jews died when Jewish parents slaughtered their own children and hus-
bands their wives and then themselves, as died at the hands of the
Christian attackers.[32]

What about actual violence against Christians? For the most part
medieval Jews were simply not in a position to harm their neighbors in
any significant numbers, and the frequent charges of ritual murder of
Christian children remain in the realm of fantasy and projection. Let
us, however, turn back to an enigmatic and troubling incident, a historical moment that is not part of the shared memories of either
Christians or Jews.

For almost three centuries following the conversion of
Constantine (with the exception of a few heady years under the pagan
emperor Julian, known to Christians as "the Apostate"), the Byzantine
Christians controlled the Holy Land. They continued the Roman policy
of prohibiting Jews from living in Jerusalem; they used the Temple
Mount, site of the ruins of the ancient Temple, as a garbage dump. In
the early seventh century, civil war in Byzantium provided an opportu-
nity to break the stalemate between the two superpowers of the age, the
Byzantine and the Sasanian Persian Empires. The Persians invaded
Byzantine territory, swept into Palestine, and conquered Jerusalem.

Many Jews read these contemporary events as fraught with messianic significance, a recapitulation of that ancient Persian, Cyrus the
Great, who defeated the Babylonians and allowed the exiled Jews to
return to their Holy City. Contemporary Christian documents indicate
that the Jews allied themselves with the Persian forces in fighting
against the Christian armies. But these sources go beyond this, recount-
ing a massacre of tens of thousands of Christian civilians in which the
Jews are said to have played a leading role. According to the Jerusalem
monk Antiochus Strategos, the Jews of Palestine offered money to their
Persian allies to desist from their own massacre and allow the Jews to
take control of the fate of the surviving Christians, who were hiding out
in the cisterns of Mamilla. They offered the Christians an opportunity
to save their lives by denying Christ and becoming Jews. The

Christians refused, preferring to "die for Christ's sake rather than to live in godlessness." And the Jews then continued with the massacre, killing priests and monks, fathers, mothers, and tender infants, and demolishing "with their own hands...such of the holy churches as were left standing."[33]

What are we to make of this text? In a stunningly provocative study, Elliott Horowitz has reviewed the Jewish historiographical tradition on this incident, from the nineteenth century to our own day, emphasizing those who present an apologetic, sanitized version of the event.[34] Some, indeed, dismiss the Christian sources completely as fantastic, or as a Byzantine precursor of the "blood libel" that would not appear in Christian Europe for another five centuries. But is it inconceivable, whether because of temperament or tradition, that Jews could ever have been the murderers and Christians the martyrs?

Imagine for a moment that Constantine the Great had converted not to Christianity but to Judaism—a choice not at all unreasonable at the time—and that Judaism had become the religion of empire, wedded to the awesome power of imperial Rome, while Christianity remained a small sect at the margins of society. What would the history of Jewish-Christian relations for the next fifteen hundred years have looked like then? Would it have been a story of openness and brotherhood between mother and daughter faiths? I have to confess skepticism about that scenario. No people is immune to the corruption wrought by the marriage of military and political power with fervent faith. We expect Christians to confront the anti-Jewish elements in Christian tradition with candor and remorse. We should be just as forthright about the exclusivist, intolerant, fanatical elements in our own.

Does the historical record of the past provide any basis for supplementing and perhaps transcending the model of persecution, hostility, polemical disputation, isolation—the terms that so readily spring to mind when we speak of the premodern era? Did Jews and Christians ever actually learn from each other? Are there signs of influence by neighbors of the other faith? Did members of these competing religious traditions ever recognize anything of value in the religion or society of the other? My answer to these questions is a cautious, limited, yet emphatic yes.

I could illustrate this with examples of Christian openness to Jewish culture, especially in the areas of *biblical studies,* where Christian scholars consulted with medieval Jews to learn more about

the original text of the Hebrew Scriptures, what they called the
"hebraica veritas";[35] in *scholastic philosophy,* where Maimonides's
Guide for the Perplexed was translated into Latin so that it could be
used by Thomas Aquinas, who frequently cites "Rabbi Moses the
Egyptian" with accuracy and respect; and in the Jewish mystical doctrine called *Kabbalah,* where Renaissance Christian intellectuals hired
Jewish tutors to provide them access to this arcane yet powerful tradition.[36] To be sure, the motivations of the Christian Hebraists varied
from intellectual curiosity to a desire to exploit Jewish sources for con-
versionary purposes. Nor does it follow that greater scholarship
devoted to Jewish sources necessarily led to warmer relations or deeper
tolerance.[37] But the interest on the part of many leading Christian intellectuals in contemporary Jews and their culture is undeniable.

I will, however, concentrate on examples of Jewish openness to
Christian influences—an openness that betokens not a weakness of
Jewish faith or an eagerness to abandon it, but rather a confidence that
it could accommodate the best in its rival religion while remaining
absolutely faithful to Jewish commitments. There is no time for
detailed exploration; I can give just a few brief examples.

I might begin with a small yet influential movement within
medieval Judaism known as Hasidei Ashkenaz, or "German Pietists,"
that emerged in the second half of the twelfth century, in the period following the massacres of the First and Second Crusades. It is perhaps
not surprising that the teachings of this group express extreme hostility
toward Christianity and its sancta.[38] This is clearly not a movement of
rapprochement with Christianity. Yet among the most important teachings of this movement is a distinctive doctrine of repentance, a theological category at the heart of rabbinic Judaism.

Quite at variance with the classical formulation of Maimonides,
the German Pietists appear to have introduced into Judaism an elabo-
rate system of penances. For example, a Jew who is guilty of forbidden
sexual relations:

> must suffer pain as grievous as death. He should sit in ice or
> in snow once or twice for an hour, and in the summer he
> should sit among flies or ants or bees, so as to suffer afflic-
> tions as painful as death....He must weep and confess each
> day, and suffer all manner of affliction, because he made the
> woman forbidden to her husband.

Here we have an extreme form of asceticism, including mortification of the flesh, that has no parallel in Maimonides's Code and at best ambiguous grounding in the rabbinic literature.[39] This appears to be a dramatic example of the influence of the medieval Christian penitential literature, which ordains many of the same penances.[40] It is as if the Jewish writers felt on some level that a purely internal transformation was not enough; the standards set by their Christian neighbors were higher, and for Jews to have what appeared to be an easier way to repentance was psychologically intolerable.

But there is something more. Maimonides spoke of individual confession to God, a confession that must put vague feelings into words but should not be public and not necessarily even out loud. Indeed, the Talmud explicitly states that, "one is impertinent [to God] in proclaiming one's sins [to others]" (*b.Ber.* 34b), indicating that disclosing one's sins to other human beings can, paradoxically, be an egotistical act of calling attention to one's own behavior. Yet the Pietists finessed the Talmudic statement while introducing a new practice: individual confession of sins to a sage who instructs the penitent about the appropriate acts of penance. And this precisely at the time when confession to the priest was being made mandatory for all Roman Catholics (through an ordinance of the Fourth Lateran Council in 1215); a rather dramatic example of openness to the dynamic environment of medieval Christianity.[41]

Another doctrine of obvious centrality both to Judaism and to the Jewish-Christian debate is the doctrine of the Messiah. We find differences not just on the identification and timing of the Messiah but on his nature and function. For Christians, the Messiah came as an incarnation of the divine, who took upon himself the sins of the world and, through his suffering and death, provided atonement for all who believe in him — atonement that cannot be achieved through human initiative alone. For Jews this idea of vicarious atonement — that the Messiah takes upon himself suffering that would otherwise come as punishment to the people for their sins — seems totally alien. The people themselves are directly accountable to God, who may forgive as an act of divine grace, and need no Messiah to suffer in their stead.

Let us turn to a passage in the *Zohar,* the classical text of medieval Jewish mysticism or kabbalah. The passage begins by describing the destiny of souls in the Lower Paradise. At times, we are told, they roam about the world in which we live, observing the suffering of human beings, "the bodies of sinners undergoing their punishment" as victims of pain and disease. They observe also the undeserved suffering of those Jews who "suffer for their belief in the unity of [God]. They then return [to their place in the Lower Paradise], and make all this known to the Messiah," who, the Kabbalists believed, exists at present in the supernal realm, awaiting the signal from God to enter our world. The passage continues:

> When the Messiah hears of the great suffering of Israel in their dispersion, and of the wicked amongst them who seek not to know their Master, he weeps aloud on account of those wicked ones amongst them, as it is written, *But he was wounded because of our transgression, crushed because of our iniquities* (Isa. 53:5).

The use of the famous verse from Isaiah 53 captures our attention, for the normative medieval Jewish interpretation—to safeguard against the Christian use of this passage—was to insist that it did not refer to the Messiah but to a prophet in antiquity or to the personification of the Jewish people. The passage then continues, after the intelligence report from the peripatetic souls to the Messiah,

> The souls then return to their place. The Messiah, on his part, enters a certain Hall in the Garden of Eden, called the Hall of the Afflicted. There he calls for all the diseases and pains and sufferings of Israel, bidding them settle on himself, which they do. And were it not that he thus eases the burden from Israel, taking it on himself, no one could endure the sufferings meted out to Israel in expiation on account of their neglect of the Torah. So Scripture says *surely our diseases he did bear* (Isa. 53:4)....As long as Israel were in the Holy Land, by means of the Temple service and sacrifices they averted all evil diseases and afflictions from the world. Now it is the Messiah who is the means of averting them from mankind until the time when a man quits this world and receives his punishment.

Once again a proof text from the "suffering servant" passage in Isaiah 53, but here the "vicarious atonement" doctrine is unmistakable.

The Messiah takes upon himself the suffering deserved by Jews, thereby removing much of it from them.[42] Note the difference from the Christian doctrine: the suffering messiah does not remove individual accountability in life after death. His suffering occurs before he enters the world, not after. But the insistence that it is part of the Messiah's role to suffer and thereby to remove affliction from the Jewish people is unmistakable and dramatic, and it seems to me undeniable that this reveals the power of the contemporary Christian model. The message to thirteenth-century Jews is clear: if you are prospering, it is not because you are blameless but because the Messiah is suffering the afflictions that you deserve; if you are suffering, know that what you really deserve for your sins is actually far, far greater. In either case, your religious failures cause the Messiah untold anguish and pain.[43]

I mentioned above the influence of Jewish biblical scholars on Christians interested in the meaning of the original Hebrew texts. But Christians influenced Jews as well. In the late thirteenth century, Jewish exegetes began to work with the idea of four levels of biblical interpretation, known by the acronym *pardes: peshat,* the simple meaning; *remez,* philosophical allegory; *derash,* homiletical interpretation; and *sod,* mystery or Kabbalistic symbolism. There is a consensus among scholars that this crystallization reflects in Jewish terms the Christian doctrine of four levels of meaning that had been formulated some centuries earlier.[44]

Elsewhere I have written about the influence of Christian models on the forms of medieval Jewish writing, especially the new thematic sermon patterned by late medieval Sephardic preachers after the "modern" scholastic sermon of the thirteenth century and the appearance of formal, scholastic "disputed questions" in Jewish preaching.[45] Here I will provide one concrete example of the impact of Christian values on the substance of Jewish exegesis. This is the problematic and disturbing story of Jephthah's daughter, found in Judges, chapter 11. About to undertake a military campaign against the Ammonites, Jephthah makes a vow to God that if he prevails, "then whoever comes out of the doors of my house to meet me, when I return victorious from the Ammonites, shall be the LORD's, to be offered up by me as a burnt offering" (11:31). When Jephthah did return, his daughter came out to meet him. Constrained to fulfill his vow, he allowed her to go with her companions for two months to "bewail her virginity," and then "did with her according to the vow he had made" (11:39).

It seems absolutely clear that Jephthah sacrificed his daughter as a burnt offering. Yet there is a Jewish exegetical tradition that spared the daughter's life. It depends on two things. First, a grammatical, semantic point: the *vav* in *ve-ha'alitihu,* usually translated "and I will offer it," can mean "*or* I will offer it." Precedent is in Exodus 21:15, *makkeh 'aviv ve-imo mot yumat,* which the rabbis interpret to mean not just "Whoever strikes his father *and* his mother will be put to death," but "whoever strikes his father *or* his mother."[46] So in this case, Jephthah vows two alternatives: as the thirteenth-century commentator David Kimhi paraphrased, "whatever comes forth from my house to meet me shall be the Lord's consecrated to God if it is *not* appropriate for a burnt offering, *or* I will offer it as a burnt offering."

More relevant to our subject, the interpretation depends also on an understanding of what it could mean for a young woman to be "devoted to the Lord" other than being sacrificed. So Kimhi wrote, "Jephthah made her a house and put her in it, and there she was separated from other human beings and the ways of the world.... Throughout the year she lived in isolation, just as those recluses who are shut off in certain houses." He is referring here not to a model in Jewish society but to Christian world-renouncing hermits. If this is not clear enough, here is the late fifteenth-century Spaniard Don Isaac Abravanel:

> She had to be secluded in one house and not to emerge from it all the rest of her life....She said, "I will bewail my virginity," meaning that she would not be able to marry. He also had to go and choose a place where she would stay in her seclusion. I believe that from this the Christians learned to make cloisters for women, into which they would enter, never to set forth again for the rest of their lives and never to see a man as long as they live.[47]

Now clearly the Christians did not learn about cloisters from this ambiguous passage. Rather, Jewish intellectuals derived their interpretation from the Christian practice of nuns in cloisters.[48] What is striking is that the biblical phrase in the vow, "devoted to God," is interpreted to be fulfilled through a life of seclusion and virginity. It is impossible to derive this from an internal Jewish tradition of celibate eremiticism.[49] What it shows is that this aspect of Christian spirituality, far removed as it was from most Jewish sources and actual behavior, apparently had some impact.

The examples provided above are of openness on a relatively high cultural level. The extent of interaction on lower levels of society, both social and cultural, especially in the areas of popular beliefs and superstition, is one of the most exciting areas of recent research, although much of the evidence—by its very nature nonliterary—has been lost to the historical record.[50]

I conclude with one final expression of this theme of openness. Some time ago I started collecting passages in which, in the context of self-criticism, particularly in sermons, Christian writers point to areas of religious life where Jews are doing better, and Jewish preachers identify those aspects of Christian behavior from which their listeners could well learn. To summarize my conclusions, medieval and early modern Christian preachers (occasionally) spoke with a grudging admiration about the Jews' devotion to the Sabbath and holy days, their abhorrence for blasphemous language and profanity, their commitment to education, and their willingness to suffer and sacrifice for their faith.[51] As for Jewish writers, I will share just two passages, among my favorites.

First is an early fifteenth-century Spanish Jew, who denounced the shortcomings of Jewish religious society following the catastrophic pogroms of 1391. Eventually he turns to behavior in the synagogue:

> Look what happens when a congregation [of Jews] gathers
> to hear words of Torah from a sage. Slumber weighs upon
> the eyes of the officers; others converse about trivial affairs.
> The preacher is dumbfounded by the talking of men and the
> chattering of women standing behind the synagogue. If he
> should reproach them because of their behavior, they con-
> tinue to sin, behaving corruptly, abominably. This is the
> opposite of the Christians. When their men and women
> gather to hear a preacher, they stand together in absolute
> silence, marveling at his rebuke. Not one of them dozes as
> he pours out his words upon them. They await him as they
> do the rain, eager for the waters of his counsel. *We have not
> learned properly from those around us.*[52]

Two centuries later, the leading rabbi of the recently established Portuguese Jewish community of Amsterdam berated his congregation by citing and then exemplifying a statement from the Talmud, "You have followed them in their corruption, you have failed to emulate their good" (*b.Sanh* 39b):

> Look at the Gentiles among whom we live. We learn from them styles of clothing and arrogance, but we do not learn from them silence during prayer. We are like them in consuming their cheeses and their wine, but we are not like them with regard to justice, righteousness, and honesty. We are like them in shaving our beard or modeling it in their style, but we are not like them in their refraining from cursing or swearing in God's name. We are like them in frequenting underground game rooms, but we are not like them in turning from vengeance and refraining from bearing hatred in our hearts. We are like them in fornicating with their daughters, but we are not like them in conducting business affairs with integrity and fairness.[53]

Needless to say, contemporary Christian moralists, whether in Spain or in Amsterdam, painted a considerably less rosy picture of their own societies. The point here is not so much the reality of the other as the perception: there were areas in which the competition appeared to be doing better. As part of the rhetoric of rebuke, it was effective to be able to argue that, measured against the actual behavior of Christian neighbors, Jews should find themselves to be wanting.

I hope I have succeeded in presenting an alternative to the regnant, totally dismal picture of intergroup relations in premodern times. In most areas of medieval Europe, Jews were not sealed off from the world around them. Despite the occasional outbursts of persecution, despite their own hostility toward much of the Christian world, they were open to positive influences of the external, Christian culture, capable of incorporating aspects of this culture in Judaism. More than this, it might be argued that Judaism survived and flourished not because of its insularity but precisely because of this openness.[54] Indeed, each side was capable of learning from the other, of using the other not just as a dangerous or demonic adversary, but as a challenge to creative competition in ethical and religious living. Perhaps that is a model that can help us set our agenda today.

NOTES

1. *Boston Globe,* July 16, 1999, A13: "This evil century which we are leaving started with those evil events of 900 years ago....Now, after the Holocaust, which is unforgettable, we have no authorization to forgive."

2. Statement in May 2000 by President Duane Litfin on Wheaton College website (http://www.wheaton.edu/alumni/mascot/ [content as of May 2000; no longer online]). Dr. Litfin's statement mentioned Christians massacring Muslims and Western Christians killing Eastern Christians, but not the massacre by some Crusaders of Rhineland Jews. An article by E. J. Dionne Jr. in the *Washington Post,* May 2, 2000, A23, cited a student newspaper editorial: "What does proudly dubbing a Wheaton student as a Crusader communicate to Jews (the land belonged to the Jews as well) and Arabs?" It is not clear from this that they were aware of the Rhineland massacres or that the Crusaders reimposed the earlier Christian policy of excluding Jews from Jerusalem, while the Muslims both before and after the Crusader conquest permitted Jews to live in the Holy City.

3. Eric J. Greenberg, "Interfaith Affairs," in *New York Jewish Week,* July 23, 1999.

4. To take just one example of how this verse was actualized and applied to Jews removed in space and time from ancient Jerusalem, here is John Chrysostom, condemning late fourth-century Christians for observing or participating in the holy day observances of Jewish neighbors in Antioch: "Consider, then, with whom they are sharing their fasts. It is with those who shouted, 'Crucify him, Crucify him!' with those who said, 'His blood be upon us and upon our children.'...Is it not strange that those who worship the Crucified keep common festival with those who crucified him?" (*Discourses against Judaizing Christians,* trans. Paul W. Harkins [Washington, DC: Catholic University of America Press, 1979], discourse 1, section 5, p. 18).

5. Acts 6:8–15; 7:54–60 (many of the medieval depictions of the martyrdom of St. Stephen signify the perpetrators as Jews). Christian historiography, beginning with St. Justin Martyr, preserved a tradition that Bar Kokhba had persecuted and killed Christians who refused to deny Jesus and who refused to help in the revolt against Rome. See the sources from Eusebius quoted in Yigael Yadin, *Bar Kokhba* (New York: Random House, 1971), 258.

6. On this, see the classic essay by Gavin Langmuir, "Thomas of Monmouth: Detector of Ritual Murder," in *Toward a Definition of Antisemitism* (Berkeley: University of California Press, 1990), 209–36. A critical passage from the primary text is conveniently accessible in Jacob Marcus, *The Jew in the Medieval World,* rev. ed. (Cincinnati: Hebrew Union College Press, 1999), 137–39.

7. Martin Luther, *On the Jews and Their Lies, in Luther's Works,* 55 vols. (St. Louis: Concordia, 1955–1986; Philadelphia: Fortress Press, 1955–) vol. 47 (1967), 264.

8. See Bernard Lewis, *Semites and Anti-Semites* (New York: W.W. Norton, 1986), 194; David Shipler, *Arab and Jew: Wounded Spirits in the Promised Land* (New York: Penguin Books, 1986), 175, 317–18.

9. In addition to the statement by David Yager cited above, the blood libel rhetoric has occasionally been used by Jewish spokesmen. An example that seemed particularly shameless to many was the statement issued by Prime Minister Begin's cabinet on September 19, 1982, following the initial report of the massacres at Sabra and Shatila, beginning "On the New Year [Rosh Hashana], a blood libel was leveled against the Jewish state, its government and the Israel Defense Forces." This was published as an advertisement in many American newspapers under the title, "Blood Libel" (e.g., *New York Times*, September 21, 1982, col. B9).

10. Simon Wiesenthal, *Every Day Remembrance Day: A Chronicle of Jewish Martyrdom* (New York: Henry Holt, 1986), introduction (my italics). How "the calendar shows" this is not explained. The model for Wiesenthal may have been Leopold Zunz's *Die Monatstage des Kalendarjahres,* published in 1848; see Nils Roemer, "Turning Defeat into Victory: *Wissenschaft des Judentums* and the Martyrs of 1096," *Jewish History* 13, no. 2 (1999): 73–74.

11. See the discussion by S. W. Baron, *A Social and Religious History of the Jews: High Middle Ages, 500–1200,* 2nd ed. (New York: Columbia University Press, 1957), 4:105.

12. David Gross, *1001 Questions and Answers about Judaism* (New York: Hippocrene, 1987), 200. A more recent publication reflecting this position is Dan Cohn-Sherbok, *The Crucified Jew: Twenty Centuries of Christian Anti-Semitism* (London: HarperCollins Publishers, 1992).

13. James Parkes, *The Foundations of Judaism and Christianity* (London: Vallentine Mitchell, 1960); cited in Sian Jones, Tony Kushner, and Sarah Pearce, eds., *Cultures of Ambivalence and Contempt* (London: Vallentine Mitchell, 1998), 2.

14. See the masterful discussion of this and the sources cited in Ismar Schorsch, *From Text to Context: The Turn to History in Modern Judaism* (Hanover, NH/London: University Press of New England for Brandeis University Press, 1994), 376–88.

15. For a compelling statement of this issue, see Yosef Yerushalmi, "Response to Rosemary Ruether," in *Auschwitz: Beginning of a New Era?*, ed. Eva Fleischner (New York: KTAV, 1977), 98–101.

16. Shlomo Simonsohn, *The Apostolic See and the Jews*, 8 vols. (Toronto: Pontifical Institute of Mediaeval Studies, 1988), 1:373 (*ut nullus*

Christianus eorundem Iudeorum personas....vulnerare aut occidere, vel suas illis pecunias auferre...presumeret ullo modo....); Edward Synan, The Popes and the Jews in the Middle Ages (New York: Macmillan, 1965), 133; Diana Wood, *Clement VI: The Pontificate and Ideas of an Avignon Pope* (Cambridge: Cambridge University Press, 1989), 196–200.

17. Particularly striking is the formulation by Rudiger, bishop and feudal overlord of Speyer, in the introduction to his charter offered to the Jews in 1084: "When I wished to make a city out of the village of Speyer, I Rudiger...thought that the glory of our town would be augmented a thousand-fold if I were to bring Jews." See Robert Chazan, *Church, State and Jew in the Middle Ages* (New York: Behrman House, 1980), 58.

18. R. I. Moore, *The Formation of a Persecuting Society: Power and Deviance in Western Europe, 950–1250* (Oxford: Basil Blackwell, 1987).

19. John Boswell, *The Royal Treasure: Muslim Communities under the Crown of Aragon in the Fourteenth Century* (New Haven, CT: Yale University Press, 1977); Mark Meyerson, *The Muslims of Valencia in the Age of Fernando and Isabel: Between Coexistence and Crusade* (Berkeley: University of California Press, 1991); David Nirenberg, *Communities of Violence: Persecution of Minorities in the Middle Ages* (Princeton, NJ: Princeton University Press, 1996).

20. Joseph Shatzmiller, *Shylock Reconsidered: Jews, Moneylending, and Medieval Society* (Berkeley: University of California Press, 1990), esp. 71, 95–103. Compare the Christian sermonic exemplum cited in Joan Young Gregg, *Devils, Women, and Jews: Reflection of the Other in Medieval Sermon Stories* (Albany: State University of New York Press, 1997), 180.

21. See, e.g., Yom Tov Assis, "Sexual Behavior in Mediaeval Hispano-Jewish Society," in *Jewish History: Essays in Honour of Chimen Abramsky,* ed. Ada Rapoport-Albert and Stephen Zipperstein (London: Peter Halben, 1988), 42: "in the Crown of Aragon we have much archival evidence demonstrating that sexual relations between Jews and Christians (as well as Muslims) were prevalent." For literary sources, see Marc Saperstein, *Decoding the Rabbis* (Cambridge, MA: Harvard University Press, 1980), 246 n. 101.

22. Sara Lipton, *Images of Intolerance: The Representation of Jews and Judaism in the Bible Moralisée* (Berkeley: University of California Press, 1999), 27.

23. A recent study of the fifteenth-century fiscal records of the Florentine commune yields an average life duration of about thirty-five years. The authors note that this represented a decline from about forty years in 1300 and 1450, though a rise from about twenty years in the second half of the fourteenth century. The thirty-five-year average is "higher than the life expectancies of English peers over the same period (pp. 30–31) probably because the

death of babies is insufficiently noted in the *ricordi*." David Herlihy and Christiane Klapisch-Zuber, *Tuscans and Their Families: A Study of the Florentine Catasto of 1427* (New Haven, CT: Yale University Press, 1985), 83–85. I know of no comparable data on life expectancy in the contemporary Jewish communities.

24. The late eminent Israeli historian Jacob Katz rejected comparisons between Jews and other groups in medieval Christian society such as those made by Baron, though conceding that "the conditions of their lives were worse than those of the Jews," because of the unique Jewish condition of "eternal foreignness" (*A Time for Inquiry, a Time for Reflection: A Historical Essay on Israel through the Ages* [in Hebrew] [Jerusalem: Merkaz Zalman Shazar, 1999], 56).

25. See the influential though nonauthoritative Sefer Hasidim: "One should not teach a Christian cleric the [Hebrew] alphabet"; see Jacob Katz, *Exclusiveness and Tolerance: Jewish-Gentile Relations in Medieval and Modern Times* (New York: Schocken Books, 1962), 95. On this general issue in the legal literature, see J. David Bleich, "Teaching Torah to Non-Jews," *Tradition* 18 (1980): 192–211.

26. The legacy of this doctrine can be seen in classical Hasidic texts. For a refreshingly honest discussion of this issue, see Arthur Green's introduction to *Menahem Nahum of Chernobyl* (New York: Paulist Press, 1982), 19–20. See also the Hebrew discussion of Jewish sources emphasizing the essential gulf between Jews and Gentiles by Moshe Greenberg, "Atem Keruyim Adam," *Shedemot* (1980): 67–76.

27. E.g., Moshe Idel, "The Attitude toward Christianity in *Sefer ha-Meshiv*" (in Hebrew), *Zion* 46 (1981): 77–91, translated in *Immanuel* 12 (1981): 77–95. Israel Yuval, "Vengeance and Damnation, Blood and Defamation: From Jewish Martyrdom to Blood Libel Accusations" (in Hebrew), *Zion* 58 (1993): 33–90. (This extremely controversial article inspired a number of heated responses in *Zion* 59 [1994]).

28. This tradition includes such figures (many of them converts) as Nicholas Donin, Anthony Margarita, Johann Pfefferkorn, Andreas Eisenmenger, Canon August Rohling. The litany of anti-Gentile and "amoral" statements from the Talmud still appears in antisemitic websites. The late Rabbi Meir Kahane was unique, to my knowledge, as a Jewish scholar who relished citing such statements and presenting them as authentic Judaism, while condemning all "liberal" positions taken by Jews as showing the contamination of an alien, Enlightenment ideology.

29. On this statement and the controversy over its interpretation involving Maimonides, Spinoza, Mendelssohn, and others, see Alexander Altmann, *Moses Mendelssohn: A Biographical Study* (University: University of Alabama Press, 1973), 217–18.

30. A classic expression of this kind of apologetic-polemical presentation of Judaism can be found in the commentaries of the Hertz Pentateuch, still widely used in synagogues throughout the English-speaking world. See the recent study by Harvey Warren Meirovich, *A Vindication of Judaism: The Polemics of the Hertz Pentateuch* (New York: Jewish Theological Seminary of America, 1998).

31. See, e.g., Jacob Bazak, *Jewish Law and Jewish Life* (New York: Union of American Hebrew Congregations, 1979), 32, 37, 164, 191, 198, 203; for the archival sources, Yom Tov Assis, *The Golden Age of Aragonese Jewry: Community and Society in the Crown of Aragon, 1213–1327* (London: Littman Library, 1997), 292–93. Cf. Ariel Toaff, *Love, Work and Death: Jewish Life in Medieval Umbria* (London: Littman Library, 1998), 105–12. For violence in Jewish memoir literature, see Mark R. Cohen, ed., *The Autobiography of a Seventeenth-Century Venetian Rabbi: Leon Modena's Life of Judah* (Princeton, NJ: Princeton University Press, 1988), 118–20.

32. See Robert Chazan, *European Jewry and the First Crusade* (Berkeley: University of California Press, 1987), esp. 109–14. The scholarly literature on this subject is enormous.

33. For the primary account by the historian Antiochus Strategos, see F. Conybeare, "Antonius Strategos' Account of the Sack of Jerusalem (614)," *English Historical Review* 25 (1910): 506–8. (I found this on the website http://www.fordham.edu/halsall/source/strategos1.html.) This story was used by modern antisemitic writers in an effort to demonstrate the murderous hatred of Jews for Christians. See, for example, Johannes Eisenmenger in *Entdektes Judentum,* in *Antisemitism in the Modern World: An Anthology of Texts,* ed. Richard S. Levy (Lexington, MA: D. C. Heath, 1991), 34, citing Cluverius as his source.

34. Elliott Horowitz, "'The Vengeance of the Jews was Stronger than their Avarice': Modern Historians and the Persian Conquest of Jerusalem in 614," *Jewish Social Studies* 4, no. 2 (1998): 1–39.

35. See on this the path-breaking studies by Beryl Smalley, Aryeh Grabois, and Michael Signer, listed in Lipton, *Images of Intolerance,* 184 n. 77.

36. Gershom Scholem, "The Beginnings of the Christian Kabbalah," in *The Christian Kabbalah,* ed. Joseph Dan (Cambridge, MA: Harvard College Library, 1997), 17–51; Chaim Wirszubski, *Pico della Mirandola's Encounter with Jewish Mysticism* (Cambridge, MA: Harvard University Press, 1989). A full conference was sponsored by the Center for Advanced Judaic Studies at the University of Pennsylvania in May 2000 entitled "Christian Hebraists, Jews, and the Study of Judaism in Early Modern Europe."

37. For an argument to the contrary, see Jeremy Cohen, "Scholarship and Intolerance in the Medieval Academy: The Study and Evaluation of

Judaism in European Christendom," *American Historical Review* 91 (1986): 592–613.

38. See Katz, *Exclusiveness and Tolerance,* 95.

39. On precedents in earlier Jewish literature, see Moshe Beer, "Acts of Atonement by Penitents in Rabbinic Literature" (in Hebrew), *Zion* 46 (1981): 161–76.

40. The question of whether the penitential practice of the German Pietists was derived from the influence of medieval Christian practice or from application of traditional Jewish texts has generated a significant debate in the past two generations, with the earlier scholars (Yitzhak Baer, Gershom Scholem) asserting Christian influence, and the consensus shifting in the following generation (Joseph Dan, Ivan Marcus, Peter Schaefer) toward an internal Jewish dynamic. For a fine review of this controversy and, in my judgment, a proper shift back to the obvious role of Christian influence, see Talia Fishman, "The Penitential System of *Hasidei Ashkenaz* and the Problem of Cultural Boundaries," *Journal of Jewish Thought and Philosophy* 9 (1999): 1–29. I believe that Fishman overemphasizes the extent to which the Pietists explicitly justified their penances by appealing to rabbinic sources (pp. 21–22), although she is correct on the dynamics of appropriation from the external context, anxiety, and resulting desire to root in traditional texts.

41. On confession to the sage among the German Pietists, see Ivan Marcus, *Piety and Society: The Jewish Pietists of Medieval Germany* (Leiden: Brill, 1981), 49, 74–79. On the later development of this practice among the Polish Hasidim, see Ada Rapoport-Albert, "Confession in the Circle of R. Nahman of Braslav," *Bulletin of the Institute of Jewish Studies* 1 (1973–1975): 65–96. This article notes that in the medieval confession, unlike its Christian counterpart, the function of confession is merely to receive knowledge of the appropriate penitential act from an expert, not to receive absolution from the confessor. The Hasidic doctrine is more radical: confession to the *tsaddik* is what effects atonement for the sin even before any penitential act is performed (pp. 66–67, 86–87).

42. Earlier Jewish sources do express the idea of a suffering Messiah, including a passage that looks quite close to vicarious atonement. See, especially, *Pesikta Rabbati,* 2 vols., trans. William Braude (New Haven, CT: Yale University Press: 1968): *Piska* 36, p. 679, where the Messiah, at the time of his creation, is warned by God that he will suffer terribly because of the sins of future Jews, is given the option of avoiding this pain if God should destroy the souls of the sinners before they come into the world, and responds "with joy in my soul and gladness in my heart I take this suffering upon myself, provided that not one person in Israel perish." The verses from Isaiah are not used in this context. For the question whether this midrashic passage reflects Christian influence, see Braude's note, p. 678 n. 5. For later expressions of the suffering

messiah, see Moshe Idel, *Messianic Mystics* (New Haven, CT: Yale University Press, 1998), 34.

43. *Zohar* 2:212a. On the possibility of influence of the Christian Trinity on the *Zohar*, see Yehuda Liebes, "The Messiah of the Zohar" (in Hebrew), in *The Messianic Idea in Jewish Thought* (Jerusalem: Israel Academy of Sciences and Humanities, 1982), 130–31 n. 182.

44. See, e.g., Gershom Scholem, "The Meaning of the Torah in Jewish Mysticism," in *On the Kabbalah and Its Symbolism* (New York: Schocken Books, 1965), 61–62; see also Frank Talmage, "Apples of Gold: The Inner Meaning of Sacred Texts in Medieval Judaism," in *Jewish Spirituality: From the Bible through the Middle Ages,* ed. Arthur Green (New York: Crossroad, 1989), 319–21.

45. On the new mode of Jewish sermon structure, see my *Jewish Preaching 1200–1800* (New Haven, CT: Yale University Press, 1989), 66–73; a recent review of the Christian thematic sermon is in M. Michèle Mulchahey, *"First the Bow is Bent in Study...": Dominican Education before 1350* (Toronto: Pontifical Institute, 1998), 400–419 (to be sure, the forms are not identical, but the influence is unmistakable). On the "disputed question," see my *"Your Voice Like a Ram's Horn": Themes and Texts in Traditional Jewish Preaching* (Cincinnati: Hebrew Union College Press, 1996), 17–18, 84–86, with a fine example on 200–207.

46. *Mekilta,* ad loc., ed. Jacob Lauterbach, 3 vols. (Philadelphia: JPS, 1935), 3:42.

47. Isaac Abravanel, *Perush 'al Nevi'im Rishonim* (Jerusalem: Torah ve-Da'at, 1955), 130.

48. See the *Biblical Encyclopedia* (in Hebrew), 9 vols. (Jerusalem: Mosad Bialik, 1955–1988), 3:751: Kimhi was "apparently influenced in his interpretation by the eremitical practices *(minhagei nezirut)* of those days." Few modern commentaries even refer to this alternative interpretation of the story. For an exception, see David Marcus, *Jephthah and His Vow* (Lubbock: Texas Tech Press, 1986), 8–9, 43. Marcus refers to "a number of Christian exegetes" who adopted this interpretation, but does not identify any premodern Christian commentator in his notes. Martin Luther stated that "some affirm that [Jephthah] did not sacrifice her, but the text is clear enough" ("Man wil, er habe sie nich geopffert, aber der Text stehet da klar"), but whether there was already such a Christian exegetical tradition at the time of Kimhi remains to be established.

49. In the worldview of the *Zohar,* failure to marry and engage in procreation was an extremely serious sin (at least for a man): see Liebes, "Messiah," 203. Some Jewish philosophers, by contrast, wrote about sexuality, even within marriage, as an unwelcome detraction from the ideal devotion to God: see Saperstein, *Decoding the Rabbis,* 89–102.

50. E.g., Joseph Dan, "Demonological Stories of R. Judah the Hasid" (in Hebrew), *Tarbiz* 30 (1961): 273–89; Ivan Marcus, *Rituals of Childhood: Jewish Acculturation in Medieval Europe* (New Haven, CT: Yale University Press, 1996), esp. 83–111; Emily Taitz, "Jewish-Christian Relations in the Middle Ages: The Underside of a Shared Culture," in *Yakar Le'Mordecai: Jubilee Volume in Honor of Rabbi Mordecai Waxman,* ed. Zvia Ginor (Hoboken, NJ: KTAV, 1998), 189–201.

51. Marc Saperstein, "Christians and Jews: Some Positive Images," in *"Your Voice Like a Ram's Horn,"* 46–50.

52. Solomon Alami, *"Iggeret Musar"* (St. Petersburg, 1912; repr. Jerusalem, 1965), 5151 (emphasis added).

53. Saul Levi Morteira, *Giv'at Sha'ul,* end of *Devarim* (Vilna, 1912), 129a.

54. On this, see Gerson Cohen, "The Blessing of Assimilation," in *Jewish History and Jewish Destiny* (New York: Jewish Theological Seminary of America, 1997), 145–56.

3
The Bible in Future Jewish-Christian Relations

John F. A. Sawyer

As a Christian who has been engaged in various aspects of Jewish studies since 1958 when I first visited Israel and started teaching myself Hebrew, I have thought a great deal about the past history of Jewish-Christian relations, especially in relation to the Bible. A substantial chapter of my book entitled *The Fifth Gospel: Isaiah in the History of Christianity* was devoted to the subject of Isaiah and the Jews, and how the church has used the Bible down the ages to provide scriptural authority for all manner of anti-Jewish writing, not to mention outright hatred and violence.[1] More recently I spent four months in Rome reading sixteenth- and seventeenth-century sermons by specially trained Christian preachers whose job it was to deliver conversionist sermons to enforced Jewish congregations in various churches in Rome and elsewhere.[2] I looked in vain for counterexamples: Did Christian scholars ever find anything good in all the Jewish literature they were encouraged to study? I tried in vain to find excuses for Christian attitudes to Judaism: The world was a very different place in those times — maybe I was wrong to expect more enlightened attitudes in those days? Was I wrong to apply modern ethical criteria to Christian attitudes and assumptions of a bygone age? However that may be, my study of the long history of ignorance and prejudice shown by the vast majority of Christians, scholars and laypeople, ancient and modern, toward Judaism makes me all the more eager to tackle the question of the future challenge of the Bible in Jewish-Christian relations.

I begin with a few general remarks about the Bible in Judaism and Christianity, which may seem blindingly obvious, but in my experience they are still so widely misunderstood and so fundamental that I make no apology for stating them now. First, Jews and Christians do not share the same Bible. The *Tanach* or the Hebrew Bible is not the same book as the Christians' Old Testament and if you underestimate the differences between them, you have a distorted view of both. We ought not to call the Old Testament the Hebrew Bible and pretend it is the same thing. It is true that the term *Old Testament* can be and often is used quite wrongly in a derogatory and supersessionist way: "Old Testament ethics" often means pre-Christian (i.e., primitive or inferior), and the God of the Old Testament is mostly portrayed as a bloodthirsty warrior God of justice and vengeance, irrespective of the fact that there are, for example, far more texts about God as mother in the Old Testament than in the New. But that must not blind us to the differences.[3]

The contents of the two books are different: most of the world's Christians have the books of Ecclesiasticus, the Wisdom of Solomon, Judith, Tobit, and 1 and 2 Maccabees in their Old Testaments. The structure of the two books is *completely* different: the Hebrew Bible starts with the Torah and ends with the Writings, an arrangement obviously designed to place the Torah in a position of special honor and authority at one end and to indicate a line of descending authority to the Writings at the other. The Christian canon reverses this order completely, beginning with Genesis, in the dim and distant past, and progressing systematically and pointedly toward the Prophets who point with increasing urgency and specificity toward the fulfillment in the Gospels to which they are attached. The language of the two books is different. Who has ever seen an Old Testament in Hebrew? Parts of it maybe, and in a different order, but I doubt whether a complete Old Testament in Hebrew exists anywhere in the world. A modern translation of the New Testament into Hebrew has sometimes been appended to the Hebrew Bible in a single volume, but that is a curious hybrid published for clearly defined purposes.[4] So if the contents, structure, and language of the two books are different, I need not say anything about the totally different context in which the two operate: the one in the inexhaustible context of rabbinic, medieval, and modern Jewish exegetical tradition,[5] the other in the equally inexhaustible, and for the most part quite separate, context of patristic, medieval, and modern Christian exegetical tradition.[6]

This leads me to my second preliminary remark: Judaism is just about as far removed from the Hebrew Bible as Christianity is. Yet despite this obvious fact it is not uncommon to find that Christians studying the Old Testament think they are studying Judaism. Just as the history of Christian doctrine is hardly the same thing as a history of biblical interpretation, so the study of Jewish thought is completely different from the study of the Hebrew Bible. This is mainly because the Written Torah cannot be read apart from the Oral Torah, as recorded in Talmud and *Midrash.* Both go back to Sinai; both are authoritative; in fact the Oral Torah is more authoritative than the Written Torah. So the fact that in modern times large numbers of Christians and non-Jews now learn Hebrew and study the Hebrew Bible, from divinity students to people interested in ancient Near Eastern history, archeology, Semitic philology or the like, has very little effect on Jewish-Christian relations. Christians studying the Hebrew Bible (or rather their Old Testament in Hebrew) seldom come anywhere near an appreciation of Jewish beliefs and practices. To achieve that you have to immerse yourself in Talmud and *Midrash,* the medieval exegetical tradition and all the rest of Jewish literature in which the Hebrew Bible plays only an ancillary role. It is no coincidence that Jews have Talmudical Colleges and Christians Bible Colleges.

Third, for most of the last fifteen hundred years or so, Judaism and Christianity have developed independently, and with a few conspicuous exceptions, Jewish and Christian biblical interpreters worked in separate worlds. Christian theologians and preachers worked in state-sponsored Christian institutions using the ancient versions, especially Greek and Latin, and other influential translations like King James Authorised Version and Luther's Bible. Jews for the most part worked in isolation from Western culture, using the original Hebrew and Aramaic text, and had no interest in Christian interpretations of scripture whatsoever, which they regarded, often quite rightly, as completely erroneous. Almost the only exceptions where Jewish scholars read or commented on Christian interpretations occurred when they were forced to engage in dialogue with Christians, as in the medieval disputations. The speeches of Ramban or Nahmanides, Rabbi Moshe ben Nahman, at the Barcelona Disputation of 1263 are a good example of this, readily accessible in Haim Maccoby's marvelous account in *Judaism on Trial.*[7] Until quite recently, only a relatively small number of Christian scholars, either for political reasons as in the case of the professional "Preachers to the Jews" mentioned above or out of academic interest as in the case of Andrew of St. Victor, Nicholas of Lyra, Erasmus, Alexander Geddes, and other Christian Hebraists, crossed the gulf between the two religions, and the influence of their work on Jewish-Christian relations was minimal.[8] Their Hebrew studies were in any case mostly restricted to biblical Hebrew: scholars such as George Foot Moore, R. Travers Herford, Herbert Danby, Emil Schürer, and Hermann Strack, who took the rabbinic literature seriously, are a very recent phenomenon.

Before looking toward the twenty-first century, I must say something about the twentieth, a century marked by at least three crucial events in the history of Jewish-Christian relations. First, the central event of our century, and not just in the history of Jewish-Christian relations, is the Holocaust. Yet, a striking feature of much non-Jewish biblical scholarship, especially here in Britain, is the almost complete absence of references to the Holocaust.[9] This applies even to discussions of sacrifice, suffering, theodicy, and the like in relation to such key passages as the Aqedah, Isaiah 53, Lamentations, and the Book of Job. Commentaries written by the professional biblical scholars on these and other texts seldom make any reference to the Shoah, focusing their attention exclusively on how things were in antiquity, apparently unaware of contemporary uses of scripture or, at any rate, without showing any interest in them. Like those Orthodox Jews who believe that the Shoah changes nothing in their tradition, many biblical scholars have until recently ignored the fact that for many Jews and Christians, Auschwitz is as much a watershed in the history of their religion as Sinai or the crucifixion. There are other reasons for this in addition to prejudice or insensitivity on the part of Christians, as we shall see shortly.

The second new factor in the situation is the establishment of the State of Israel. Modern Zionist uses of the Bible and Israeli literature, especially since 1967, constitute a fertile area of contemporary biblical interpretation. I devoted a few pages of my chapter entitled "Isaiah and the Jews"[10] to this topic and suggested that the role of Isaiah in the origins and development of Zionism would make a good subject for a PhD thesis or a very interesting monograph. This is not the place for me to discuss the biblical roots of Bilu, a nineteenth-century Zionist movement whose name is an acronym derived from Isaiah 2:5, or Mapu's novel *Ahavat Tziyyon*[11] or the numerous place-names, institutions, and monuments bearing biblical names or mottoes, or the many works of literature, music, and art, both religious and secular, inspired by biblical language and imagery. This is another aspect of biblical interpretation almost totally ignored by non-Jewish biblical exegetes.

A conspicuous exception, motivated more by ideological passion than the pursuit of truth, is the pro-Palestinian tirade against Zionist imperialism by the late Michael Prior, a Roman Catholic priest and biblical scholar, in his books *The Bible and Colonialism*[12] and *Zionism and the Bible*.[13] He looks only at the negative influence of the Bible, in particular the Book of Joshua, in the hands of modern Jewish writers and leaders. Another example where non-Jewish scholars take an interest in the contemporary situation is the suggestion by Keith Whitelam and others that Zionism and Israeli politics have had a detrimental effect on biblical historiography.[14] But these are up to now exceptions to the rule. The rich and powerful Jewish interpretations of scripture, inspired by the establishment of a Jewish state after centuries of forced diaspora, have had little effect on mainstream biblical scholarship.

Third, the official attitude of the churches toward the Jews and Jewish-Christian relations has undergone some important changes in the second half of the twentieth century. Catholics, since the Second Vatican Council, for example, are now officially instructed to abandon their traditional, negative, supersessionist beliefs about Judaism and to seek a new appreciation of Jewish tradition and its relationship to Christianity.[15] It is not long ago that the charge of deicide against the whole Jewish people was dropped and some offensive language removed from the Christian liturgy at the behest of Blessed Pope John XXIII. The question of removing the word *Jew* from New Testament translations has even been discussed, and alternatives like *Judaeans* or even just *the people* proposed as more accurate or appropriate in some contexts.[16] There have been efforts on the part of most, though not all, of the main Christian institutions, to recognize officially the horrific errors of the past when biblical texts were used to justify violence and hatred toward the Jews, and to encourage Christians to become aware of how much we can learn from Jewish writers, ancient and modern, about our own faith as well as theirs. Again the influence of this enormous sea change in the history of Christianity has yet to be fully appreciated and implemented within biblical studies.

This brings me back to the world of modern scholarship and what I believe to be a sea change almost comparable in its significance for Jewish-Christian relations to some of the other twentieth-century developments referred to above. I am convinced that what we may loosely refer to as postmodern biblical scholarship will substantially change the way we approach the Bible and in particular the way in which we understand its role in the multicultural, largely secular, global village we are currently moving into.[17] The gulf between the world of biblical scholarship and the real world in which we live is being bridged in new ways. Biblical scholars are now studying the patristic and rabbinic literature, medieval art history, contemporary film, and the like with the same degree of enthusiasm and scholarly skill as they formerly devoted to archaeology, textual criticism, and various exotic ancient Near Eastern languages. Many factors have played a role in this: new insights from linguistics, literary, and critical studies, new applications of the social sciences, disillusionment with the quest for original meanings. Whatever the reason, I think there are three aspects of this revolution in biblical studies that are destined to be of enormous significance to Jewish-Christian relations in particular.

The first is a recognition of the fact that texts have more than one meaning. Not that this is a new idea: both the rabbis and the early church fathers knew this well enough. Origen believed that, like a human being, scripture is made up of body, soul, and spirit, and consequently has three meanings—literal, moral, and spiritual.[18] According to the rabbis, "the Torah can be interpreted in forty-nine ways."[19] Among modern scientific scholars, however, it is a relatively new idea that biblical interpretation is not necessarily a search for the one and only correct meaning of a text but rather a critical examination of different readings, each in its own context, each with its own nuances and associations, each worthy of careful consideration in its own right. The relevance of this for Jewish-Christian relations is obvious.

I am lucky to be involved in a major new series of commentaries devoted to just this aspect of biblical interpretation, designed to provide the reader with access to the many meanings that each text has and has had in the history of its interpretation down the centuries.[20] We are at the stage of commissioning authors for each book and the sheer size of the task confronting them has meant that a number of volumes will be written jointly by two people. What I must confess we did not think of at first is that the ideal solution would be to have a Jew and a

Christian working on each book. So far only the volume on the Song of Solomon falls into this category, but the aim is to allow Jewish and Christian interpretations to speak for themselves side by side. In some cases the Jewish interpretation will be the more interesting or more appealing to the modern reader than the Christian, as in the case of the story of Jephthah in Judges 11 in which the hero is roundly condemned for sacrificing his daughter (had he never heard of *piqquah nephesh?*);[21] while in other passages such as Isaiah 7:14 in which Christian interpreters prefer the Greek παρθένος, "virgin," to the Hebrew *'almah,* "young woman," the Christian interpretation is obviously far richer and historically far more influential than the Jewish. Heightened awareness of the potential of texts to have more than one meaning, including traditional Jewish and Christian meanings, it seems to me, is going to be a characteristic of future biblical studies and one that will revolutionize Jewish-Christian relations.

As a matter of fact, even before this change of emphasis, access for non-Jews to many traditional Jewish interpretations had not been all that difficult: *Midrash Rabbah* in English is easily accessible,[22] as are some of the commentaries of Rashi, Kimhi, and Ibn Ezra and other exegetical works.[23] Another less systematic way into Jewish exegetical tradition is through modern Jewish scholars: literary critics such as Robert Alter and Michael Fishbane.[24] More narrowly biblical critics such as Jacob Milgrom, Moshe Greenberg, Alex Rofé, and others frequently introduce rabbinic or medieval Jewish material into their commentaries[25] (far more frequently, incidentally, than their opposite numbers in Christian scholarship, who seldom show any interest in patristic and medieval interpretations of the texts they are discussing, however interesting, important, or helpful they are). So it has not been so hard to access many interesting Jewish interpretations or indeed many Christian ones: what is new is that more scholarly attention is now being given to such alternative meanings and Jews and Christians can effortlessly learn about each other in a new atmosphere of respect and tolerance.[26]

Second, there has been a shift away from the historical-critical quest for the original meaning of a text toward the reception history or *Wirkungsgeschichte* of the text, that is to say, the history of its impact on Western culture. What people, Jews and Christians, believe the text means and how they have used it in politics, literature, art, music, and film is important and can be studied with as much scholarly skill and sensitivity as its original meaning is studied. There have been numerous scholarly studies of this kind of material from Jeremy Cohen's *"Be Fertile and Increase; Fill the Earth and Master It" (Genesis 1:28): The Ancient and Medieval Career of a Biblical Text* (1989) and William Holladay's *The Psalms through 3000 Years* (1993), to Margarita Stocker's *Judith, Sexual Warrior: Women and Power in Western Culture* (1998) and David Clines's "Why Is There a Song of Songs and What Does It Do to You If You Read It?"[27] There are also several major reference works like David Jeffrey's extraordinarily interesting and useful *Dictionary of Biblical Tradition in English Literature* (1992) and more recently John Hayes's *Dictionary of Biblical Interpretation* (1999).[28] Once again this move away from the ancient prehistory of Judaism and Christianity to the study of how real people have read the text, and still read it, has obvious implications for Jewish-Christian relations.

A rather special example of this approach to biblical interpretation is Göran Larsson's *Bound for Freedom: The Book of Exodus in Jewish and Christian Traditions* (1999).[29] Larsson was director of the Swedish Theological Institute in Jerusalem, a center of international scholarship dedicated to improving Jewish-Christian–Muslim relations. Unlike my own study *Isaiah in the History of Christianity,* which is arranged thematically (Isaiah and Christian origins, the cult of the Virgin Mary, the man of sorrows, Isaiah and the Jews, women and Isaiah, the Peaceable Kingdom and so on), Larsson's book on Exodus is in the form of a commentary. He works through the text passage by passage, discussing each topic or phrase or image in the light of a variety of interpretations gleaned from the Jewish and Christian literature (mostly Jewish to redress the balance) down the ages. The bibliography is short but very revealing and, for present purposes, really encouraging. Alongside the more traditional commentaries of Umberto Cassuto, Nahum Sarna, and Brevard Childs, the emphasis is entirely on *Midrash,* Rashi, the *Siddur,* the Passover Haggadah, and modern responses to Exodus by such writers as Martin Buber, Jon Levenson, and Michael Walzer. The result is a fascinating treatment of the text devoted to how people have understood the text and applied it to their lives, rather than what actually happened or what the original author meant. Section titles such as "Three Women," "Love Your Enemies," "The Sanctuary of Freedom," and "The Fall and the New Covenant" give an idea of Larsson's approach. It is easy to point to omissions or oversimplifications or personal bias in such a work, but it opens the way for us to see the text for what it is: not only an ancient Near Eastern text like the Code of Hammurabi, but a source of inspiration and authority that changed the world.

This brings me, finally, to a third characteristic of the latest approaches to biblical interpretation: a greater awareness of the ethical, political, and ideological implications of biblical exegesis. It has taken many centuries for scholars to recognize the extent to which the Bible has been used to authorize social injustice, hatred, oppression, and even violence. The Jews, alongside heretics, blacks, women, and the poor, have often been the victims of Christian biblical interpretation. I collected hundreds of examples in my work on Isaiah.[30] Isaiah provided the church with scriptural authority to hurl at the Jews every kind of insult: if its prophet criticized them for their blindness (Isa 6:9–10), their incredulity (65:2), and their deicide ("your hands are full of blood" 1:15; cf. Matt 27:25), then the church had a right to do that too. When St. Justin Martyr (ca. 100–165), St. John Chrysostom (ca. 347–407), St. Augustine (354–430), and many others called the Jews "rulers of Sodom" (1:9), "dogs" (56:10), and "drunkards" (29:9), and accused them of "blindness" (6:9–10), "obstinacy" (65:2), and "treachery" (3:9–11), they quoted Isaiah. When they wanted to say that it was their own fault that they had been rejected (29:13–14), their cities destroyed (3:11), their lives ruined (57:1–4), they cited Isaiah. More recently and more insidiously, as Charlotte Klein showed in her invaluable little book *Anti-Judaism in Christian Theology,* renowned and highly influential biblical scholars make statements on postexilic Judaism or *Spätjudentum,* "late Judaism," that are offensive in the extreme.[31] In some instances maybe these were unintentional, due to ignorance rather than prejudice, but that certainly does not apply to them all.

Nowadays with the appearance of ideological criticism, ethical criticism, feminist criticism, postcolonial criticism, and the like, alongside (not in place of) form criticism, source criticism, textual criticism, and the other tools of traditional biblical scholarship, such abuses are exposed and condemned us unethical. Books such as Göran Larsson's *Bound for Freedom* mentioned above, Sugirtharajah's *The Postcolonial Bible,* Raymond Brown's *Unexpected News: Reading the Bible with Third World Eyes* (1984), and a host of others are heightening our awareness of what we are doing when we read and interpret the Bible.[32] To end with a specific example, it seems to me that Christians interpreting Isaiah 53 in a post-Holocaust world will no longer be able to ignore the Holocaust. The myth of the Jew as "suffering servant" is now seen by many as morally and indeed historically unacceptable.[33] Indeed many would put it even more strongly: in Irving Greenberg's words, nothing can be said about suffering that cannot be said in the presence of the burning children.[34] So how are we to understand Isaiah 53? In particular we have to ask, What has the "prophet of consolation" to say, if anything, to survivors of the Holocaust and their children? This is, in my view, the kind of question biblical scholars will be asking in the future. I can only imagine what the results will be, but I am sure they will be beneficial.

NOTES

1. John F. A. Sawyer, *The Fifth Gospel: Isaiah in the History of Christianity* (Cambridge: Cambridge University Press, 1996), 100–125.

2. C. Roth, *The History of the Jews in Italy* (Philadelphia: Jewish Publication Society, 1946), 315–17; A. Milano, "Un sottile tormento nella vita del ghetto di Roma: La predica coatta," *Rassegna Mensile di Israel* 18 (1952): 517–32. Also J. F. A. Sawyer, "Isaiah and the Jews: Some reflections on the Church's use of the Bible" in *Reading from Right to Left. Essays on the Hebrew Bible in Honour of David J. A. Clines,* ed. Cheryl Exum (Sheffield, UK: Sheffield Academic Press, 2003), 390–401.

3. Cf. J. F. A. Sawyer, "Combating Prejudices about the Bible and Judaism," *Theology* 94 (1991): 269–78.

4. N. H. Snaith, ed., *Torah, Nebi'im u-Ketubim* (1961, 1967) with *Berit Hadashah,* trans. F. Delitzsch (1891), published in one volume (London: British and Foreign Bible Society, 1968).

5. See R. Loewe, "Jewish Exegesis," in *Dictionary of Biblical Interpretation,* ed. R. J. Coggins and J. L. Houlden (London: SCM Press, 1990), 346–54.

6. See J. L. Houlden, "Christian Interpretation of the Old Testament," in *A Dictionary of Biblical Interpretation,* ed. R. L. Coggins and J. L. Houlden (London: SCM Press, 1990), 108–12; Sawyer, *Fifth Gospel.*

7. H. Maccoby, *Judaism on Trial: Jewish-Christian Disputations in the Middle Ages,* 2nd ed. (London: Valentine Mitchell, 1993).

8. B. Smalley, *The Study of the Bible in the Middle Ages,* 3rd ed. (Oxford: Basil Blackwell, 1983), 112–94; W. McKane, *Selected Christian Hebraists* (Cambridge: Cambridge University Press, 1989).

9. For some exceptions, see T. Linafelt, "Biblical Interpretation and the Holocaust," in *Dictionary of Biblical Interpretation,* ed. J. H. Hayes, 2 vols. (Nashville: Abingdon Press, 1999), 514–15; see also the essays in

T. Linafelt, ed., *Strange Fire: Reading the Bible after the Holocaust* (Sheffield: Sheffield Academic Press, 2000).

10. See Sawyer, *Fifth Gospel.*

11. Avraham Mapu, *Ahavat Tziyyon* ("Love of Zion") (Vilna, 1853); English translation by A. M. Schapiro, *In the Days of Isaiah* (New York: Translator, 1902), and *The Shepherd Prince* (New York: Translator, 1922, 1930).

12. M. Prior, *The Bible and Colonialism: A Moral Critique* (Sheffield: Sheffield Academic Press, 1997).

13. M. Prior, *Zionism and the Bible* (London: Routledge 1999).

14. K. Whitelam, *The Invention of Ancient Israel: The Silencing of Palestinian History* (London: Routledge, 1996).

15. E.g., "Guidelines on Religious Relations with the Jews (No. 4, 1 December 1974)," reprinted in A. Flannery, OP, ed., *Vatican Council II: The Conciliar and Post-Conciliar Documents* (Leominster, Hereford: Fowler Wright, 1981), 743–49.

16. See R. Kysar, "Anti-Semitism and the Gospel of John," *in Anti-Semitism and Early Christianity: Issues of Polemic and Faith,* ed. C. A. Evans and D. A. Hagner (Minneapolis: Fortress Press, 1993), 113–27.

17. See, e.g., E. Castelli et al., eds., *The Postmodern Bible, The Bible and Culture Collective* (New Haven, CT: Yale University Press, 1995); and J. Barton, ed., *The Cambridge Companion to Biblical Interpretation* (Cambridge: Cambridge University Press, 1998), part 1.

18. F. Young, "Origen," in *Dictionary of Biblical Interpretation,* ed. R. L. Coggins and J. L. Houlden (London: SCM Press, 1990), 501–3.

19. *Pesikta Rabbati* 14:20.

20. J. F. A. Sawyer, J. L. Kovacs, and C. C. Rowland, eds., *Blackwell Bible Commentary Series* (Oxford: Blackwell, 2002–). Four volumes have appeared so far (Exodus, Judges, John, and Revelation).

21. L. Ginzberg, *Legends of the Jews* (Philadelphia: Jewish Publication Society, 1947), 4:43–47.

22. *Midrash Rabbah,* 2nd ed., 10 vols. (New York/London: Soncino, 1951).

23. E.g., M. Rosenbaum and A. M. Silbermann, eds. and trans., *The Pentateuch with Targum Onkelos, Haphtaroth and Rashi's Commentary* (Jerusalem: Silbermann, 1973); *The Longer Commentary of David Kimhi on the First Book of Psalms,* trans. R. G. Finch with an Introduction by G. H. Box (London: SPCK, 1919); M. Friedlander, ed. and trans., *The Commentary of Ibn Ezra on Isaiah,* (London: Trubner, 1873–1877).

24. R. Alter, *The Art of Biblical Narrative* (London: Allen & Unwin, 1981); M. A. Fishbane, *Biblical Text and Texture: A Literary Reading of Selected Texts* (Oxford: One World, 1998).

25. J. Milgrom, *Numbers: The Traditional Hebrew Text with the New JPS Translation and Commentary* (Philadelphia: Jewish Publication Society, 1989); M. Greenberg, *Ezekiel 1–20: A New Translation with Introduction and Commentary,* Anchor Bible Series 22 (New York: Doubleday, 1983); A. Rofé, *Prophetical Stories* (Jerusalem: Magnes Press, 1989).

26. See S. A. Handelman, *Slayers of Moses: The Emergence of Rabbinic Interpretation in Modern Literary Theory* (Albany: State University of New York Press, 1982); H. Schwartz, *Reimagining the Bible: The Story-Telling of the Rabbis* (Oxford: Oxford University Press, 1998).

27. J. Cohen, *"Be Fertile and Increase; Fill the Earth and Master It" (Genesis 1:28): The Ancient and Medieval Career of a Biblical Text* (Ithaca, NY: Cornell University Press, 1989); W. Holladay, *The Psalms through 3000 Years* (Minneapolis, MN: Fortress Press, 1993); D. Cohn-Sherbok, ed., *Using the Bible Today,* Canterbury Papers 3 (London: Bellew, 1991); M. Stocker, *Judith, Sexual Warrior: Women and Power in Western Culture* (New Haven, CT: Yale University Press, 1998); D. J. A. Clines, ed., *Interested Parties: The Ideology of Writers and Readers of the Hebrew Bible* (Sheffield: Sheffield Academic Press, 1996), 94–121.

28. D. L. Jeffrey, ed., *A Dictionary of Biblical Tradition in English Literature* (Grand Rapids, MI: Eerdmans, 1992); J. H. Hayes, ed., *A Dictionary of Biblical Interpretation,* 2 vols. (Nashville, TN: Abingdon, 1999).

29. G. Larsson, *Bound for Freedom: The Book of Exodus in Jewish and Christian Traditions* (Peabody, MA: Hendrickson, 1999).

30. Sawyer, *Fifth Gospel,* 108–15.

31. C. Klein, *Anti-Judaism in Christian Theology,* trans. E. Quinn (Philadelphia: Fortress Press, 1978).

32. R. S. Sugirtharajah, ed., *The Postcolonial Bible* (Sheffield: Sheffield Academic Press, 1998); R. A. Brown, *Unexpected News: Reading the Bible with Third World Eyes* (Philadelphia: Westminster Press, 1984); A. Brenner and C. Fontaine, eds., *A Feminist Companion to the Bible* (first series), 10 vols. (Sheffield: Sheffield University Press, 1993–1998).

33. E. Berkovits, *Faith after the Holocaust* (New York: Ktav, 1973), 125–27; I. Greenberg, "Cloud of Smoke, Pillar of Fire: Judaism, Christianity and Modernity after the Holocaust," in *Auschwitz: Beginning of a New Era? Reflections on the Holocaust,* ed. E. Fleischner (New York: Ktav, 1977), 54; A. L. Eckhardt and A. R. Eckhardt, *Long Night's Journey into Day: A Revised Retrospective on the Holocaust* (Oxford: Pergamon Press; Detroit: Wayne State University Press, 1988), 93, 146.

34. Greenberg, "Cloud of Smoke," 34.

4
The Orthodox Churches in Dialogue with Judaism

Nicholas de Lange

BACKGROUND

The remarkably rapid growth of understanding and trust between Jews and Christians of the Latin tradition, particularly since the 1960s, has thrown into relief the very slow rate of progress in dialogue between Jews and Christians of the Greek tradition.

The relatively sparse achievements may be briefly catalogued. It is worth mentioning a series of four formal meetings of academics and leading figures on both sides, held in 1974, 1979, 1993, and 1998. The first two of these meetings involved mainly Greek theologians, as the times were not propitious for the participation of Christians from the Communist world and the Middle East. However, the third meeting, held near Athens in 1993, and the fourth, held in Israel in 1998, brought together a far broader range of participants and marked a very considerable advance in terms of both academic study and real dialogue. In Russia, an international conference was held in St. Petersburg in January 1997 entitled "Theology after Auschwitz and the Gulag: Attitudes to Jews and Judaism of the Orthodox Church in Communist Russia"; it was followed a year later by a second conference, "Theology after Auschwitz and Its Correlation with Theology after the Gulag: Consequences and Conclusions."

Despite such meetings, and despite some very helpful pronouncements by leading Orthodox churchmen, there is simply no comparison with the current state of play in the Roman Catholic and Protestant churches.

To some extent the uneasy relationship of the Orthodox churches with the Jewish people echoes the state of their involvement in the ecumenical movement too, and it would no doubt be unreasonable to expect Orthodox Christians to be more forward in seeking reconciliation with the Jews than with their own Christian brethren. No doubt also there are other specific factors that may be identified, some of a local character and some more general. I do not have time to attempt an analysis of the reasons for the present disparity between the Western and Eastern churches in this respect. But I do want to draw your attention to it and emphasize it, because Orthodox–Jewish dialogue does not exist in a vacuum. Nowadays if I go into a Catholic or Protestant church I am very often (though not always) struck by relevant pamphlets on display, by visible signs of cooperation with nearby synagogues, or by positive words from the pulpit. I have yet to experience any of this in an Orthodox church. Nor is there much Orthodox input into the discussions and publications of the Council of Christians and Jews and other analogous organizations. And at a higher level, there does not seem to be a firm and clear commitment to dialogue with the Jews in the pronouncements of the ecclesiastical leadership. Even when positive statements are occasionally heard (and I do not belittle the courage of those, such as the ecumenical patriarch Demetrios or Metropolitan Damaskinos of Switzerland, who *have* spoken out), too often they are met with hostility or rejection among their own followers, underlining how much uphill ground has still to be covered in the years ahead.

A NECESSARY STRUGGLE

But this ground must be covered, however arduous the work. After all, we are not dealing with a minor or marginal component in the Christian family of churches. Not only numerically but historically, theologically, and in every other respect the Orthodox churches occupy a major position at the heart of Christendom. Without wishing to reactivate old wars, in the Orthodox Church we are brought face-to-face with authentic Christian traditions going back without interruption to the early church (indeed in some ways this is a real problem in dialogue with Judaism). Numerically, I do not know if reliable statistics exist but

I imagine there must be well over two hundred million baptized members of the various Orthodox churches. A small but growing number of these are our neighbors here in Britain, in western Europe, and throughout the English-speaking world. North America is the meeting ground of very significant communities of Jews and Orthodox Christians. Christian-Jewish dialogue cannot afford to ignore or exclude the Orthodox churches; and if we imagine that the great progress that has been made with the Catholic and Protestant churches means that we are approaching the goal of fuller debate and understanding, as if the Orthodox churches can somehow be left out of the picture, we delude ourselves. Orthodoxy is an essential, an indispensable partner within the encounter between Jews and Christians.

Let me mention briefly some other considerations that are relevant to this argument. A majority of the Jews in the world today, if they do not actually live in countries where Orthodoxy is dominant or at least very vocal, have a sense that they have strong family or personal roots in such countries. I am referring mainly, of course, to territories that belong to the former Russian empire, but we should not overlook Romania and the Balkans. Nor should we ignore the strong Orthodox presence in the Middle East, and particularly in Jerusalem, one of the ancient patriarchates of the church, singled out for special honor at the Council of Nicaea because of its place in the life of Christ and the primitive church, as well as the spiritual heart of the Jewish world throughout history. The historical and sentimental history of Orthodoxy and of Judaism overlap, and are wedded to each other to a far higher degree than we are normally aware.

I believe personally that there are also affinities between Orthodoxy and Judaism on the level of religious practice and belief. This is dangerous territory, particularly at this early stage of discussion, but in the course of the academic meetings that have taken place some very suggestive comparisons have been drawn, and it is my experience that Jews experiencing Orthodox Christian worship for the first time are frequently struck by something familiar, an intangible element that they often describe as being somehow "Jewish," and that is lacking in Catholic or Protestant worship.

What all this means from a Jewish perspective is that we need encounter and dialogue with the Orthodox churches every bit as much as we need dialogue with the Western churches, if not more so. We need this dialogue because our relationship with Christianity is incomplete without it. We need this dialogue because of the special historical bonds that link us to these churches. Jews and Orthodox Christians today inhabit the same world, the same nations, the same local communities, and this compels us to speak to each other and to try to confront and, if possible, overcome our barriers. And of course for those Jews who live as minorities either within nominally Orthodox countries where the church has real power over their lives (like Greece), or in countries where the dominant form of Christianity is Orthodox, there are real and practical consequences that may flow from greater mutual understanding and meeting.

OBSTACLES TO DIALOGUE

It would be shortsighted to overlook the obstacles that stand in the way of dialogue. I shall mention these briefly under three headings: theological or religious factors, historical problems, and contemporary issues.

Theological or Religious Factors

I shall focus on factors existing on the Christian side, either general characteristics of Orthodox belief and practice or specific attitudes to Jews, because on the Jewish side I do not think there are distinctive problems relating to Orthodoxy that are different from those that have already been addressed in the wider context of Christian-Jewish relations since the Second World War and have been amply dealt with. Similarly, I shall not dwell on the broader questions of Trinitarian theology, Christology, or the special place accorded to the Mother of God, difficult though these are for Jews and Orthodox Christians to discuss together, because broadly speaking they do not mark the Orthodox out from other participants in Christian-Jewish dialogue.

However, there are some aspects of Orthodox theology that, while not peculiar to Orthodoxy, pose particular problems, because they stand at the heart of the church's teaching on the Jews and the attitude toward Jews that it is proper for Christians to adopt. Chief among these are *supersessionism* and the accusation of *deicide*.

Supersessionism is the name that has come into use for the belief, which can be traced back to the early church, that the coming of Christ and the establishment of Christianity render Judaism obsolete and redundant. I have called it a belief, and it is indeed a belief that is expressed with great power and rhetorical skill by the fathers of the church and by later writers. But it is also an attitude of mind, and as such it is perhaps just as dangerous and perhaps even harder to dislodge. However venerable its pedigree, supersessionism must be dislodged if there is to be any true meeting between Christians and Jews. Otherwise there is simply not enough common ground for a discussion to take place. This has been widely recognized by Catholics and Protestants involved in dialogue, even if it has yet to take root in the minds of a wider Christian public, and it needs to be understood clearly by all Orthodox participants in the encounter with Judaism. Moreover, the basic conditions for interreligious dialogue are lacking when one side is of the belief, rightly or wrongly, that the aim of the other in engaging in dialogue is evangelical. This has been one of the gravest obstacles to dialogue between Christians and Jews in the past.

"Murderers of the Lord" or "God-killers" is an epithet for Jews in general in the writings of the church fathers and in the Orthodox liturgy for Holy Week. The historical as well as the theological justification for such an expression is dubious in the extreme, but more importantly it has been used as the excuse for violent acts perpetrated by Christians against Jews through the ages to our own time, and it is a serious barrier to encounter between Christians and Jews. It is not alone. Many other adjectives that would not be admitted in polite conversation and are deliberately calculated to provoke hatred are applied to "the Jews" by the fathers and by subsequent Orthodox preachers. The Western churches have finally recognized the need to avoid such language and where necessary to excise it from liturgies (for example, the removal of the phrase "perfidious Jews" from the Good Friday liturgy), but nothing of the sort has been done on the Orthodox side.

When one begins to discuss these issues with Orthodox theologians, it immediately becomes apparent that the fundamental problem is not so much that of ingrained prejudice as of the place of *tradition* within Orthodoxy. Tradition is one of the fundamental pillars of Orthodoxy, and I believe that Jews, particularly Orthodox Jews, must be sensitive to the problems that this raises. These problems are far from being confined to the relations between Jews and Christians but stand in the way of all change. In Orthodox Christianity, as in Orthodox Judaism, tradition has come to be venerated for its own sake, and there is consequently felt to be blanket license to reject all reform or change.

I do not know how this extreme attitude can be overcome, either in
Christians or in Jews, but unless it is overcome I do not see how any
real dialogue or rapprochement can take place.

Indeed one of the most potentially fruitful areas of dialogue is
how as Christians and as Jews we can combine our respective religious
traditions, which we feel to a large extent serve to define our identities
as well as our beliefs, with the demands imposed on us by the modern
societies we inhabit. How much progress may we or indeed ought we
embrace, and where should we draw the lines? I strongly believe that
one of the fruits of dialogue is that we can enrich each others' deliberations and support each others' stands on such questions. Jews and
Christians both know how to value and uphold tradition. But unless we
can abandon a blind and inflexible attachment to whatever has been
expressed in our traditional sources, even if it is blatantly inappropriate
to our present real-life situation, then I fear we shall merely isolate ourselves from each other and from the world around us.

Historical Problems

It hardly needs to be pointed out that, in general, the Jewish experience of Christianity down the ages has been anything but positive.
Within the collective Jewish memory some of the bleakest examples of
this have nothing to do with Orthodoxy—for example, the Spanish
Inquisition or the attacks on Jewish communities in Germany and the
Rhineland. However, other very traumatic experiences that have left a
lasting mark on Jewish memory took place in Orthodox lands (e.g., the
Chmielnicki massacres in the seventeenth century and, more recently,
the Black Hundreds and the pogroms), and even if the churches'
involvement in some of them may be contested, the lasting *impression* is
that the churches at the least did nothing to help the Jewish victims and
at worst that Christians encouraged the violence and even participated
actively. The experience of dialogue with the Western churches suggests
that there is a need to confront these wounds from the past together. The
same might apply to the Christian resentment at a supposed Jewish participation in the persecution of the early Christians, although here it is
hard to find much in the way of concrete historical evidence.

The Nazi genocide stands at the forefront of contemporary Jewish
views of the past, often seeming to block more remote events from view.
The Nazi genocide is a problem for Orthodox–Jewish dialogue from
two different and somewhat contradictory angles. In the first place,

there are memories of Orthodox Christians assisting the Nazis. Nazi sources themselves comment on the willingness and even enthusiasm with which this was done.[1] On the other hand, most Russian Christians who can remember the Second World War had no direct experience of what has been called the "War against the Jews" and today in Russia, largely thanks to deliberate Soviet policies, the public is largely unaware of what took place; this contrasts starkly with a preoccupation with Nazism on the Jewish side that verges on the obsessive. The recent conferences on Auschwitz and the Gulag revealed what a gulf exists in this respect. This gulf too needs to be overcome if there is to be a dialogue, so that Jews and Christians can learn to have sympathy and respect for the other's memory of suffering. In this regard I think there is a definite contrast with the dialogue between Jews and Western Christians: in discussions between Jews and Eastern Christians, suffering has the potential to be a very productive starting-point.

Contemporary Issues

Two concerns within contemporary politics have a direct bearing on Christian-Jewish relations: political antisemitism and the Arab-Israeli conflict. While they properly belong to the realm of politics, both issues spill over into religion. Antisemitism, which has lost all respectability in the West since the war, is still very much alive in Russia, Belarus, the Ukraine, and other Orthodox lands—and sadly the church has not been immune to it. This is a major obstacle to progress. Jews, for obvious reasons, are highly sensitive to antisemitic language and arguments wherever they occur, and it is essential for the church to be purged of antisemitism if there is to be any dialogue with Jews. There is also an intellectual muddle in the minds of many Christians, quite understandably, in that the language of political antisemitism often converges with the traditional Christian theological invective against the Jews, so that less educated Christians may instinctively feel that this invective is somehow justified and rendered relevant by the support it receives from respected sources outside the church. This is most regrettable and demands a special effort from responsible Christian leaders. Needless to say, much political antisemitism in Russia has nothing to do with Christianity and indeed is profoundly hostile to Christianity.

As for the Arab–Israeli conflict, it is hard for people who have been subjected to all kinds of propaganda for fifty years to separate truth from falsehood and sense from nonsense. Antisemitism has been at work here too, cleverly manipulating preexisting anti-Jewish attitudes in relation to the politics of the Middle East. Precisely because the Middle East is so vitally important to Christianity and to Judaism alike, the destiny of the region is a matter on which Jews and Christians ought to be reflecting together, but external political factors render such a dialogue extremely problematical.

OVERCOMING THE OBSTACLES

All these obstacles, needless to say, have to be overcome before there can be a dialogue, and, as I have tried to argue, it is essential for such dialogue to take place. We should bear in mind not only the appalling consequences of the historic antagonism between the church and the Jewish people but also the positive benefits that can accrue from greater openness and encounter. In the first place, there is an opportunity to heal a rift in our societies that, while it may appear of limited significance in some countries, has a very harmful effect in others. Second, the experience with Western churches has demonstrated how much Jews and Christians have to learn from one another, and I believe this to be particularly true as far as relations with the Orthodox churches are concerned. Third, we should not overlook the ecumenical dimension. The ecumenical adventure is revealing to the churches how much they have to gain from exploring together their shared Jewish roots, and the dialogue with present-day Judaism can enrich this process of exploration. At the same time, the revision of traditional attitudes toward Judaism is a topic within ecumenical debate, and there is a two-way relationship between ecumenical dialogue and Jewish-Christian debate.

Given, then, that there is a need for such a dialogue, how can the obstacles be overcome? The theological obstacles, and particularly the unhelpful doctrines of supersessionism and deicide, can only be tackled by a concerted effort of Orthodox theologians and bishops. It would be wrong to underestimate the effort that is required, precisely because both attitudes are so deeply ingrained in the traditional thinking of the churches and are enshrined in venerable texts going right back to the early fathers. But to do nothing, and to permit the ancient poison to continue to do its destructive work, is unthinkable. The groundwork laid in the Western churches, which encompasses a very painful and thorough confrontation with the patristic, and indeed biblical, texts, will be of immeasurable value here, but the Orthodox theologians need to bring their own distinctive perspective to bear. Above all, they have to have the will to make the effort, and this first step is perhaps the hardest one.

While the initial moves on the Christian side must come from bishops and theologians, in Orthodox Christianity the consent of the laity is a crucial element in any progress, and so there is a great task of education and persuasion to be undertaken. The role of liturgy is not to be underestimated. There is an obvious and entirely understandable reluctance to revise ancient and cherished prayers and hymns for the sake of political correctness. However, liturgies have a vital teaching role, and they inculcate theological attitudes in the minds of the "simple faithful" with great effectiveness. It is therefore essential that the liturgies reflect the thinking of the church, and when aspects of that thinking are revised or restated it is vitally important that the changes of emphasis should be reflected in prayers and hymns, and not only in sermons and publications. As the experience of the Western churches has shown, there is a very serious problem with the lectionary too. Scriptural readings have an unrivalled commanding authority, and it is painful to note that certain readings, particularly those for Holy Week, have played and continue to play a part in fostering anti-Jewish attitudes among simple Christians. The answer, in my view, does not lie in censoring scripture but in interpreting and explaining it so that the message derived from the readings is always healthy and beneficial—I believe that this approach is in keeping with the perennial teaching of the church.

In terms of the historical problems I have outlined, I believe that both sides have a part to play. Orthodox Christians need to understand the part played today by the Shoah in the collective Jewish consciousness. This is not difficult in countries such as Greece or Bulgaria that witnessed the deportations and in which some Christians, both bishops and ordinary believers, stood out from the mass and actively helped the Jewish victims, frequently at the risk of their lives. In other countries, however, there is less understanding of the issues—this is a particular problem in Russia, where the numbers of Christians, and indeed Jews, are greater than elsewhere and where the Christian memory of the Gulag can occupy such a primordial place that it can interfere with any effort to understand the memory of Jewish suffering. But here we are not speaking about a prerequisite for dialogue but rather a barrier that will gradually be eroded as Christians and Jews come to know each other better and share their feelings about the past. In due course the memory of the involvement of Christians as persecutors of Jews will need to be confronted as indeed will be the accusations (however ill or well founded) on the Christian side that Jews have taken part in persecutions of Christians. This work is best undertaken once the ground for dialogue has been securely laid.

Contemporary antisemitism is another matter. This hateful doctrine is far too prevalent in political life today in Russia and neighboring countries, and needs to be eradicated for the good of society as a whole not just for the sake of the Jewish minority. It is appalling that the irrational rhetoric of hate and the false historical claims associated with this movement are found within some of the Orthodox churches, including most notably the Russian Orthodox Church. (One need only mention in this connection the book *The Autocracy of the Spirit* by a leading thinker of the Russian Orthodox Church, the late metropolitan John Snychev of St. Petersburg, published in 1994, which gives an authoritative contemporary voice to the discredited *Protocols of the Elders of Zion* and other antisemitic writings.[2] This book was warmly welcomed and endorsed by other leading figures of the church.) The Orthodox churches owe it to their own dignity and self-respect to purge themselves of the traces of this monstrous and alien creed, which is regrettably given a foothold within their bosoms by the venerable tradition of theological anti-Jewish rhetoric to which I have already referred.

The presence of Orthodox churches in the Middle East and the challenge this presence presents for Christian-Jewish relations will have to be confronted within the framework of an interreligious dialogue. The only precondition is that both sides should adopt a reasonable and reasoned approach and endeavor to let the facts take precedence over prejudices. There is much suspicion and misinformation on both sides, and this can gradually be broken down by personal encounter as well as by appropriate publications, including the present book.

CONCLUSIONS

The wounds of the past need time to heal; that much is certain. We need to face up to the memories of the past, but it is a mistake to rake over the ashes while the fire is still burning. The problem of resentments founded on history has been faced already in dialogue between Jews and Roman Catholics, particularly. The resentments, notably of the treatment of Jews in the past at the hands of Catholics, were very deep, and yet with time and goodwill it has been possible to achieve a strong sense of reconciliation, which bodes well for a future dialogue between Jews and Orthodox Christians.

Naturally it takes two to dialogue. So far, however, neither side has expressed much interest in opening a dialogue; I have tried to suggest some reasons why this situation must change. The churches have a vital part to play in this dialogue, and it would be good if they could be seen to initiate it and not be dragging their feet as unwilling partners. On the Jewish side I am not sure that there is any specific reluctance; the lack of initiative is probably to be ascribed to lack of interest.

Once the obstacles I have mentioned are overcome (as they must be if dialogue is to proceed), I believe there is scope for a very fruitful exchange. Leaving aside the historical and organizational questions, there is very rich potential for theological dialogue. Whereas in the case of dialogue with the Western churches the initiative on the Jewish side has lain mainly (though by no means exclusively) with the theologically progressive wing of Jewry, in the case of Orthodox Christianity there is real scope for Orthodox Jewish theologians to become involved because of the analogous problems facing Jewish and Christian Orthodoxy in today's world. Both alike are confronted with pressure to adapt to modernity, and this pressure conflicts forcefully with their deeply rooted commitment to tradition. As I have suggested above, this commitment to tradition is of a different order from that which is present, to a greater or lesser degree, in all long-established religions, because it is part of the very fabric of Orthodoxy, an essential aspect of its unique identity. I believe that Orthodox Christian theologians and Orthodox Jewish thinkers are in a position, if they so desire, to teach each other from the standpoint of their respective experiences of modernity, and this debate can help them also in articulating their positions to their own co-religionists.

All this is still a pipe dream, however. True dialogue lies far in the future and will entail a great effort, particularly, as I have tried to argue, on the Christian side. But already there are small beacons of light — local initiatives that have begun to bear small fruits and the meetings of academics to which I referred at the beginning. What is needed now is a framework for dialogue that will build on the foundations that have been laid and ensure that progress can be achieved.

There is also a great need for education, on both sides. Christians tend to derive their knowledge of Judaism from Christian, not Jewish, sources. Inevitably what they learn is distorted. The same is true of Jews: they tend to learn about Christianity from Jewish publications, which cannot present an authentic picture. There is a great need for Jews and Christians to educate each other about their respective faiths. This is part of what dialogue is about.

I realize that some may regard my outlook as excessively optimistic. I do not underestimate the difficulties, and I have spelled out obstacles to dialogue that are enormous. However I have also tried to argue that the times we live in demand that we make the effort to overcome these obstacles. The horrors of the Shoah brought home clearly to some far-sighted individuals that the rift between Jews and Christians had to be healed if similar monstrosities were to be avoided in the future. The resurgence of antisemitism in Russia today is a warning of the urgency of extending this healing work to the Orthodox churches.[3]

NOTES

1. See in brief on this period Jane Ellis, *The Russian Orthodox Church: A Contemporary History* (London: Routledge, 1986), 4, 14.

2. *The Autocracy of the Spirit* [Samoderzhaviye dukha] (St. Petersburg: Tsarskoye delo, 1994). The book is discussed in a review by I. Levinskaya, "Ranny Gitler, Pozdny Stalin, niezlobivy Ivan Grozniy i drugiye," *Barier* (St. Petersburg 1994), 11–13 (English translation in *Churchman* 109 [1995]; 171–80); and by Y. Tabak, "Relations between the Russian Orthodox Church and Judaism: Past and Present," at www.jcrelations.net/en/?id=787 (posted 2000).

3. For further reading on Jewish–Orthodox relations, see Nifon Mihaita, ed., *The Christian Orthodox–Jewish Consultation II (Bucharest, October 29–31, 1979)* (Bucharest, 1979); Zvi Ankori, "Encounter in History: Jews and Christian Greeks in their Relation through the Ages" [in Hebrew] *Yehude Yawan le-dorotam* 1 (Tel Aviv: University of Tel Aviv, 1984); George C. Papademetriou, *Essays on Orthodox Christian–Jewish Relations* (Lima, OH: Wyndham Hall Press, 1991); Malcolm Lowe, ed., *Orthodox Christians and Jews on Continuity and Renewal (Immanuel 26/27)* (Jerusalem, 1994); and Thomas Kratzert, *Wir sind wie die Juden: Der griechisch-orthodoxe Beitrag zu einem ökumenischen jüdisch-christlichen Dialog* (Berlin: Inst. Kirche und Judentum, 1994).

5
Jewish–Russian Orthodox Christian Dialogue

Irina Levinskaya

If we look at the contents of this book we can see that the dialogue between Jews and Orthodox Christians is marked as a separate issue. This singling out of a particular Christian denomination in a work on Jewish-Christian relations is wholly justified. While Jews and churches of the Roman tradition have come a long way down the road of mutual understanding and respect, and can now discuss particular and subtle issues in a dialogue, Orthodox Christians are only on the threshold of starting a dialogue with Judaism. For many Orthodox Christians the very idea of such a dialogue seems alien. This is especially true for Orthodox Christians in Russia.

There are various reasons for this. Orthodoxy is well known for its careful and loving attitude toward its patristic heritage. It is nearly as important and sacred as scripture itself. The deep meditation over patristic tradition gives Orthodox Christians a unique feeling of presence at, and participation in, the very beginning of Christian theological thought. But the other side of the coin is that Christian theology was born on the battlefield of ideas. Under the influence of the somewhat militant writings of early church fathers and without careful attention to their historical background, the balance of modern theological thought can easily be tipped to the side of fighting. The belief that Jews were responsible for the death of God is found repeatedly in writings of the church fathers. The accusation of *deicide* appears in the writings of Melito, the bishop of Sardis, St. Augustine, and St. John Chrysostom.

The latter name is particularly important, since St. John Chrysostom is among the most respected and revered church fathers in the Orthodox tradition. It is especially difficult for Orthodox Christians to accept that John Chrysostom, whose anti-Jewish homilies were translated into Russian as early as the eleventh century, could be wrong, or to recognize the ancient rhetorical conventions or the specific historical situation in ancient Antioch for the background of his anti-Jewish sermons.

Besides patristic writings Orthodox Christians encounter anti-Jewish statements in the liturgy. The traditionalism of the Orthodox Church prevents it from editing the liturgy. In some parishes in the West the Orthodox liturgy has been purified of anti-Jewish statements, and supersessionist or anti-Judaic parts have been taken away. But this has happened *un*officially and at the initiative of certain conscientious priests, while the printed official liturgical books remain the same. In the meantime the editing of the liturgy not only is necessary, it is urgent. As Father Yves Dubois, an Orthodox priest who has introduced changes into the liturgy in his Orthodox parish in Bath, England, stresses, "the urgency of a break away from anti-Judaism in the liturgical texts of the Orthodox Church is increased by the presence of anti-semitism in our Church."[1]

An anti-Judaic and antisemitic strand in the Orthodox Church is very deep and visible at all levels. Let me give just two examples. Quite recently a book was published under the title, *The Good News according to St Paul and Jewish Rabbinical Theology.*[2] The author is Nicholai Glubokovsky, an Orthodox theologian who was a professor at St. Petersburg Theological Seminary at the beginning of the twentieth century. After the communist coup d'état he emigrated from Russia and lived in Bulgaria. The book was originally published before his emigration. I am not going to discuss it here, but it is sufficient to say that it is dated and is typical of that period, which lacked the idea of a dialogue with Judaism. But even worse than the publication of a dated book is the fact that it was published in an abbreviated form and that the abbreviations were made in such a way that the book appears to be even more anti-Judaic than the original longer version. At the end of the book there is a small glossary. I'll cite just one entry: "Pharisees—a Jewish sect, whose adherents are marked by pride, hypocrisy, pretended piety and inner uncleanness." In the modern period such language is impossible for Western Christianity. Yet, it is still quite normal for Orthodox Christians.

It is often and quite rightly stressed that the unity of the Old Testament and the New Testament and the impossibility of seeing differences in the One God of both are essential to Orthodox theology. This seems to be a promising starting point. But this unity can be and is treated by some Orthodox theologians in an anti-Judaic way. A recently published book *How They Make Anti-Semites*,[3] written by Andrej Kuraev, a deacon of the Russian Orthodox Church and one of the most widely published modern theologians, witnesses to this. "Without Christ the Old Testament is perhaps the most terrible book in the religious history of humankind," writes Kuraev. "You should not read the Bible as a national chronicle, i.e. through Jewish eyes. One can respect this book only after it is taken away (or rather pulled out) from the Jews" (65).

The actual absence of Orthodox–Jewish dialogue can be and usually is explained by the traditionalism of the Orthodox Church, which incorporates the anti-Judaism that has been inherited from tradition. This sort of explanation is undoubtedly correct, but much remains to be said.

I suggest that we should take a sociological perspective on the problems of Jewish–Orthodox Christian dialogue. It is usually the intellectuals—theologians, religious thinkers, scholars—who push for the dialogue between different religious traditions. It is worthwhile remembering that most members of this social stratum in Russia have no religious background. They were brought up in an atheistic environment. For those who did become religious in the Soviet period, religion was their personal choice and a kind of challenge not only to themselves but also to society. It was a symbolic act of rejecting the values of the inhuman state in which they were born. Now that Russia is in a period of transition many people feel frustrated and lost, and they turn to religion in an attempt to find their identity. Both Jews and Christians in Russia are trying to reestablish their roots—we are in reality talking about a dialogue of neophytes. And this is important.

Such a situation has both advantages and disadvantages. It is easy to see the advantages. One could use the positive experience of other traditions and therefore not have to start from scratch. The disadvantages are, however, rather serious. People who look into the past in an attempt to find out something crucially important to them usually see this past in a rather idealized way, and they tend to lack the necessary critical attitude toward their tradition. They feel themselves bound by it. They do not feel intellectually free to introduce any changes. They are looking for answers to present-day questions in the books of those whom they see as their spiritual authority, that is, in the books of nineteenth- and twentieth-century Orthodox religious philosophers. This complicates Jewish–Orthodox relations even more, since nineteenth- and twentieth-century Orthodox thought does not encourage dialogue.

For Russian religious thinkers of this period the issue of Judaism was crucially important. The most famous of them, such as Solovyev, Berdyaev, and Karsavin, were deeply preoccupied with it.[4] This preoccupation was fatal but understandable given the fact that the Orthodox tradition is much closer to Judaism than any other Christian denomination. The liturgy of the Orthodox Church has retained more traditional ancient features than the liturgy of Western Christians. This similarity between Judaism and Orthodox Christianity was deeply felt by many distinguished Russian theologians.

The first name that should be mentioned in this connection is Vladimir Solovyev. He was born in 1853 to the family of a distinguished historian. He died at the age of forty-seven. Vladimir Solovyev was a religious philosopher, theologian, mystic, and poet. He was, perhaps, the most important figure for Orthodox Christian thought in Russia in the nineteenth century. His impact on the development of religious philosophy in the twentieth century cannot be overestimated, representing a creative understanding of the Orthodox tradition. He knew Hebrew and had many Jewish intellectuals among his friends. He even raised his voice in defense of the civil rights of Jews. But for him, as for his contemporaries, the future of Jewish-Christian relations was not in a dialogue. As he wrote in his article "Jews and the Question of Christianity," "the best part of Israel would join the Christian Theocracy."

Solovyev lived in the nineteenth century. Let us look at a more modern authority. Lev Karsavin was a philosopher and theologian who tragically perished in the Gulag and whose heritage has recently become very influential. Much of his work is now accessible, including an article entitled "Russia and the Jews," which was originally published in 1928. In this article he describes the similarities between Orthodox Christianity and Judaism. In his view, both Russians and Jews are essentially religious and have as their aim the triumph of their faiths. The Orthodox idea of *sobornost* (catholicity, collegiality, *koinonia*) is the purified Jewish idea of *kahal* (community). Both Judaism and Christianity try to fill their everyday life with religion.

The Russian messianic idea is similar to the Jewish. For Karsavin, Judaism was an ontological rival of Christianity and this heavily influenced the attitude toward Judaism on the part of many Russian religious philosophers. It was the basis of their preoccupation with Judaism, the reason why they again and again returned to discussions about Judaism versus Christianity. If there is only one truth and one God, and if Christ is the Savior, how is it possible for both Jews and Christians to be the people of God, to be the True Israel? The philosophers conclude that Jews *must* convert to Christianity.

The article by Karsavin is a provocative text. As the author made clear at the very beginning, he was well aware of the fact that he would be accused of antisemitism. And he did give grounds for such an accusation. Karsavin divided all Jews into two groups: the ones who had lost their national identity and the ones who had preserved it. He insisted that Jews who belong to the first category must be vigorously tackled, since he thought that they were a real threat to both Jews and Christians. They were the destructive force that stood behind the Russian revolution. Those Jews who belong to the second category, although the natural and eternal enemies of Orthodoxy, must be treated differently. The only acceptable form of struggle with them is love. But love, as Karsavin puts it, is an active force, which has as its aim the good of the beloved, and, since the real goal is for Jews to convert to Orthodox Christianity, Orthodox Christians must wish for their conversion. Of course, he added, conversion must be voluntary and Jews must form a separate Jewish Orthodox Christian Church. However, this is not a suitable starting point for Jewish-Christian dialogue. In fact, it prevents such a dialogue from happening at all!

Now, imagine people who are neophytes in the world of religion and who therefore at the same time feel themselves bound by tradition. On the one hand, in the patristic texts and in their church they find traditional anti-Judaism and antisemitism, while on the other hand, in the books produced by the most influential religious thinkers and theologians of the past, they discover that sympathetic feelings toward Jews sit side by side with a belief that the best fate for Jews is to convert to Christianity.

With all these difficulties in mind is there any future for real dialogue? I think that there is. The starting point for real dialogue could be theological reflection on suffering. The Holocaust made the problem of suffering central to Jewish religious thought. Questions such as: How could the all-loving God fail to intervene to prevent the tragedy to happen? or, Does human suffering question the power of God? continue to be raised. These are precisely the questions that Russian religious thinkers struggled with in the nineteenth century and that are now once more on the agenda after the tragic Russian history of the twentieth century. Sometimes this preoccupation with suffering could be viewed from outside in a rather peculiar way. I remember reading an article in the British newspaper *The Independent* in which a journalist seriously maintained that Russians simply love to suffer. He treated the Russians as a nation of masochists.

Not being masochists, Russian religious writers have, however, again and again asked the same questions: How could the world be so evil? How can evil and suffering exist if God is all loving and merciful? The problem of suffering is a burning issue in Russian religious thought. This is epitomized by Dostoyevsky in Ivan Karamazov's rejection of a harmony in God's plan for the world should it be based on one tear of one tortured child. In my youth there was a group of Christian intellectuals in St. Petersburg who took Ivan Karamazov's position as a personal challenge. They exchanged letters as they reflected on this problem and tried to find an answer. Not surprisingly they did not find an answer that could be accepted as satisfactory, but a number of important issues emerged from their discussions and helped fill the gap between personal experience and philosophical abstraction. I think that taking a central human problem, one that is of concern to every religious person, is surely a promising way to begin a dialogue.

NOTES

1. H. P. Fry, ed., *Christian-Jewish Dialogue: A Reader* (Exeter: University of Exeter Press, 1996), 35.

2. Nicholai Glubokovsky, *The Good News according to St Paul and Jewish Rabbinical Theology* (St. Petersburg: Svetoslov, 1998).

3. Andrej Kuraev, *How They Make Anti-Semites* (Moscow: Odigitria, 1998).

4. For a recent study in English of Solovyev's thought, see P. Valliere, *Modern Russian Theology—Bukharev, Soloviev, Bulgakov: Orthodox Theology in a New Key* (Edinburgh: T&T Clark, 2000).

6
Catholic-Jewish Agendas

Remi Hoeckman, OP

The introduction written by the editors of this volume could not have been clearer when it stated the aims of the book, the questions that it intends to address, and the kind of authors that the editors were looking for. With regard to the last item, the introduction reads as follows, "The choice of authors here has been guided by a selection of those who are able to combine an academic perspective on the subject with real practical experience of Jewish-Christian relations." I can assure you that Jewish-Christian relations have filled my days, and at times also my nights, for the past seven years. I shall reflect on the theme from that perspective.

I would first of all like to state that the theme is both relevant and timely as far as the Holy See's Commission for Religious Relations with the Jews is concerned. As a matter of fact, the question of agenda has preoccupied our minds for quite some time.[1] Looking back at our experience in this regard, one can say that our partnership with IJCIC (the International Jewish Committee on Interreligious Consultations) in the ILC (the International Catholic-Jewish Liaison Committee), a body that was set up toward the end of 1970, has undoubtedly been fruitful in the past. The ILC was an official linking body between the Catholic Church, through the Holy See's Commission for Religious Relations with the Jews, and the Jewish community, insofar as the Jewish community at large felt that IJCIC (i.e., the organizations and agencies of which IJCIC is composed) was in fact representing them. Over the years, especially the past five years, many Jews have come to

69

tell us that it is not. However, since the specifically religious component of IJCIC, that is, the Synagogue Council of America, disappeared
from the IJCIC scene a few years ago, IJCIC became a body of secular
organizations, each bringing its own agenda to the dialogue table—an
agenda that we refuse to accept any longer as the basis for an encounter
that should respect the aspirations and sensitivities of *both* parties
involved. Moreover, we find a "partnership" with bodies and individuals that have engaged in a destructive campaign against us, and the situation is unacceptable.

An American Jewish leader, Rabbi Henry Siegman, already saw
the point being addressed in a paper thirty years ago. In the reassessment of "Ten Years of Catholic-Jewish Relations" that he presented
to the ILC meeting in Jerusalem in 1976, he made the following
remarks:

> If the past ten years have taught us anything, it is that we
> come to each other with different agendas....Taking full
> advantage of the prerequisite of the injured party, Jews have
> successfully managed the dialogue so that it has focused
> entirely on what we consider to be Christian failings....
>
> I suppose that Christian forbearance with this one-
> sided situation is compounded of a sense of guilt and of
> *noblesse oblige*. However, it is a situation which cannot per-
> sist for long...because our Christian partners are not likely
> to continue the dialogue on these terms....
>
> I say all of this with diffidence and even trepidation,
> not only because, even now, sensitivities are still raw on
> both sides..., but primarily because I do not wish to encour-
> age the notion that the *Shoah* be exploited as a device to
> generate Christian guilt, and thereby to manipulate the rela-
> tionship in ways that give the Jewish side an advantage.
> Such manipulations must be seen as a desecration of the
> memory of the victims and utterly destructive of the real
> hope which the dialogue holds.[2]

On the same occasion Rabbi Siegman also made a reference, quite
rightly—and courageously in my opinion—to a tendency among Jews
to "weigh the volume of public statements made by Christian officials in

support of Jewish causes," and to their use of pressure through the mass media. "I have come to the conclusion," he said:

> that there is something particularly distortive of the relationship, and misleading of its genuine character and depth in the frenetic efforts in which we engage with such monotonous regularity to extract public statements from Christian officials at every turn in Jewish affairs. Indeed, it seems to have become a major industry of American Jewish life, whose major beneficiaries, insofar as I can tell, are the advertising agencies and metropolitan newspapers. Of course, Jewish existence continues to be fragile and vulnerable, and we need understanding friendship and public support as desperately as we ever did. But if these are to have any meaning and practical consequence, then they must be spontaneous expressions rather than ritualistic responses to heavy-handed pressure exerted by Jewish organizations, including my own.[3]

This is plain language, and it is with the same diffidence that Rabbi Siegman felt thirty years ago that I am quoting it to you today.

At a symposium held at the Van Leer Institute in Jerusalem in February 1997, Daniel Rossing, a Jewish educator with a long record of experience in Jewish-Christian dialogue in the West and in Israel, has been outspoken too. "I think it is obvious to all who have labored in the vineyard of Jewish-Catholic relations that nearly all of the changes which have brought about the vast improvements in relations have taken place on the Catholic side," he said, and "in the light of the historic record of the Church's relations with the Jewish people, it is fully understandable that the dialogue in the West has for the most part been a one-way street, at least in terms of the re-examination of traditional attitudes." However, Rossing expressed the hope that today the "historic changes" that have occurred since the Second Vatican Council, "will also enter the consciousness of the inhabitants of this land [Israel], and most especially the hearts and minds of Jews."

At a symposium held at the Columbus School of Law at the Catholic University of America in Washington, DC, in April 1997, I addressed the same issue, then quoting in a footnote some of the above-mentioned observations made by Henry Siegman. Today, unfortunately, they need to be stated in the text itself. In fact, I did do this one year later, in April 1998, when I addressed an international conference on the Holocaust at the University of Notre Dame, Indiana.

In Washington, DC, when I was a little more optimistic than I am now with regard to relations with Jewish agencies and organizations (and I am speaking not about a great number of Jewish individuals, local community leaders, and scholars to whom we relate very well indeed), I insisted on the need to be truthful in our dialogue, the need for transparency in proposing (or imposing) agendas, the need to respect the feelings and understanding of *both* sides. Our relations, I said, must become far more a reciprocal discovery of one another, of one another's heritage and tradition, of one another's values and spiritual potential, as well as of one another's aspirations and fears. Such a venture, I insisted, rooted in a common spiritual patrimony and in respect for one another's faith convictions, but also in the human friendship that we can share could—far from being short-term opportunism—become a blessing to both ourselves and the rest of the world. A question that Rabbi Siegman had already asked twenty years before, namely, "what impels us to dialogue, and what does each of us seek to get out of it?" I had quite often asked myself with regard to the agendas of certain Jewish organizations that were in contact with us, agendas that were often disguised as, or wrapped up in, "interfaith dialogue."

At Notre Dame, where I spoke on the theme "The Jewish-Christian Encounter: A Matter of Faith?" I looked at the meaning of those terms (dialogue, encounter, faith) in the realm of the Jewish-Catholic relations that I experience day after day. I stated then, as I do now, that before anything else I am a person of faith who does believe in interfaith encounter and interreligious dialogue, but I have a problem with what I feel is an ambiguous use of these words. There is great potential inherent in sharing and discovery, growth and promise, especially in the realm of Jewish-Christian relations and dialogue, which provide a space where hearts meet hearts and minds meet minds, and where these can be informed and transformed in the process. But this is all too easily emptied of its religious content and filled with something else. In my dealings with interfaith affairs, interfaith institutes, interfaith programs, interfaith relations, interfaith dialogue, interfaith groups, and interfaith directors, I often have difficulty with finding any religious content in those affairs, programs, or dialogues. I warned then, as I do now, that excessive concern for bolstering organizational and private ambitions, agendas, and policies, and for the lobbying and media campaigns that go with it—at the expense of what I believe to be a genuine encounter between equal partners in which mutual trust and respect for sensitivities are essential—can easily become counterproductive. As a matter of fact it *is* becoming counterproductive. An increasing number of Catholic people who are quite open to the new spirit that is slowly growing between Catholics and Jews, and to which we in our commission are totally committed, are tired of unrelenting pressure in matters and issues that not only pertain to Jewish concerns but that also deeply touch *their own* concerns, convictions, and sensitivities. They refuse to be continually forced into producing so-called lasting answers to nagging doubts[4] by people who, they suspect, are doing their best to keep those nagging doubts alive. What Rabbi Siegman had so clearly warned his fellow Jews about in 1976 (and which went unheeded) is unfortunately happening today.

However—and I would like to underline that I am entering now that part of my assessment that really matters—when I listen to people such as the Orthodox chief rabbi Jonathan Sacks or the Reform rabbi Tony Bayfield in the United Kingdom, both representing quite different traditions in Judaism, I realize that Jewish persons of *faith,* in spite of their differences, do in fact share with us an agenda for the future. Also the Orthodox rabbi David Rosen, the president of the International Council of Christians and Jews, pointed to this in an interview with the ecumenical news service of the World Council of Churches on September 17, 1998, spelling out what, in his opinion, the agenda is. "I think we have to try to have a deeper communion," he said, "while respecting the very fundamental differences. I see us as partners in divine destiny with two different models of the message." In spite of the serious problems and difficulties that both faith communities find themselves coping with, including their very relationships with each other, I too am convinced that we are able to move ahead in genuine dialogue and, in many instances, in giving common witness to the religious values that we share, the moral principles placed in our hands by the One who created this world and that are set down in the Holy Scriptures that both our faith communities revere.

The president of our commission, Edward Idris Cardinal Cassidy, made the same point on February 10, 1997, on the occasion of the above-mentioned symposium at the Van Leer Institute in Jerusalem, which reflected on the theme "The Future of Catholic-Jewish Relations in Israel." Speaking on what our commission believes to be the current issues in those relations, the cardinal stated that in our opinion the present task is to determine precisely what it is that we can do, what we should do, and *with whom* we should be in partnership in order to take forward the good work that has been done in the past. We must, it seems to me, he said, move on from the constant examination of difficulties in our bilateral relations to joint action in favor of the moral values that as *faith* communities we share. In fact, at this point in the history of our relations, our commission is convinced of the need for a dialogue that goes beyond the discussion of problems and enters into the very heart of what constitutes our identities as faith communities, in order to allow us to proceed – on that basis – along the path of common action in today's society.[5]

This direction in Jewish-Catholic relations had already been jointly decided upon (i.e., by Jews and Catholics together) at the thirteenth meeting of the ILC, which took place in Prague in September 1990. The statement that the Prague meeting made public began by acknowledging the monumental role of the Second Vatican Council's declaration *Nostra Aetate* as well as the role of later efforts by the popes and church officials to bring about a substantial improvement in Catholic-Jewish relations ("*Nostra Aetate* created a new spirit in these relationships," the statement says). It then proceeded to call for a deepening of this spirit, "which emphasizes cooperation, mutual understanding and reconciliation; goodwill and common goals to replace the past spirit of suspicion, resentment and distrust." Moreover, the joint statement insisted, this new spirit should also manifest itself in the work that our two faith communities could do together to respond to the needs of today's world. These needs were spelled out too, "This need is for the establishment of human rights, freedom and dignity where they are lacking or imperiled, and for responsible stewardship of the environment." The statement concluded on a hopeful note:

> After two millennia of estrangement and hostility, we have a sacred duty as Catholics and Jews to strive to create a genuine culture of mutual esteem and reciprocal caring. Catholic-Jewish dialogue can become a sign of hope and inspiration to other religions, races, and ethnic groups to turn away from contempt, toward realizing authentic human fraternity. The new spirit of friendship and caring for one

another may be the most important symbol that we have to offer to our troubled world.[6]

What a worthwhile agenda this is!

The ILC Jerusalem meeting in 1994 embraced and reconfirmed this view in its conclusions by adopting Pope John Paul II's message to the people of his native land, Poland, on the occasion of the fiftieth anniversary of the Warsaw Ghetto Uprising: "As Christians and Jews, following the example of the faith of Abraham, we are called to be a blessing for the world (cf. Gen. 12:2 ff). This is the common task awaiting us. It is therefore necessary for us, Christians and Jews, to be first a blessing to one another," he said.[7] In fact, the agenda we had before us in Jerusalem was intended to carry forward what took place at the Prague meeting and what had been confirmed two years later at the ILC meeting in Baltimore, where we decided to seek to become more effective instruments to respond to and indeed to anticipate a variety of challenges in today's world, to which both our faith communities are called to respond. The Baltimore statement emphasized our common duty to build together on a new world "in which differences are addressed in quiet and constructive dialogue rather than fractious accusations."[8]

At the 1994 Jerusalem meeting (in which, as in the previous meeting, Orthodox Jewish scholars also participated), we were able to produce a *Common Declaration on the Family,* and we started to work on a *Common Declaration on the Environment* that was published in the spring of 1998 at the last ILC meeting that took place in the Vatican.[9] In the meantime the ILC steering committee, meeting in Geneva, had jointly prepared the draft of what I thought to be an excellent *Common Statement on Violence,* which was expected to be approved by the ILC at its sixteenth meeting, scheduled to take place in Buenos Aires in April 1996. However, this meeting had to be cancelled at the very last moment because—in my personal, but I believe informed, opinion—some of our IJCIC partners seemed to fear that someone else also belonging to IJCIC might steal the show. In fact, another Catholic-Jewish meeting was going to take place in Buenos Aires more or less at the same time. In any case, you might be interested to read the text of the *Common Statement on Violence,* which, as it turned out, was never stated at all.[10] I must confess, however, that I have resented the fact that by the cancellation of the Buenos Aires meeting, on rather trivial grounds, the common good had been sacrificed on the altar of personal ambition, and the Catholic-

Jewish dialogue hijacked by an organizational agenda. On the other hand, it is also true that incidents such as this one contribute to a major transparency of certain dynamics at work. Far more important, however, is the fact that we in the Catholic Church, together with the many Jewish friends who do believe in the possibility of and the need for a common agenda, have continued to work in the meantime in fields such as education, knowing that *both* Jews and Christians badly need to be informed about the new reality that, in spite of destructive actions in some quarters, is emerging between us but that still needs to be received by the majority of the people in our respective communities. "We well know the abyss of ignorance in both our communities concerning the other, which includes dangerous myths and prejudices," the late Geoffrey Wigoder of the Jewish Council of Interreligious Consultations in Israel admitted in his keynote address to the participants of the 1994 ILC Jerusalem meeting. In those situations, though, where the process of reception does take place and where, therefore, a genuine interfaith encounter between Jews and Christians can really happen, Christians and Jews are enabled to discover an agenda that, I believe, is offered to us from above. Rabbi Irving Greenberg, an Orthodox theologian, has put it like this: "If committed and believing Christians and Jews can discover the image of God in each other, if they can uncover and affirm each other's proper role in the overall divine strategy of redemption, surely the inspiration of their example would bring the kingdom of God that much closer for everyone."[11] The point is that we are talking here about Jews and Christians of *faith,* believing people who are—in faithfulness to their respective faith traditions—committed to the will of God.

Cardinal Cassidy has spoken on this important matter also—important because it signifies a turning point in our relations with the Jews—in his opening address to the ILC meeting on March 23, 1998. "We have as our heritage twenty-seven years of difficult and important work done by the ILC," he said,

> At the same time, there are serious questions that call for our common reflections. Has the ILC still a valid reason for existing? And if so, what should be our future role in regard to Jewish-Catholic relations? Now we need to set ourselves common goals, rooted in our separate but in many aspects similar faith traditions. We are called to be a blessing to the world. That is our common destiny. To do that effectively,

however, we must—as Pope John Paul II has pointed out—firstly be a blessing to each other. And for that we need mutual understanding, reconciliation and good-will. I should like that we ask ourselves, Jews and Catholics, if we are satisfied with the progress made in this connection. Have we, in fact, a *deep mutual understanding,* one of the other? Or, rather, do we not continue in some ways to cling to "the past spirit of suspicion, resentment and distrust"? The work of mutual understanding is not easy, yet it is essential if we are to build a solid relationship that will be able to resist whatever difficulties the future may hold. I can honestly say that we have tried to base our dialogue on this basis. Not everyone in our Church has fully absorbed the new spirit of mutual understanding. We continue our efforts. But I have to ask our Jewish friends, if they are making the same kind of effort to understand the Catholic Church and its position on [certain] matters.[12]

On quite a number of issues our positions converge because of the common heritage that Jews and Christians have. We do have a message, a vision, that we can share with the world, but as Rabbis Jack Bemporad and Michael Shevack have pointed out in their good little book *Our Age,* "this work has been weakened, because we have been unable to feel comfortable with the fundamental theological differences that have separated us, or because we have still been entrenched in past pain."[13]

As far as our commission is concerned, this awareness, this experience and vision, must set the agenda for the future, and we know that many of our Jewish friends share this vision with us. That is why we wish to relate to these Jewish brothers and sisters, to engage in a constructive and enriching dialogue with them, on a *religious* basis. We will gladly, and I am quite sure also fruitfully, work together with believing Jewish partners with whom we can *share* the agenda, whatever religious tradition within Judaism they belong to. Hence, Christians and Jews will be able to find one another on a far deeper level than has been the case until now, able to stand together in responding to the serious challenges that both faith communities have to face in today's society—rising secularism, religious apathy, and moral confusion in a world in which there is little room for God.

Moreover, as Cardinal Cassidy has pointed out in an address to the American Jewish Committee in May 1998, it may be wise to keep in mind the possibility that a society with little room for God may one day have little room for those men and women who believe in God and wish to live according to his law and commandments.[14] In fact, the cardinal had already expressed this concern of ours at the last ILC meeting. Against a background of continuing pressure and lamentations on the part of some of the Jewish organizations that were rather eager to use the meeting for their own purposes, and undoubtedly having in mind the good resolutions of the 1990 ILC Prague meeting, he stated:

How much better would our world be were Catholics and Jews to come together better to know each other, and in common cause to act in order to uplift their communities! In most of the societies in which we live, the basic philosophy of life has in the past been firmly established on Judeo-Christian traditions and values. But that is becoming less and less the case. Is there anything that we should seek to do together in order to preserve these traditions that are so often threatened...?

The erosion of the fundamental God-oriented pillars of our Western civilisation will necessarily have a negative effect eventually on respect for human rights. The denial of the existence of God and a consequent understanding of good and evil result inevitably in a loss of respect for the other. What makes a man or woman valuable, irrespective of race or social standing, if there is no divine plan, if each man and woman is not created in the image of God ?

Belief in the divinity and in the divine creation of human nobility are fundamental to Catholic and Jewish traditions. Here we have the possibility of building together, of standing together against ideologies and systems that can lead once again to men and women, children of the one God, being despised just for what they are, and even for the world to be considered a better place without them....Let us not forget that there is still evil in the world. Those who created the gas-chambers and the gulags were atheists who, while denying the existence of a God, acted as though they themselves were God! There is no reason to feel comfortable that future atheists will not again consider themselves equal to God.[15]

These phrases clearly spell out our vision and understanding. We do believe in the need for Jews and Christians to have a more profound knowledge of one another as faith communities, while maintaining their distinct identities, to witness together to a new conscience of *partnership* founded on a common nucleus of faith as contained in the Holy Scriptures that we share. It is indeed time for us to go "beyond apologies."[16] Our communities need it, and the world in which we live needs it.

Rabbi Ismar Schorsch, a conservative Jewish scholar and professor at the Jewish Theological Seminary in New York City, has put it even more strongly at a seminar on *Nostra Aetate* at Fordham University on November 20, 1995. "The time has come for us to move beyond dialogue," he said, so that Catholics and Jews can "address the weakening of the moral fiber of...society."[17] In a different context, Pope John Paul II expressed a similar conviction in an address to the Diplomatic Corps accredited to the Holy See. "What the international community perhaps lacks most of all today is not written conventions or forums for self-expression," he said, "but a moral law and the courage to abide by it."[18] Therefore, in Jewish-Christian relations the polemics and hurtful rhetoric should be left behind; instead, putting it in the words of Marcus Braybrooke, "religions should meet where religions take their course, in God."[19]

The well-known Jewish scholar David Novak has illustrated this "religious need," which is the point being made here, in the wake of the publication by our commission of the document *We Remember*. Addressing the Jewish criticism of this document, Novak writes, "My own view is that the Jewish response [to the document] is largely mistaken, and that it reflects a misunderstanding not only of Catholic theology but of Jewish theologies as well." After having analyzed the document theologically, he concludes (and this is quoted as a mere illustration of the point):

> The document asserts [that] "the Nazi regime was determined to exterminate the very existence of the Jewish people, a people called to witness to the one God and the law of the covenant." No Jewish statement could have enunciated more precisely why Jewish people exist in the world.

Jews are committed to survival. Much of our language, uttered both to ourselves and to others, is the language of survival. Surely, that is quite understandable considering what the Jewish people have suffered, especially in this century. But survival for Jews is not enough. Jews always have to understand *for what*—better, *for whom*—we are surviving. Perhaps the true source of the Nazi venom against the Jewish people is that for which or for Whom the Jews are to survive.

This statement of the Catholic Church recognizes the chosenness of the Jewish people, the vocation of the Jewish people, a fact nothing short of *qiddush ha-shem,* "the sanctification of the name of God." If the Church, from the top down, recognizes this as the reason for the survival and continuing strength of the Jewish people, then, despite any reservations, Jews have to see this document as making a positive contribution to the always complex relationship between the Jewish people and the Catholic Church. It is a document Jews can and should embrace because its theological argument and conclusions have a resonance in our own theology and law. It is by no means the last word—nothing is in this world—but its integrity and wisdom should not be missed because of moral and political antagonism stemming from those having less integrity and less wisdom.[20]

As mentioned above, Novak's essay is an illustration of the fact that a religious, and indeed theological, appreciation of one another can help us further along the road of dialogue, common discovery, and cooperation on the condition, though, that both parties are nourished by their own faith, feel realized in their own faith community, and feel secure in their own faith commitment. That is what Pope John Paul II meant when he said at the start of the World Day of Prayer for Peace in Assisi in October 1986, addressing persons of other faiths, "It is, in fact, my faith conviction which has made me turn to you."

When Jews and Christians meet each other in a religious "space," that is, under the gaze of God, and feel blessed by it, they enter on a road that may be one of struggle but also one of mutual discovery. In September 1997, addressing a conference of the International Council of Christians and Jews at Rocca di Papa, near Rome, Chief Rabbi

Jonathan Sacks spoke about the story of Jacob and Esau, and the strange encounter that Jacob had with the One who gave him his new name, and he commented:

> At that moment, Jacob is cured of wanting to be Esau. For the first time he can meet Esau without aggression or deception or fear. He says to Esau, "I have seen your face as one sees the face of God," meaning I have recognized your otherness, and I have let it go. You are not me. I am not you. It is in our mutual otherness that we can have relationship. If I am I and you are you, we no longer threaten one another, for we each have our own blessing. We are affirmed in our otherness by Him who is ultimately Other. The Torah signals that this was not an easy discovery. It took many years, it took a deep inner struggle; after it Jacob limped. But after it Jacob became Israel—he who is content to be different, not to be Esau.
>
> Judaism and Christianity, each in their different ways, have had to undergo that inner struggle, and we still do.... Yet it is only by being ourselves and not another that we create space for the other to be himself and not us. Only when I-am-not-Thou and Thou-are-not-I, can there be relationship. And because God lives in relationships, He lives in difference.
>
> We are others. We are also brothers. We have been so for a long time.... When we look back on our past, we find much that we have in common.... We have shared origins, though our paths diverged.... Looking back on this long, strange story of two brothers, we stand hushed for a moment in awe....
>
> It took a long inner struggle, and the darkest night of all, for Jews and Christians to reach the moment when we could meet without fear, each secure in our own blessing, each faithful to our particular truth.... We have reached that stage today, and we must never regress. For it is only if we are true to our separate vocations, if Christians are not Jews, and if Jews are not Christians, that we bring our respective truths to the world, and live, as brothers, in peace.[21]

Looking back on the past we realize, for instance, that too often Christians have pictured the law of the covenant as a burden rather than as a delight. Too often they have also forgotten that when Jesus was crucified by the Romans, with the complicity of some Jews, other Jews have mourned and lamented over him.[22] They had forgotten what *Nostra Aetate* has reminded them of, namely, that "the Jews still remain most dear to God" who "does not repent of the gifts He makes nor of the calls He issues."[23] They had forgotten that Jesus was a faithful Jew and "that from the Jewish people sprang the apostles," the foundation stones and pillars of the church who "draw sustenance from the root of that good olive tree onto which have been grafted the wild olive branches of the Gentiles."

On the other hand, Jews too have forgotten that Jesus was a fellow Jew (their "great brother" as Martin Buber has described him),[24] that they can know him in a way that remains inaccessible to the Gentiles who follow him.[25] Jews have failed to "come to terms with the historical significance of the figure of Jesus," to "see the great parallel in our two religions on essential religious issues," to recognize and appreciate "the remarkably unique manner in which Christianity has expressed Jewish teachings," to "recognize that a place must be given to the reality that Christianity has been a vehicle through which the promises made to Abraham have to a large extent been realized," and to "recognize the degree to which Christianity has been and continues to be a vital influence on Jewish history, practice and self-understanding."[26]

We need to remember though that if today we are able to talk about these things, it is because we are the beneficiaries of the changes that took place forty years ago, because, as Rabbi James Rudin has once put it, "we are all the children of Vatican II."[27] On the other hand, if today we can realistically hope to become a blessing to one another and thus a blessing to the rest of the world—"we should be taking holiness into the streets," is how Rabbi Irving Greenberg has beautifully expressed it[28]— it is because of changes that are taking place right now, and the key to these changes is a *religious* one: it is religious faith. It is my conviction that the more we, Jews and Christians, "seek the face of God" (Ps 27:8), the nearer we will come to each other; in this encounter we will encounter God in a new way.[29] If we do believe this, and if we dare to act on this belief, our hope will certainly exceed our present experience.

Another key to the changes in Jewish-Christian relations that are badly needed today is a joint reflection on the meaning of history and on history itself, particularly the history of the parting of the ways. We need to reflect on history itself because, to put it in the words of the Jewish historian Ellis Rivkin in his classic study *What Crucified Jesus?*, "as seekers of truth, we would wish to know what occurred, why it occurred, and who was responsible for its occurrence; as seekers of reconciliation between the mother and the daughter religions, we would wish to build this reconciliation on the facing of facts rather than on the dissolving of them." For example, "it is tragic indeed," he writes, "that the birth pangs of Christianity were occasioned by an event [the crucifixion of Jesus] in which Jews were directly implicated. It is tragic because it spawned intense hostility between mother and daughter religions," and he then sets off on a historical study that he describes as "an odyssey from human bitterness, hate, and blindness to divine love, reconciliation, and enlightenment."[30] Father John T. Pawlikowski has made the same point, as indeed have other Christian and Jewish scholars: "Certainly there is a long history to overcome in transforming Good Friday into a period of Christian-Jewish reconciliation. But if we better understand the concrete political dynamics that brought Jesus to Calvary, we will be well underway toward beginning that process of transformation."[31] The same is true with regard to any other period of history.

Also a joint reflection on the meaning of history could be very helpful. For instance, some of the insights that Irving Greenberg shared with us at the Jerusalem Conference on Religious Leadership in Secular Society, have greatly helped me to understand better certain Jewish attitudes, for example, what he calls the Jewish temptation of triumphalism of powerlessness (and what Rabbi Leon Klenicki calls the triumphalism of pain). To quote Greenberg:

> Jewish Christianity was born within the body of the Jewish people—shortly before Jewry experienced catastrophic destruction, exile and powerlessness. For Judaism, over the course of the next few centuries, this became a moment of covenant renewal, the flowering of rabbinic Judaism....In the course of history, the Rabbis developed an ethic of powerlessness which gave dignity and meaning to Jewish life. The rabbinic way sustained the patience to wait for a redemption that would some day sweep aside the secular and religious earthly rulers alike and restore Israel to its past

glory. This ethic became even more urgent and central as Christianity came into power and aggressively persecuted Jewry. To put it bluntly, the Rabbis wrote off history.

On the other hand, I am well aware that Christians also have often been tempted to write off this world and its history and to withdraw into spiritual security. Today, however, both sides are caught off guard by the upsurge of modernity. "The history which both religions denied in order to claim their absolute validity came back to haunt them," Greenberg said, and echoing the words of Pope John Paul II he added,

> Whatever Judaism and Christianity try to do, they will have to do together and to each other first. Their moral and cultural credibility depends on overcoming the legacy and image of their mutual hatefulness, it depends on their ability to set a standard of mutual respect....Whatever the differences and conflicts between them, they are lumped together in the same part of the cultural spectrum from the perspective of the secular majority in the West. Thus their authority is hopelessly tied one to the other by what they have in common and the gulf between that and the view of religion's cultured despisers.[32]

I would like to conclude with a paragraph taken from a paper, *Catholics and Jews: Confronting the Holocaust Together,* written in December 1987 by Judith Banki, who was then the associate director for interreligious affairs of the American Jewish Committee. It summarizes my vision of the future of Jewish-Christian relations rather well:

> Let us resolve to pursue [our efforts] toward the goal of understanding and combating the pathology of group hatred and persecution, in an atmosphere free of polemics. We are not responsible for the prejudices of the world into which we were born, but we are responsible for fighting them. We are not accountable for past events over which we had no control, but we are accountable for the future. We are jointly responsible for facing history and for forging new traditions of human and spiritual solidarity—for the sake of our children, our world, and the sanctification of the One who is Holy to all of us.

NOTES

1. At the time of writing I was the executive secretary of the commission.

2. International Catholic-Jewish Liaison Committee, *Fifteen Years of Catholic-Jewish Dialogue 1970–1985* (Rome: ILC, 1988), 27–28. See also the opinion of David Klinghoffer in his article "Anti-Semitism without Anti-Semites," *First Things* 82 (April 1998): 10–13.

3. ILC, *Fifteen Years of Catholic-Jewish Dialogue,* 27–28. In an address on the theme "Catholic-Jewish Relations—The Unfinished Agenda," given in Baltimore on February 18, 1999, Cardinal Cassidy remarked: "Recent Jewish attempts to influence decisions concerning the internal life of the Catholic Church are strongly resented. Persons very dear to the Catholic faithful are condemned without proof, simply because they are not 'personae gratae' with the Jewish community."

4. See the Institute of the World Jewish Congress's *Policy Dispatches* 23 (November 1997) and 36 (November 1998). With regard to the latter, Ralph Leinoff, Jewish cochairman of the Rockaway Catholic Jewish Council (U.S.), reacted very strongly in a letter dated December 8, 1998, endorsed by Rabbi Joseph I. Weiss of the RCJC Advisory Board, and addressed to the Institute of the World Jewish Congress:

> Gentlemen,…if the goal of this document was to call a halt to dialogue and further efforts to encourage the Catholic Church's march towards confronting the bitter history of its relations with the Jewish people, then I must congratulate you on your success. You could not have done a better job of instilling a sense of dismay and futility in all who have been engaged in the process of dialogue over the last two and a half decades. Your document reeks with half truths, innuendo, gossip and a total lack of appreciation for all the good that has been accomplished since *Nostra Aetate* in 1965.…All your grudging acknowledgments of fundamental changes for good in the Church's teachings on Judaism are designed to minimize their great importance. Instead, you elevate unresolved lesser issues to high importance, thereby justifying the failing grades you give the Church for all the changes it has made and indeed, is still making. Your accusation that the Church is trying to "Christianize" victims of the Shoah is a point of view not shared by most Jews at this time. However, we do not doubt your capacity to peddle that kind of nonsense to those who are in ignorance about what has taken place in the last third of this century or to those who have a distrustful fear of any kind of dialogue.…Your we'll-tell-you-how-to-run-your-religion attitude is an onerous distortion of what dialogue is all

about....It will be interesting to see how you will continue to discount first hand eye witness reports of historical facts in favor of highly fictionalized Broadway productions about the Church's complete failure in WW-II....Catholics also have sensitivities....In a world where Jews find themselves so vastly outnumbered and besieged by so many enemies, why do we have to go out of our way to add another billion Christians by biting off their outstretched hands in fellowship?

5. In his above-mentioned address delivered in Baltimore, Cardinal Cassidy spelled it out:

The possibilities for common witness and co-operation are immense. Is there any reason why we cannot work together for a better, more just society? Or fight together against every form of evil in our societies, and especially every manifestation of racism and anti-Semitism? Are we not called by our common heritage to promote together the defense of the weak and oppressed? Have we not motives for defending together the family, protecting our children, and helping the young in their search for meaning, nurturing the hearts of all by sharing the treasures of our respective spiritualities? Could we not, for example, say something together to a world in which millions lack the basic necessities of human existence, while nations spend billions of dollars on armaments and weapons of mass destruction? Then there are challenges for us in the field of human rights, for the protection of the rights of religion, for dialogue with the other great religions of the world—with a special place in this context for dialogue with the believing followers of Islam—and for collaboration in the realm of culture....As two faith communities with common roots, I am convinced that the time has come for us to move beyond the agenda of the past 35 years and begin to examine more closely the spiritual bonds that unite us, while at the same time seeking to deepen our understanding of the various teachings of our faiths that constitute our separate identities...Will not a dialogue that goes beyond a discussion about problems and concentrates rather on what can bring us to a deeper understanding one of the other be valuable also in helping us to proceed further and more securely along the path of common action?

6. See *Information Service,* the official bulletin of the Pontifical Council for Promoting Christian Unity, 75 (1990).

7. See *L'Osservatore Romano,* April 17, 1993.

8. See *Information Service* 82 (1993). At that meeting I delivered a paper entitled "The Teaching on Jews and Judaism in Catholic Education," published in *Seminarium* 2 (1992).

9. See *Information Service* 98 (1998). It was at the 1994 Jerusalem meeting that a confidential progress report on the work we were doing in preparation for an official Catholic statement on the Shoah was immediately leaked to the media, in spite of our explicit request to keep it confidential for the time being. This incident was very serious because it not only meant a brutal breach of trust on the part of some of our Jewish dialogue partners (although other Jews who were present were as much disgusted about it as we were), but because it undoubtedly harmed our work and delayed the publication of the document *We Remember: A Reflection on the Shoah* considerably. It was precisely those who leaked our report prematurely who, after the document came out in 1998, labeled it as "too little too late."

10. *Common Statement on Violence* of the ILC: In today's world, violence is an all-pervasive phenomenon. There is violence in the heart of persons. There is violence in families and communities. There is violence within and between nations and states. There is violence in fanaticism and especially in a religious fanaticism which distorts and destroys the message of peace inherent to religious belief.

We remember the violence and death that sought to annihilate not only individuals but entire peoples, including our own, our brothers and sisters. We stand here on the eve of *Yom Hashoah,* having this afternoon visited the site of the tragic attack on the Jewish Community Centre in this city. We cannot forget these horrors, also because we see today other peoples being systematically destroyed. We want, therefore, to stand together in strongly condemning such acts that are still occurring today, never forgetting those of the past. We want to stand together in preventing such atrocious evil from happening in the future.

We join our voices to those of many of our leaders, to the voices of all men and women of goodwill and reason, to the voices of millions of innocent victims of violence, past and present, and we proclaim together with all the conviction of our faith in God and in the equal dignity of all human persons, whatever their race or color, religion or culture, that violence is evil, that violence is totally unacceptable as a solution to problems, that violence is utterly unworthy of the human person.

Violence is a lie, because it goes against the truth that our religions profess, the truth of our humanity. Violence destroys what it claims to defend: the dignity of life, the freedom and the rights of human beings. Violence breaks down persons and relationships.

Today, we turn to one another in order to help one another to overcome violence wherever it may occur. We cannot do it alone; we do not want to do it alone, for we firmly believe and proclaim that peace must be built on justice and trust and that this will happen only when we act together.

We, therefore, proclaim that we must stand together in choosing life, not death. We take this commitment together.

11. Eugene J. Fisher, "Judaism and Christianity: Their Respective Roles in the Strategy of Redemption," in *Visions of the Other: Jewish and Christian Theologians Assess the Dialogue,* ed. Eugene J. Fisher with Frank DeSiano, Studies in Judaism and Christianity (Mahwah, NJ: Paulist Press, 1994), 27.

12. C. C. Aronsfeld, author of the book *The Text of the Holocaust: A Study of the Nazi's Extermination Propaganda 1919–1945* (Marblehead, MA: Micah Publications, 1985), wrote in an article ("Jews and Christians in England," *Midstream* 39, no. 8 [November 1993]: 17):

> I sometimes have the feeling that the Council of Christians and Jews [in Great Britain] tends to regard itself as a Society for the Enlightenment of Christians about Jews. This of course is legitimate and necessary, but it seems to me no less legitimate and necessary to enlighten Jews about Christians....The fact is that any suggestion that for example Jews get to know the contents of the New Testament is resented by them....If Jews may legitimately refuse to read the New Testament and be enlightened about it, I cannot help wondering what the future of Jewish-Christian relations will be.

13. J. Bemporad and M. Shevack, *Our Age: The Historic New Era of Christian-Jewish Understanding* (Hyde Park, NY: New City Press, 1996), 9.

14. See *Catholics Remember the Holocaust,* published by the Secretariat for Ecumenical and Interreligious Affairs of the National Conference of Catholic Bishops, Washington, DC, 1998.

15. *Information Service* 98 (1998).

16. David Novak, "Jews and Catholics: Beyond Apologies," *First Things* 89 (January 1999): 20–25.

17. Peter Feuerherd, *National Catholic Register,* December 17, 1995, p. 10.

18. On January 13, 1997.

19. In Marcus Braybrooke, *Time to Meet: Towards a Deeper Relationship between Jews and Christians* (London/Philadelphia, PA: SCM Press, 1990), 152.

20. Novak, "Jews and Catholics," *First Things* 89 (January 1999): 20–25.

21. The text of his address is published in *From the Martin Buber House* 25 (Heppenheim, Germany: ICCJ, 1998), 31–41.

22. Braybrooke, *Time to Meet,* 50.

23. Quotations from *Nostra Aetate* taken from W. M. Abbott, SJ, ed., *The Documents of Vatican II, with Notes and Comments by Catholic, Protestant and Orthodox Authorities* (New York: America Press, 1966).

24. In the foreword to his study of the relationship of Judaism and Christianity, *Two Types of Faith* (London: Routledge & Paul, 1951), 12. See also Byron L. Sherwin, "'Who Do You Say That I Am?' (Mark 8:29): A New Jewish View of Jesus," *Journal of Ecumenical Studies* 31, nos. 3–4 (summer–fall 1994): 255. In this essay Sherwin proposes a radical reassessment of the place of Jesus in Jewish theology. He describes this place in traditional Jewish theology as follows:

> Though the twentieth-century philosopher Martin Buber called Jesus his "brother," much of classical Jewish theological teaching considered Jesus an "other" (*otoh ha-ish;* literally, a derogatory term for "that man")—an apostate who subverted the teachings of Judaism, a Jew whose teachings were utilized by his followers as a justification for the persecution of the Jewish people in many lands over many centuries, and the paradigmatic false messiah. Jews, in effect, excommunicated Jesus from the Jewish faith and from the Jewish people.

25. Martin Buber, *Two Types of Faith,* 13, as quoted by G. Vermes in *Jesus the Jew: A Historian's Reading of the Gospels* (London: Collins, 1973), 223. See also Jack Bemporad, "Jesus for Jews," *Church* (spring 1997): 11.

26. Jack Bemporad, "Jesus for Jews," 11–12. See also Michael Hilton, *The Christian Effect on Jewish Life* (London: SCM Press, 1994).

27. *New York Times,* January 23, 1985.

28. In his address "Jews and Christians: Facing the Modern World," given in Jerusalem on February 2, 1994, at the International Jewish-Christian Conference on Religious Leadership in Secular Society.

29. See Rabbi Albert Friedlander in E. Wiesel and A. H. Friedlander, eds., *The Six Days of Destruction* (New York: Paulist Press, 1988), 61, cited by Marcus Braybrooke, *Time to Meet,* 158.

30. E. Rivkin, *What Crucified Jesus? Messianism, Pharisaism, and the Development of Christianity* (New York: UAHC Press, 1997), 3–6 (originally published, Nashville: Abingdon Press, 1984). With regard to the need for Jews and Christians to reflect together on history and on the meaning of history, the Jewish authors Harold Troper and Morton Weinfeld, in the introduction to their book *Old Wounds* (London: Penguin Books, 1989), justly state that Christians and Jews "do not share a common historical memory. Both groups have confronted the same forces of history. But in the process whereby experience becomes memory and the memories of many converge to become communal

historical understanding, both....have inherited very different and distinct understandings of the past and the role played by the other in that past."

31. "Christian-Jewish Bonding and the Liturgy of Holy Week," *New Theological Review* (February 1997): 104.

32. Ibid.

7
Institutional Relations in Jewish-Christian Relations

Friedhelm Pieper

1. INSTITUTIONAL RELATIONS — AN ISSUE FOR INTERFAITH RELATIONS?

Rabbi Leon Klenicki, director of the Anti-Defamation League's (ADL) Department of Interfaith Affairs in New York, once stated in a dialogue with Jay T. Rock, director of Interfaith Relations and Christian-Jewish Concerns for the National Council of Churches of Christ in the United States: "Inter-religious dialogue often starts with personal friendships among lay people, clergy or professionals in the field of interfaith relations. This is the very heart of the dialogue relationship. Interfaith dialogue is essentially an encounter."[1] Against the background of the experience described in this quotation, one can question whether within the framework of Jewish-Christian dialogue it makes sense to deal with institutional relations.

My perspective on the topic is formed on the basis of my work in the International Council of Christians and Jews (ICCJ) — the oldest of today's international organizations in Christian-Jewish dialogue — where I am privileged to serve as general secretary. Reviewing the more than fifty years of work of the International Council of Christians and Jews I can only agree with Rabbi Klenicki: Jewish-Christian dialogue started as personal encounters. And in thinking about persons, I would like to recall the remarkable pioneering work in England of James W. Parkes, William W. Simpson, and, a little later, Rabbi Hugo Gryn.

In October 1998 I visited London at the invitation of Sir Sigmund Sternberg to some festive events arranged by him on the occasion of Hans Küng's seventieth birthday and in recognition of the publication of his latest book in England. When I listened to Hans Küng addressing the audience I noticed how much he stressed the role of individuals in the process of bringing about change. Of course he talked particularly about Pope John XXIII and the decisive role he played during his pontificate in the enormous changes that led to the Second Vatican Council and the declaration *Nostra Aetate*.

Listening to Hans Küng it occurred to me that he spoke about the influence of individuals without even mentioning the religious institutions of which many of us are members and that play an important role in any interfaith relation, whether positive or negative. On questioning him about this, I received the reply that he does not in fact rely on religious institutions when it comes to changing global interfaith relations and global ethics. Institutions by their very nature are intent on continuity not on change. And he again referred to his experiences during the deliberations of Vatican II and the role played by individuals such as Pope John XXIII. While appreciating his point, I felt that I could not entirely agree.

We must also deal with religious institutions when we are looking for changes in interfaith relations. It is true that the start of such changes is indeed almost always set in motion by individuals, but, if we want to have these changes take root and endure, we have to work for their implementation in the religious life of the faith traditions, and we have to look at the religious institutions for their implementation.

Second, we have to deal with religious institutions, because faith traditions and their institutions, instead of being sources for peace, justice, and fruitful interfaith relations, have been, and continue to be, to some extent major sources of misunderstanding, prejudice, and even hatred. To reach the level of implementation, however, one has to prove that the envisaged changes are a legitimate interpretation of the respective faith tradition so that they are rightly incorporated into the given religious institution.

Looking back on more than fifty years of the ICCJ's work and on the many endeavors in bringing about new relations between Christians and Jews, I am glad that I can say: the Christian-Jewish dialogue has at long last reached the level of religious institutions. And speaking for the network of the ICCJ member organizations I can only say that we do feel gratitude for all that has been achieved in recent decades. The late Geoffrey Wigoder in a survey about Jewish-Christian interfaith relations stated,

> Whereas relations between Jews and the many streams of Christianity have been characterised by hostility for millennia, recent decades have witnessed the cultivation of a dialogue based on mutual respect and tolerance. In spite of the pluralism within both Judaism and Christianity, one can speak of a general Christian re-thinking of the way the Christian world today understands Judaism.[2]

I believe that Wigoder said this because of his perception that changes in the Christian understanding of Judaism are today increasingly implemented in Christian religious institutions, namely, the different churches. As a result we can indeed speak today of a "general Christian re-thinking" toward Judaism beyond the encounter of individuals. Institutional relations will be an important and growing issue in the future development of Christian-Jewish relations.

2. THE INTERNATIONAL NETWORK OF THE ICCJ

Approaching the theme of this study from the perspective of the international work of the ICCJ, it is necessary to talk about the present situation of this international network of Christian-Jewish associations. Established in 1947, the ICCJ today embraces thirty-one member organizations in twenty-nine countries worldwide from Canada to New Zealand, from Argentina to Russia and Israel. At present, however, we have no member organizations in Africa and Asia.

But the worldwide movement of Jewish-Christian cooperation within the framework of the ICCJ is growing, and we are aiming at the creation of new and sustainable relations between the two faith groups in mutual respect and understanding. It is growing in size and in the range of issues being addressed in the different member organizations, thereby also creating an increasing diversity of approaches within its network. And not least it is the relationship with Muslims and the cooperation with them that is a growing issue in the ICCJ.

This reflects the situation in the countries of some ICCJ member organizations. In Israel, dialogue with Muslims has been central to the work of the Israel Interfaith Association from the very beginning. In the United States and Canada, cooperation with Muslims is a natural consequence of the prevailing interreligious and intercultural situation. In Europe, we realize that the Muslim communities are growing. They are in the process of establishing Muslim communities within the legal framework of religious communities in the European countries and of finding a status equal to that of the Jewish communities or the churches. To engage in a growing dialogue with Muslims also reflects the theological awareness that the "House of Ishmael" (as Islam defines itself) is the next neighbor to both of us: Jews and Christians.

Within the ICCJ there has been an ongoing discussion about how to relate the Christian-Jewish dialogue to the encounter with Islam. One important step has been the establishment of the ICCJ Abrahamic Forum Council, which held its first international ICCJ trilateral conference for Jews, Christians, and Muslims in Berlin in October 1999. The theme of this conference was "The Concept of Monotheism in the Abrahamic Traditions."[3]

The first chairman of the ICCJ Abrahamic Forum Council is Sheikh Dr. Zaki Badawi, head of the Muslim College in London, so that for the first time in the history of the ICCJ one of its major bodies is being chaired by a Muslim. I will return to the important question of dialogue with Muslims later.

Another focus of interest for the ICCJ is the situation in central and eastern Europe. The 1999 ICCJ international conference in Kiev, Ukraine, entitled "Destruction and Renewal—The Role of Religion in Changing Society," again indicated how the ICCJ continues to focus its attention on central and eastern Europe.[4] The need to do so has obvious reasons for us all. The first is that the societies in that region are going through a process of dramatic changes. We only need to look at the former Yugoslavia to realize that ethnic and religious divisions can (but do not have to) lead to violent conflicts through the preaching of prejudices resulting in a collective mania. Looking at Northern Ireland, we see that this is not a problem unique to central and eastern Europe; and being a German myself, aware of the history of my own people, I know for sure that this is not so. But these societies today are challenged in a special way while their countries try to find their role in a changing world. The people working to further dialogue and understanding between the different religious and cultural communities in this region are doing vitally important work. We should be very much aware of this and should encourage it by all possible means.

The second reason is that we should also continue to deepen the relations with Orthodox churches. In the past years ICCJ member organizations were able to establish contacts in Moscow, Minsk, St. Petersburg, and now in Ukraine. Also, our Israeli member organization has throughout been engaged in dialogue with representatives of the Orthodox churches in the Middle East, as have other ICCJ member organizations in the west with Orthodox Christians in their countries. Without a doubt the relationship between the various Orthodox churches and the Jewish people is one of the most important challenges for the future development of Christian-Jewish dialogue and cooperation. Therefore, I have included a section on dialogue with the Orthodox churches below, considering it from the particular position of relations between organizations rather than the theological questions already discussed by Nicholas de Lange and Irina Levinskaya.

Before dealing with religious institutions from the perspective of Christian-Jewish relations I would like to conclude this section about the ICCJ with a personal remark. I feel blessed to experience that, while bearing responsibility for the course of the ICCJ, I can be a witness to the fact that the visions of the founders of the ICCJ today continue to find men and women in different regions of this world who feel committed and obliged to act in engaging in real dialogue and cooperation and trying to overcome the obstacles that still trouble and disturb the relations between Christians and Jews, as well as with Muslims. Indebted to all these men and women we have to move on and be sensitive to the place of dialogue within and among the different religious institutions.

3. RELIGIOUS INSTITUTIONS

When we begin to consider the role of religious institutions we do of course have to acknowledge first the manifold pluralism within each of the major faith communities. On the Christian side, besides the Catholic Church, there are more than three hundred Protestant and Orthodox mainstream churches as member churches of the World Council of Churches (WCC), and in addition to these there are many other evangelical and charismatic churches. On the Jewish side there are different streams of Judaism each with its inner Jewish discussions and conflicts. The focus here will be on the major Christian institutions, beginning with the Vatican.

3.1. The Catholic Church

In January 1999 ICCJ honorary president, His Eminence Carlo Maria Cardinal Martini, Archbishop of Milan, visited the ICCJ headquarters at the Martin Buber House in Heppenheim, Germany. In a public lecture during that visit Cardinal Martini reminded the large audience that it was the ICCJ conference in Seelisberg that paved the way for the changing attitude in the Catholic Church. It was this route that brought about the declaration *Nostra Aetate* at the Second Vatican Council, a declaration that subsequently fostered the renewal of Christian-Jewish relations in the different churches worldwide.

When considering religious institutions we acknowledge the fact that it has been the Catholic Church with its declaration *Nostra Aetate* that has given the most important impulse for this historic change and the general Christian rethinking of Judaism in the troubled twentieth century. The declaration can be seen as a breakthrough for the new era of dialogue within the context of the Christian churches. It was especially Pope John Paul II who, from the early years of his pontificate, proclaimed on countless occasions his theological insight deriving from the apostle Paul's letter to the Romans (chapter 11) that God's covenant with the Jewish people has never been broken and still retains lasting validity, since God does not revoke his promises.[5]

On the question of institutions we should acknowledge that the Vatican to this day is the leading international religious institution to promote new relations between Christians and Jews. In addition to the pope's own work, this is promoted by the important work of the Pontifical Council for Promoting Christian Unity and its Commission for Religious Relations with the Jews, chaired by His Eminence Edward Idris Cardinal Cassidy and its secretary, Father Dr. Remi Hoeckman. To this day there has not been on the international level an impulse by any religious institution equal to that of *Nostra Aetate*. It is my hope that the impulse set by the Catholic Church will encourage the community of Protestant and Orthodox churches within the WCC to deepen the ongoing process of deliberation about the relations of their respective churches to the Jews. Looking at the documents that have been published by various churches in recent years, we can see that this process has already shown some results and will lead eventually to a declaration by a WCC General Assembly regarding renewed relations with the Jewish community.

In the meantime the Vatican published in 1998 its well-publicized paper on the Holocaust, *We Remember.* At the 1998 ICCJ conference in Erlbach, Germany, delegates of the worldwide community of Christian-Jewish dialogue organizations were able to discuss in person with Cardinal Cassidy the controversial reaction that it had received. The wide-ranging discussion on this document, continued in papers around the world, showed in my opinion that even after many years of dialogue we still have to learn much about each other.

We Remember is the first of its kind teaching Christians through-out the world to acknowledge the fact that the Shoah has taken place in the midst of so-called Christian civilization. This is probably the most important part of the Vatican document.

The question of the responsibility of the Catholic Church as an institution in times of Jewish persecutions, and in particular during the Nazi dictatorship, is a major issue in the controversial discussions about the declaration. But it would be better not to criticize the state-ment in this respect. I suggest that we must do more to try to understand the background of the Catholic Church over the issue of an institution acknowledging its own mistakes. To gain a more accurate picture we should try to understand it in the light of the implications of the theo-logical concept of the Catholic Church as the mystical body of Christ. A Catholic approach toward dealing with institutional failures needs to be able to relate to this concept. We can witness that on the level of the national bishops' conferences it was obviously possible to formulate different statements, such as those that have recently been issued from the French and the German bishops. They expressed in clear words the guilt of the church as an institution regarding its role in the develop-ments that finally led to the Shoah. A declaration by the German and Austrian bishops in 1988 states that, "the Church, which we proclaim holy and which we honour as a mystery, is also a sinful Church and in need of conversion."[6]

Pope John Paul II himself in the letter by which he introduced the Vatican statement on the Shoah asserted that, "the Church encourages her sons and daughters to purify their hearts through repentance...and examine themselves on the responsibility which they too have for the evils of our time." I hope that these moving words are also being heard beyond the Catholic Church and are being taken seriously by other church leaders.

When dialogue reaches the level of institutions we of course have to take into account that institutions generally are not very eager to deal with their failures. The American Catholic theologian Father Richard McBrien in a comment on the Vatican paper stated, "the Catholic Church almost never acknowledges mistakes institutionally" and even went on to compare his church with American politicians who, as he says, would never admit personally that they had done anything wrong.[7] It seems to be clear that one can find a reluctance to examine critically the history of ones own organization in almost any institution. I have experienced this in many discussions within the Lutheran churches in Germany. But it also seems to be clear that in order to ensure a common future we have to be able not only to share our different memories of history but also to confess explicitly the failures and sins we perceive as we examine the role of our institutions and faith traditions in times of oppression and the persecution of other faith groups.

For a Christian, the most important prayer is probably the Lord's Prayer, a central part in almost every Christian service. This prayer pleads, "Forgive us our debts," or in another version, "Forgive us our sins." It is "us" not "me"; it is "our sins" not only "mine." It is not only individual but collective. It is emboldened upon us, as responsible members and leaders of institutions of our faith traditions, to declare this.

3.2. The World Council of Churches

As a Lutheran pastor I do have a specific approach toward the failures and sins of the churches. In fact one of the vital conclusions of the Reformation was that the churches can fail and that they are therefore in need of constant reformation, which has been formulated in the Latin phrase *ecclesia semper reformanda* (the need of the church for permanent reformation). But that does not mean that the picture we find when looking into the history of Lutheran and the other Protestant churches reflects this pretension, especially when we look at their relations with the Jewish community. While several Protestant churches have up to this day passed declarations showing their endeavors to come to a new relationship with the Jewish community, we do not have any declaration at the level of the General Assembly of the World Council of Churches that might reflect the insights of the renewal of Christian-Jewish relations that have been seen in recent decades. The ambivalence of the statement of the first WCC General Assembly in Amsterdam (1948) declaring a specific and unique relationship between Christians and Jews, while at the same time calling for greater Christian missionary activity to the Jews, still to some extent endures. But the present WCC guidelines, the new Ecumenical Vision, clearly incorporate interfaith dialogue within the policy of the council.

Of course we need to bear in mind that the WCC encompasses not only Protestant churches but Orthodox churches as well. We need to know that the community of more than three hundred non-Catholic churches is highly diverse so that any statement of the WCC has to undergo a very complicated process of decision making, which is often affected by the many different attitudes prevailing among the WCC member churches. Attending the Eighth General Assembly of the World Council of Churches in December 1998 in Harare, Zimbabwe, I had a chance to experience this fascinating and highly heterogeneous community. In that WCC assembly, relations between Christians and Jews, as well as Christian-Jewish dialogue, were once again not items on the assembly's agenda. Encounter with the Jewish community has been an issue only within the delegates' broader discussions of interreligious affairs, apart from the the work of the WCC Office for Interreligious Relations and Dialogue and the endeavors for Christian-Jewish dialogue by Rev. Hans Ucko of that office. Within this framework of interfaith dialogue the WCC does indeed also engage in Christian-Jewish encounter and dialogue. In fact we should recall in this context the pioneering projects of Hans Ucko to organize the first conferences for Christian-Jewish encounter in Asia and Africa, thereby putting into action the call within the WCC to include other contexts outside the western European and North American regions in the Jewish-Christian encounter.

The latest high-ranking statement of the WCC has been the document "Christian-Jewish Dialogue beyond Canberra 1991," adopted in 1992 by the Central Committee of the organization. This document states:

> [the] WCC will assist the churches to understand the theological significance of living Judaism, to examine contemporary theological affirmations vis-à-vis Judaism...and to foster implementation of the churches' recommendations in Christian teaching, mission and liturgical life.

There is still a long way to go until a joint declaration of the General Assembly of the WCC will emerge out of this process.

The presence of Orthodox churches as constituent members of the WCC has helped the organizing of meetings between Orthodox Christians and Jewish representatives; but even so, at present the participation of Orthodox Christians in Christian-Jewish dialogue seems to have become embroiled in the conflict over the role of the Orthodox churches in the decision making of the WCC within this council.

3.3. Orthodox Churches within and outside of the WCC

In order to comprehend the relations between Jews and the Orthodox churches we have to acknowledge both the obvious difficulties in this dialogue and the first steps and encounters that have been made. And again we should not forget those individuals within the framework of the Orthodox churches who cared for the Jewish community and even risked their lives during the Nazi dictatorship in order to help their Jewish neighbors. It is therefore appropriate to start with some recollections of certain individuals before turning to the contemporary difficulties in the relations between Jews and Orthodox churches.

One might recall Mother Maria (Skoptsova), who "suffered a martyr's death in Ravensbrück for saving Jews from the Nazis in France and for helping the Resistance."[8] In relating Mother Maria's story, Grigori Benevich of St. Petersburg tells that, after emigrating from Russia to France along with her family, this remarkable woman—then called Elizaveta Skoptsova—"experienced a deep crisis after the death of her daughter Anastasia in 1926."[9] She "divorced and became a nun (Mother Maria), but having renounced the world and its passion, she did not separate herself from people. She organized, together with like-minded people, a movement, 'Pravoslavnoye Delo,' helping needy Russian emigrants. A Russian Orthodox community came into being, and Mother Maria was its soul," giving warmth and help to the poor.

> Then the persecutions of Jews started. Mother Maria and other members of her community took an active part in helping the Jews. They gave shelter to the hunted and the rejected....At this time Mother Maria again was understood and helped by her husband and her mother, and her son

> Yuriy took an active part in Mother Maria's, and the whole community's, activity of saving Jews and other people persecuted by the Nazis....As her contemporaries (told)...when he accused her of loving only Jews, Mother Maria said to the Nazi Hofman, a Baltic German who came to arrest her, that she could help him too if he were in danger.[10]

Mother Maria was charged for helping Jews and was brought to Ravensbrück, where she was put to death.

We might also remember Metropolitan Andrei Szeptycki of the Greek Catholic Church in Nazi-occupied L'vov. Archpriest Dr. Sergij Hackel said this of him,

> In 1942, ignoring all risks to his position and his life, he did not hesitate to protest against the treatment of the Jews. He addressed Hitler personally and then also Himmler separately. Among other things he issued a heartfelt pastoral letter to his flock (entitled), "Thou shalt not kill"...he also risked his life to shelter potential victims of the Shoah under his own roof. Likewise he encouraged the Greek Catholic monastic communities to offer their support.[11]

It is also important to remember the many members of the Greek Orthodox Church who helped their Jewish neighbors during the occupation of Greece by Nazi Germany, and to this day this shared experience is the basis for continuing good relations between the Jewish and the Greek Orthodox community.

Nevertheless, the dialogue between Jews and the Orthodox churches is still in its infancy and faces many obstacles. At the second international conference on "Theology after Auschwitz and Its Correlation with Theology after the Gulag" in St. Petersburg, held by the St. Petersburg School of Religion and Philosophy, and supported by the ICCJ, the archpriest Dr. Sergij Hackel from England expressed very clearly the problems of specific dialogue with the Russian Orthodox Church. The difficulties he described encompass: the ignorance of the Shoah; the gradual withdrawal of Russian Orthodoxy from ecumenism, so that for instance developments in the Catholic Church "remain distant and indistinct for many of its members";[12] the endemic anti-Semitism; the reluctance toward any reform whatsoever; a "simplistic tendency to believe that scripture and tradition are both equally immutable"; and anti-Jewish expressions in the liturgy still being used unchanged to this day.[13]

The archpriest Dr. Sergij Hackel concluded his paper by stating, "We have a long way to go." An ecumenical council for all Orthodox churches has been promised for years. But Dr. Sergij saw a "lack of the scholarship, humility and persistence to reach beyond familiar norms, even in preparation for the Council." Much work needs to be done and, as he said, "For each stage of this process we shall need much daring." He saw some hope in the international conferences that had been prepared by the International Jewish Committee on Interreligious Consultations (IJCIC), Geneva, and the Orthodox Centre of the Ecumenical Patriarchate, Geneva, in some of which the WCC and the ICCJ have been involved. And especially he hoped that the words of the Greek metropolitan Damaskinos at the 1993 meeting of Christian Orthodox and Jewish representatives in Athens would be heard in the Orthodox community. Metropolitan Damaskinos said at the conclusion of the conference in Athens that Orthodox Christianity recognizes in "the theology, anthropology and cosmology of Judaism basic elements of its own corresponding teaching." This is confirmed "by a sincere respect not only for the Old Testament, but also for the spiritual experience of the chosen people in the divine plan of man's salvation."[14]

It is a sign of hope that the ecumenical patriarch of the Orthodox churches, Bartholomew I of Constantinople, sent a message of endorsement along with representatives of the different Orthodox churches to the 1993 Athens meeting of Jews and that he later expressed his commitment to Jewish-Christian Orthodox dialogue on a visit to Israel and in a moving speech at the Washington Holocaust Memorial museum stating,

> The bitter truth for so many Christians of that terrible time was that they could not connect the message of their faith to their actions in the world. We boldly proclaim to our own spiritual children and to our brothers and sisters in the entire *Oikumene,* that silence in the face of injustice, silence in the shadows of helpless suffering, silence in the darkness of Auschwitz's bitter night will never again be allowed.[15]

This is what we have to know when we are dealing with institutional relations with the Orthodox churches. We have to know the many problems that lie on the long road ahead. And we have to know the start that has been made. The next steps will have to be to increase encounters between Jews and Orthodox Christians in all our countries and regions and to work together theologically on the questions of scriptural interpretation and on the examination of liturgical traditions. One central issue will be how Christian Orthodox theology can relate its own theological concepts to the new understanding of the lasting validity of the divine covenant with the Jewish people, which is already in fact expressed in the New Testament.

4. MAJOR ASPECTS OF INSTITUTIONAL RELATIONS WITHIN THE INTERFAITH WORK

4.1. How Does Dialogue between Religious Institutions Differ from Dialogue between Communities?

Dialogue starts with individuals, often with personal friendships. To quote Rabbi Klenicki again, "Interfaith dialogue is essentially an encounter." Dialogue today has reached the communities, organizations, and associations. It has begun to reach the institutions too, evidenced for instance by a growing number of church statements. The increasing number of offices for Christian-Jewish relations and/or for interreligious relations that the different churches and the different Jewish organizations have established in recent years also witnesses to its presence on an institutional level.

This is a great step forward. Furthermore, it is a historic breakthrough. Dialogue has reached official church politics. The new theology of Judaism has been taken on board as official church theology within the Catholic Church and within a growing number of Protestant churches. It will be taken forward to the next generations. It will be part of the curriculum. There is a chance now that the renewal of the relations between Christians and Jews has reached a level of change that can be sustained. This is a *chance*—it cannot be taken for certain. As we know from church history things can develop in a different way, too. There are always new generations that may fall back and return to old attitudes and prejudices.

As I have tried to show in this paper, we can understand that there is still much work to be done before we can invite churches who are skeptical about dialogue to take part in this historic learning process between Christians and Jews. The dialogue cannot, however, be left alone in the hands of the institutions. Institutions tend to be, at best, conservative. That is one of the reasons why they exist: in order to conserve the movement, to organize it. Institutions are seldom revolutionary. They seldom demand changes. They need criticism from within and from outside their organizational framework.

Jewish-Christian dialogue still needs forums outside the religious institutions, forums where members of the respective faith communities are able to meet and discuss openly in mutual confidence. They need forums in which they can attend as members of their institutions but not as their representatives. These will be places where they can try to go further in the exploration of a common understanding even when this is to some extent heterodox to their traditions. They should be forums that can serve as some kind of think tank on the potential for and the problems of Christian-Jewish relations as well as on the new encounter with Islam. The Christian-Jewish councils are already serving in many regions of the world as forums of this kind. The combination of institutional relations with such open forums will provide the best way to further improve the Christian-Jewish dialogue and the Abrahamic interfaith relations, and will contribute to their implementation in the religious institutions.

4.2. What Should the Future Relations Be between Different Religious Institutions?

The potential of the growing number of direct institutional relations should be used for creative projects at all levels. There have been good experiences in mutual visits between members of parishes from different faith communities as well as with pulpit exchanges and shared action on ethical issues. Caring for one another has served, for example, in the Chicago region, to improve the relations between different religious communities. An established relationship leads to joint action by the faith communities involved, allowing them to respond quickly when there are cases of difficulty facing either of them. In Latin America a permanent mechanism of communication was proposed at a meeting of the World Jewish Congress (WJC), the Anti-Defamation League (ADL) and the Latin American Council of

Bishops (CELAM).[16] This kind of permanently available mechanism would be a most helpful tool for increasing institutional relations and possible common action.

4.3. Is There a Need for Greater Cooperation?

There is a need for more theological research. The number of university and college centers, such as the Centre for the Study of Jewish-Christian Relations in Cambridge, is growing. A number of similar centers are working in the United States and in other European countries. Mention has already been made too of the St. Petersburg School of Religion and Philosophy and their conferences on "Theology after Auschwitz and Its Correlation with the Theology after the Gulag."[17]

When inviting more members of the Jewish, Christian, and Muslim faith communities into the interfaith encounter, we must prove theologically that insights gained in dialogue are a legitimate interpretation of the respective faith traditions. In order to counter fundamentalist movements in our respective communities, we have to show how the engagement for peaceful relations and good neighborliness between the religions is a theological, legitimate, and even imperative consequence of our central religious convictions.

There is also the need for enhanced biblical studies and for research into liturgical traditions that reflect the new theology of Christian-Jewish relations.

There is a need for more international communication of the different findings in the area of theological research on issues of Jewish-Christian relations as well as relations with Islam.

There is a need for cooperation in the educational field so that the new theology reaches more effectively the understanding of the faith communities. It needs to be incorporated in the curricula of schools, seminaries, universities, and educational centers of the religious communities.

Common action in cases of religious suppression is yet another field where cooperation is needed.

4.4. Should There Be Relations between Religious and Nonreligious Institutions?

Interreligious relations are more and more being dealt with by political bodies at all levels, from the city councils to national governments, the European Union and the United Nations. In the midst of the secular changes in the public and private life, religion is back as an influential part of both the public and private spheres, serving as a challenge for a constructive development of multireligious and multicultural societies, but also as a danger in the reality of fundamentalist movements within all the Abrahamic religions. The latter has been described very accurately by the French author Gilles Kepel in his book *God's Revenge,* in which he shows the growth of new religious movements as a reaction to the secular modern world.[18]

We are also witnessing today the establishment of Islamic communities as an accepted religion in many European countries. There are new and controversial discussions in many European cities and countries about Islamic cemeteries, planning permission for mosques, wearing of scarves while working in public services, and so on. There is a need for cooperation between religious and nonreligious institutions with regard to such interreligious and intercultural conflicts in the neighborhoods, in the cities, and in the countries. Such cooperation must engage in advocacy and conflict resolution as well as in educational and political action to further the capabilities of interreligious and intercultural neighborliness.

5. CONCLUDING REMARKS

In his *Negative Dialectics* Theodor Adorno stated, "Only if that which exists can be changed, is that which exists not all [that exists]."[19]

How, then, can the necessary changes be brought into reality? Only by committed people, insofar as Hans Küng is correct. But they have to go beyond their personal experiences and insights and bring the necessary dialogue work and its new perceptions into the institutions.

Changes can be brought forward by people sharing a vision that the relations between our faith communities including their institutions can be better, and can be most fruitful. There is a vision to be found in the ancient texts of the prophets and in the New Testament scriptures, a vision of the kingdom of God. This vision helps to look beyond the boundaries of individual existence as well as beyond the boundaries of our given religious institutions. This vision is capable of overcoming the attitude of perceiving the institutions that one relates to as an aim in itself. This vision is still capable of motivating women and men to become engaged in interfaith cooperation, to contribute to peace and justice, to build a community in diverse societies, and to work for the renewal of institutions so that these institutions can serve people and people need not serve the institutions.

NOTES

1. ADL Interfaith Relations, Interfaith Focus, *A Dialogue: The Anti-Defamation League and the National Council of Churches,* Vol. 1, No. 1 (New York, 1994), p. 1.

2. Geoffrey Wigoder, *Jewish-Christian Interfaith Relations: Agendas for Tomorrow,* Policy Forum no. 14 of the Institute of the World Jewish Congress (Jerusalem, 1998), 3.

3. The conference proceedings have been published as *From the Martin Buber House 28: The Concept of Monotheism in the Abrahamic Traditions* (Heppenheim: ICCJ, 2001).

4. Published as *From the Martin Buber House 27: Destruction and Renewal—The Role of Religion in Changing Society* (Heppenheim: ICCJ, 2000).

5. Ibid., 6.

6. Ibid., 24.

7. Richard McBrien, in "Papal Apology," *The News Hour with Jim Lehrer,* transcript: http://www.pbs.org/newshour/bb/religion/jan-jun98/vatican_4-8.html.

8. Grigori Benevich, "Judaism and the Future of Orthodoxy," in *Theology after Auschwitz and Its Correlation with Theology after the GULag,* ed. Natalia Pecherskaya (St. Petersburg: School of Religion and Philosophy, 1998), 87.

9. Ibid.

10. Ibid., 87, 88.

11. Sergij Hackel, "The Relevance of Western Post-Holocaust Theology to the Thought and Practise of the Russian Orthodox Church," in *Theology after Auschwitz and Its Correlation with Theology after the GULag,* ed. Natalia Pecherskaya (St. Petersburg: School of Religion and Philosophy, 1998), 65–66.

12. Ibid.

13. Ibid., 70–73.

14. Ibid., 76.

15. Wigoder, *Jewish-Christian Interfaith Relations,* 16.

16. Ibid., 18.

17. Natalia Pecherskaya, ed., *Theology after Auschwitz and Its Correlation with Theology after the GULag: Proceedings of the Second International Conference, St. Petersburg School of Religion and Philosophy* (St. Petersburg: School of Religion and Philosophy, 1998).

18. Gilles Kepel, *La Revanche de Dieu: Chrétiens, juifs et musulmans à la reconquête du monde* (Paris: Seuil, 1991). Translated into English as *The Revenge of God: The Resurgence of Islam, Christianity, and Judaism in the Modern World,* trans. Alan Braley (Cambridge: Polity, 1994).

19. T. W. Adorno, *Negative Dialectics* (London: Routledge, 1990).

8
The New Europe, Nationalism, and Jewish-Christian Relations

David Weigall[†]

The term *New Europe* was coined after 1989 to embrace a range of significant developments. These included the collapse of single-party Communist governments in central and eastern Europe, the frag-mentation of the Soviet Union into fifteen independent republics, the dismantling of the Berlin Wall, and the reunification of Germany.

In western Europe there have been further, and much-debated and contested, advances in integration from the mid-1980s with the 1992 proposals and the Single European Act through to the Treaty of Amsterdam. During this period the European Community (and now Union) has incorporated the Iberian Peninsula, Austria, Finland, and Sweden and entered into association agreements with other states, with an enlargement to twenty-five states. The completion of the EU inter-nal market has been intended to create a Europe without frontiers, in which the international borders, which present barriers to the move-ment of people, goods, and capital, become anachronistic. Europe is once again undivided, but it no longer occupies the central role in world affairs it had before the Second World War.

These events have encouraged great reappraisal and introspection and offered previously unimaginable scope for the inhabitants of the European continent to reconsider their existing national, regional, and ethnic identities. The whole issue of collective identities has acquired a new, or renewed, urgency. At the same time, one has been forced in dra-matic ways to assess to what extent the novelty of the New Europe has been for the better and to what degree the early euphoria that accompanied the events of 1989 has been justified. Certainly, to begin with, there was no shortage of hyperbole. President George Bush in 1992 in his State of the Union Address referred to the events in central and eastern Europe as "miracles of biblical proportions." Pope John Paul II, who in 1987 had evoked the Gaullist vision of a "Europe from the Atlantic to the Urals"—a vision seemingly excluded with the Warsaw Pact invasion of Czechoslovakia in August 1968 and the accentuated tension in East-West relations with the "New Cold War" of the 1980s— envisaged "a world without frontiers." There was talk of a "New World Order," of the "end of history," but history reasserted itself in traditionally violent ways, with war in the Persian Gulf and Iraq as well as bloody conflicts from Bosnia and Kosovo to Chechnya.

The New World Order was forgotten with the development of a range of new, albeit previously submerged, security anxieties in Europe, including the first war on European soil since 1945 and grave instability in North Africa, with protracted economic recession, unemployment, economic hardship, political disenchantment, and an upsurge in separatist tendencies in both parts of the old divide. There was marked popular alienation from the European integration process or at least from the agenda of its most forward proponents, as witnessed in the Maastricht treaty ratification debates and the rejection of the EU constitution in 2005. The sudden collapse of Communism, which had done much to encourage the unification process in western Europe in the Cold War years, now unleashed a new wave of state particularism and cantonization right across the Continent.

Preoccupied with domestic political issues in the recession of the early 1990s, concerned with the resurgence of right-wing and radicalist extremism, and disagreeing over the question of a "wider" or "deeper" Europe, the countries of the European Union, as it became with the Treaty of Maastricht, proved incapable of agreeing on a coherent response to the dilemmas of the former countries of the Soviet Bloc and the successor states of the Soviet Union. As a consequence, as one recent account puts it: "The East European position, including that of Poland, was largely reactive and dependent, forcing the aspiring democracies into the difficult military and foreign policy limbo of a commitment to a Europe itself uncertain of its aims and boundaries."[1] Overall, complex tensions have arisen between economic modernization, transnationalism, and integration on the one hand and, on the other, the "old" Europe of nationalisms and ethnic diversity.

In central and eastern Europe after 1989 there was a conspicuous mood of anticlimax, disappointment, and apathy. As Pope John Paul II said in 1997, even after the Berlin Wall had fallen "another invisible wall" still divided Europe. It was a wall in human hearts "made out of fear and aggressiveness, lack of understanding for people of different origins, colors and religious convictions, a wall of political and economic selfishness, of weakening sensibility to the value of human life."[2] Across the Continent, in spite of all these changes, Raymond Aron's judgment of 1964 still stands: "Consciousness of the nation remains infinitely stronger than a sense of a Europe."

Not least, this alienation has expressed itself in a significant resurgence of the extreme right across Europe. While primarily voicing anger against immigration from Africa, Turkey, and eastern Europe in particular, this has predictably also carried an antisemitic message. It has meant the dissemination of Holocaust-denial propaganda and significant provocations from far-right leaders, such as M. le Pen's allusion to the Shoah as a "point of detail" in the Second World War, or the Flemish Bloc leader Dewinter's statement that Jews had a right to live in Antwerp, but that they are not part of the Flemish people.[3]

The end of the Communist period in central and eastern Europe, the failure of the promised Leninist utopia, has resulted in an emphatic return to themes of national definition, national sovereignty, and even the quest for previously defined state borders. The nationalist ideology as well as the agenda of political parties have, in some cases, called for monoethnic states. Society is invited to define itself in ethnic terms rather than as a civil society. This ethnic nationalism claims that an individual's deepest attachments are inherited not chosen, that it is the national community that defines the individual not the individuals who define the community.

Shlomo Avineri has referred to "the return of history,"[4] but this has been history with a number of illusions. The central and eastern European societies were as unprepared for the sudden collapse of Communism as were Western politicians, and it was the first time a totalitarian system had collapsed under its own weight in a noncataclysmic way. There was a strong persuasion to stress historical continuity and a belief that a natural historical process had simply been interrupted by the Nazis and then by Soviet occupation. With newfound independence,

there was the conviction that one should return to the established historical institutions that represent national continuity and specific culture—
hence, among other things, the ironic symbolism of the restoration of the
crown on the coats of arms of countries that are republics.

The consequence has been, though, some idealization of the past
and the temptation to overlook the profound changes that have taken
place since the Second World War: dramatic industrialization, urban-
ization, and secularization. With such transition and insecurity political
elites have referred to "eternal values," which are either overtly or by
implication identified with Christian values, and have articulated a nostalgic desire to retrieve the norms, patterns, and values destroyed by
Communist rule. There is a Hungarian saying: "From now on everything was different."

In their extreme forms political ethnocentrism and the ideological
fantasy that an ethnically pure state can be achieved have brought about
war and massacres, as in the former Yugoslavia. In central and eastern
Europe extremist nationalist parties have appeared, and populist
leaders—often coming from the former Communist *nomenklatura,* such
as Milosevic—are recycled as nationalists. This has inevitably led to
increased antisemitism because, even though Jewish people and communities may not be directly implicated in the various crises and debates
that have accompanied these dramatic transformations, it is observable
that when extreme nationalism is confronted with the prospect of an
open, pluralistic, and democratic society, it usually returns to traditional
antisemitic arguments of the mythological variety. To give two illustrations: the extreme nationalist Rumanian Party has singled out "Judeo-
Magyars" in its anti-Hungarian attacks. We find the Serbia correspondent
of "Tanjug" in Moscow complaining that the "Jewish lobby" in the
Russian Foreign Ministry was responsible for Russia acceding to
Croatian and Slovenian independence, helping to precipitate the atrocities in Bosnia. The permutations of such fantasies are infinite.

The differences between eastern and western Europe have in many
respects outlived the fall of the Berlin Wall. As people learned that political emancipation was not accompanied automatically by economic
improvement in their own lives, many developed nostalgic sentiments
for the bygone days of authoritarian certainties. In a period of considerable uncertainty and upheaval this radical nationalism has had a soterio-
logical, salvationist aspect. What happened in Serbia after the breakup
of Yugoslavia is the epitome of the politics of national hysteria: political

values have been subordinated to the ultimate purpose of national aggrandizement, defined through the exclusion of all those who do not belong because of blood, confession, or simply cultural preference.[5] It is a classic example of nationalism from the top down, a managed nationalism in an area, incidentally, where a quarter of the population were in mixed marriages.

From the other side of the Serb-Croatian conflict, the demands of nationalist identification in these circumstances have been clearly conveyed by the Croatian writer Slavenka Drakulic:

> Along with millions of other Croats, I was pinned to the wall of nationhood—not only by outside pressure from Serbia and the Federal Army but by national homogenization within Croatia itself. That is what the war is doing, reducing us to one dimension: the Nation. The trouble with this nationhood, however, is that whereas before, I was defined by my education, my job, my ideas, my character— and, yes, my nationality, too—now I feel stripped of all that. I am nobody, because I am not a person any more. I am one of the 4.5 million Croats.[6]

In central and eastern Europe and Russia the vestiges of long-perpetuated and jealously guarded historical fallacies and self-serving fabrications have become part of the new vindictive mythologies. Nationalist narratives of hatred have emerged or reemerged, ascribing the guilt for all that has happened to foreigners, to those who "brought Communism."[7] This is most clearly the case in Russia where the motley red-black coalition of Stalinists, fascists, Black Hundreds, and Russian Orthodox fundamentalists use the myth of "Judeo-Communism" to offer immediate scapegoats for popular discontents and economic failure. We find in uneasy harness the "white" Russian politics of heroic nationalism and imperial grandeur and the "red" exaltation of equality and social justice. In all of the post-Communist societies political operators use popular prejudice and superstition to mobilize anger and designate certain ethno-cultural or religious groups as collectively guilty for their countries' predicament.

The origins of these sentiments may be traced to the nationalist radical right. At the same time, in the circumstances since 1989, with great economic uncertainty, dislocation, and challenge, they may as likely be expressions of radical leftist hostility to multinational companies, the free circulation of capital, and so on. From state socialism the so-called new tribalism inherits the collectivist egalitarianism and anti-market disposition. At all events, it is a complex picture. As Mark Mazower has put it: "In contemporary Europe democracy allows racist parties of the Right to coexist with more active protection of human rights than ever before. It encompasses both the grass-roots politics of Switzerland and the near-dictatorship in post-Communist Croatia."[8]

Ethnic nationalism flourishes in central and eastern Europe because decades of Communist single-party rule largely destroyed whatever civic culture there had been in the region. Moreover, following the Paris Peace Settlement at the end of the First World War no single state that emerged from the collapse of four empires—the Hohenzollern, Austro-Hungarian, Ottoman, and Romanov—did not have ethnic minorities within its frontiers.

The interwar years aggravated the issue and Sovietization only swept it under the carpet. The empty slogan of "eternal friendship and unity of fraternal countries" only disguised the fact that these countries were under Soviet domination, and, as was seen repeatedly after the death of Stalin in 1953, significant assertions of nationalism would meet with forceful repression. At the same time, there is a European-wide ethnic nationalism, which is a revolt against civic nationalism, against the very idea of a nation based on citizenship rather than on ethnicity. There are also many states in which ethnic nationalism flourishes within states committed to civic democracy such as Canada and India.

A few years ago in an overview of the demographic trends of European Jewry, Sergio DellaPergola posed the question: "Is Europe striving for political integration, or is it headed for ethnic polarization and conflict? Is it Maastricht or Sarajevo that is more meaningful to an assessment of the contemporary European situation?"[9] In the same collection of essays Dr. Jonathan Webber asked: "What is it that characterizes the 'New Europe'? Is it the collapse of Communism and the new scope for the peaceful extension throughout the continent of liberal democracy—a development Jews would normally associate with good conditions for their security and well-being? Or is it the explosion of new ethnic and nationalist conflict—a development that Jews would today normally associate with the threat of antisemitism, that is, with poor conditions for their security and well-being."[10] He concluded that it would be in the interest of Jewish people to support the idea of wider European integration and indeed the notion of a European Jewish community.

The answer to DellaPergola's question depends, in part, on the extent to which the states of central and eastern Europe manage effectively to become "civic" states, that is, states of and for all their citizens, irrespective of ethnicity or religion. Civic nationalism maintains that the nations should be composed of all those—regardless of race, color, creed, gender, language, and ethnicity—who subscribe to the nation's political creed. It is called *civic* because it envisages the nation as a community of equal rights–bearing citizens united in patriotic attachment to a shared set of political practices and values. This nationalism is necessarily democratic since it vests sovereignty in all of the people.

Given the history of the area, many people have voiced skepticism, perhaps unfairly, about the longer term. It is perhaps hard to see a civic self-understanding as coming to be the prevalent ethos given the pervasively institutionalized understanding of nationality as fundamentally ethno-cultural rather than political.[11] One might remember that, with the exception of Bohemia and Moravia, these societies had never been democratic before 1989. They did have parliamentary institutions, but voting was either rigged or by open ballot. The majority of the political parties did not represent popular interests and, shortly after the war, by 1948 at the latest, the Communist takeovers had frustrated all efforts to construct a democratic multiparty system.

Another path is the way of minority rights. Here international organizations such as the Council of Europe, the European Union, and the Organization for Security and Cooperation in Europe have pressed the states to adopt and implement minority rights legislation. As a result all new states are formally committed to nondiscrimination and to protecting minority rights. Pessimists could remind us, though, that this was true of the new states of interwar Europe, which were subject to League of Nations Minorities Treaties that expressly required equal treatment and respect for minority languages. Recent history reminds us of the fragility of such undertakings in the face of rampant nationalism.

If modern ideals of liberalism and democracy cannot fill the gap left by the collapse of Communism, the evocation of the past and the emphasis on historical continuity will inevitably take over as legitimating ideas. What about the role of the Christian churches, particularly the Roman Catholic Church, in this transformation? With the resurgence of the nationalities there has been a considerable degree of identification with Christianity: emphasis, for instance, on a Christian and national Hungary, Poland, or Slovakia that puts the churches—particularly, the largest in the region, the Roman Catholic Church—in a paradoxical position. On the one hand, the churches have welcomed the restoration of religious freedom, the possibility of retrieving nationalized church property, including schools, the legally unimpeded exercises of their pastoral missions, and so on. On the other hand, over the more than forty years of Communist rule, the state and the party not only thoroughly changed society but also set out to subordinate the churches with the ultimate ambition of eliminating religion. As a result, the churches became largely isolated from the wider international ecclesiastical community; in particular, the Roman Catholic churches were isolated from important changes wrought by the Second Vatican Council.

In 1965 the Second Vatican Council issued the Declaration on the Relation of the Church to Non-Christian Religions *(Nostra Aetate)* in which it states: "The Church repudiates all persecutions against any man. Moreover, mindful of her common patrimony with the Jews, and motivated by the gospel's spiritual love and by no political considerations, she deplores the hatred, persecutions, and displays of anti-Semitism directed against the Jews at any time and from any source."[12] In an act of major symbolic value, Pope John Paul II addressed congregants in the Central Synagogue in Rome in 1986 in the following words: "The Jewish religion is not 'extrinsic' to us, but in a certain way, 'intrinsic' to our religion. With Judaism, therefore, we have a relationship that we do not have with any other religion. You are our dearly beloved brothers, and, in a certain way, it could be said that you are our elder brothers." Four years later the Vatican branded antisemitism a "sin against God and humanity" and called on the church to repent of the antisemitism that had found a place in past Catholic thought and conduct.

The attempt to subordinate churches to an atheistic totalitarian regime that claimed to modernize society only further reinforced the conservative elements within these regimes. It is not surprising, therefore, that the Roman Catholic Church in particular in central and eastern Europe was not prepared for the collapse of Communism. Whether it actively participated in bringing down the old system, as in Poland and the Czech lands, or was only a beneficiary of the change, as in Hungary, it found it hard to adapt.

More generally, in the post-Communist period the churches found that they confronted the state as institutional actors, making demands on the political process and affecting outcomes. Rather than merely the objects of policy, religious organizations have become participants in the process of shaping policy. Although under Communism much was said about political and economic reforms, little thought was given to necessary ecclesiastical reforms. This became immediately apparent when the churches faced the demands of a pluralistic society. As two recent authors put it, with reference to the Roman Catholic Church: "the Church's greatest danger lay not in persecution but indifference. The spirituality of life on the margins could hardly be expected to survive the advent of democracy, when local conflicts over issues from education to property restitution soon overshadowed the Church's wider social mission."[13]

The prestige of the churches remained high during the decades of Communism. A morality based on absolutes could and did counter the relativistic morality of Communist ideology. Moreover, churches became the focus of civil society, whether the Catholic Church in Poland or the Evangelical Church in the German Democratic Republic, for instance, and to some extent also became the focus of political opposition. The question quite simply posed by 1989 and its sequel was: Would the self-evident identification of Christian ethics with justice and freedom survive the transformation?

After 1989 the prestige of the church declined. First, the establishment of a multiparty political sphere meant that the political sphere regained its autonomy. The church lost its privileged position in this respect. Second, the church had not taken sufficient notice of the progressive secularization of society. Unprepared for the collapse of Communism, it started without a design for the new society. In Poland a heated discussion broke out about the growing clericalization. The church's efforts to Christianize the country (for example, with the introduction of compulsory religious instruction into schools) provoked the criticism of even such prominent Catholics as the poet Czeslaw Milosz. The essential point is that, if being a Pole, Hungarian, or Slovak means being a Christian, then a significant part of the population in these countries is implicitly defined as excluded from the nation in its fullest sense.

That tendency was reflected in the Roman Catholic Church's responses in central and eastern Europe after the fall of the Berlin Wall. In 1990–91 there was, for instance, desecration of Jewish cemeteries and the defacing of the statue of Raoul Wallenberg in Budapest. The

Lutheran and Calvinist churches condemned these acts. There was no official condemnation by the Catholic Bishops' Conference. By contrast, the Polish bishops in their pastoral letter on Jews and Judaism called church members' attention to the evils of antisemitism.[14]

One should neither generalize nor exaggerate. Elements within the Catholic Church and other churches too that espouse antisemitism are, as the Antisemitism World Report of 1997 comments, undoubtedly mainly on the fringes. But the development of conservative nationalism with exclusivist attitudes cannot help. Pope John Paul II was a positive influence on the mutual understanding of Christians and Jews. His strong condemnation of antisemitism, though, indicated the existence within the Polish church of divisions between xenophobic reactionaries unhappy with the line of Vatican II and those who supported dialogue and tolerance. In any case, the impact of the collapse of Communism has had ambiguous consequences for Jews in eastern and central Europe. They have been blamed both for the economic and social difficulties of the post-Communist years and for Communism itself. At the same time that the collapse of Communism has contributed significantly to the upsurge of antisemitism because of ethnic exclusivism and nationalism, it also has led to its decline because of the lifting of Communist repression and the end of official state-sponsored antisemitism.

Pope John Paul II recognized the problem with nationalism. Initially he eulogized the nation. It was not his intention to do so at the expense of ethnic minorities, which he also called on to reassert their identities. The problem was that what sounded inspirational in the Communist period could be abused as inflammatory rhetoric in the changed circumstances of the 1990s. He speedily recognized that a different language was needed for societies jealous of their newfound emancipation. This was shown in papal initiatives over the last decade, including his trip to Bosnia, braving assassination threats, and his appeal on behalf of European gypsies. It is also the case that nationalism in Russia has tended to block papal ecumenical initiatives. Russian Orthodox leaders have seen the post-Communist revival of Greek Catholic churches as a challenge to Orthodox Church jurisdiction and accused Catholics of proselytizing in traditionally Orthodox territories. Historic demarcations have militated against interfaith dialogue here too in part because of the close identification of traditional Russian nationalism and Orthodoxy.

Leszek Kolakowski in 1968 described the Roman Catholic Church in Poland as "a conservative body intent on imposing total hegemony on the whole." During the transformation Monsignor Glemp spoke of the need for a "unanimist democracy," by which he meant that Polish identity should be defined by Roman Catholicism. In practice there have been different movements and approaches, traditionalist and collectivist, and yet, like "The Sign" movement (Snak) embracing *aggiornamento*. There is a particular intensity about the experience of the Polish—a people who, having experienced partition and, in turn, absolute subordination to Germany and the Soviet Union, idealize a mythical unity. In the 1980s the Polish Catholic Church was closely associated with the democratic movement and supported pluralism.

After the installation of the non-Communist Tadeusz Mazowiecki as prime minister in August 1989, the church reversed its position, calling for, among other things—though this demand was not granted— Catholicism to be declared the state religion of Poland. There was an "unmistakable theocratic impulse."[15] Such gains as the Roman Catholic Church in Poland obtained, though, on such issues as abortion and religious education reduced the popularity of the church in Polish society. An approval rating of 87 percent in 1989 had fallen to 31 percent by 1995.[16]

All over eastern Europe, too, after 1989 the Catholic Church became a factor in political disputes. In 1990 the pope warned Czech priests and nuns not to allow the church "to close in on itself." The church's "solidarity with the persecuted has strengthened its moral authority," he claimed, and he listed the "immense historic tasks" the church now faced, which included the revival of ecumenism and the assertion of its presence in public life.[17] The transition since 1989 has meant a Catholic Church in Poland both strengthened and weakened. The collapse of the East-West polarization has imposed reappraisal on the church as well. It has had to abandon the central role that it played during the years of suppression and resistance, when it was either the focus for opposition or the mediator between state and dissidence. Psychologically as well as practically the adjustment to pluralism has not been easy for it, for as Adam Michnik, the prominent Polish intellectual, commented: "to live in pluralism is to know how to limit oneself, to know that we live with others, and to make that cohabitation viable."

One could argue that, as the countries of central and eastern Europe compete to enter the European institutional structures, in particular the European Union, liberalism will become the dominant order of the day, leaving it to marginal demagogues to voice sentiments of chauvinism and discrimination. One can speculate that nationalism will be progressively replaced by what Habermas, in relation to West Germany, called "constitutional patriotism," that tolerance will reign in an unquestioned acceptance of civic nationalism. One can point to the fact that the role of the nation-state has been changing with economic globalization and the impact of decision making by international and supranational institutions. However, it is also true that the insecurities that result both from the end of the Cold War framework of international relations and from globalization have provoked what has been called the "new tribalism." Integration has been shadowed by fragmentation, disintegration, and popular disenchantment. Demands for autonomy have been voiced in western as well as central and eastern Europe.

At the same time, it is appropriate to reflect that the New Europe cannot credibly be defined *tout court* as a Christian Europe. It incorporates a plurality of races, identities, and religions more than ever before. Very obviously and temptingly the new post–Cold War configuration since 1989 has led a number of Christians to focus on the notion of the restoration of Christendom, rather as Hilaire Belloc and those of his views did after the First World War, what has been described as the "Christendom tradition." This view was articulated by the English Roman Catholic historian Christopher Dawson in the following definition of Europe as "a community of peoples who share in a common spiritual tradition that had its origins in the Eastern Mediterranean… and which has been transmitted from age to age and from people to people until it has come to overshadow the world." In his view Europe could only be comprehended by the study of Christian culture, since "it was as Christendom that Europe first became conscious of itself as a society of peoples with common moral values and common spiritual aims."[18] This depiction of Christendom was contrasted with the baleful effects of nationalism: "To ignore Europe and to concentrate all our attention on the political community to which we belong, as though it was the whole social reality, leads in the last resort to the totalitarian state, and National Socialism itself was only this development carried out with Germanic thoroughness and Prussian ruthlessness."[19]

This line of argument would now equate Catholic Christianity with the soul of Europe and would argue that the church, having temporarily been displaced by Marxism, secularism, and materialism, will come into its inheritance. This, among other things, overlooks the extent to which Christianity has been and continues to be a perennial factor in European disunity as well as aspirations to unity. In practice, the only realistic thing is for Christians to face up to the ambiguities of the history of Christian Europe and to participate in a plural order of things.

In this respect, the end of the Cold War did not return us to the Europe of the Treaty of Versailles and the 1920s and 1930s. It is a genuinely *New* Europe, though very old problems have come to haunt it. Just as there has been a temptation to romanticize and grossly to simplify the national histories in central and eastern Europe over the last decade—something that rarely bodes well for minorities—so, too, some have romanticized the notion of Christian Europe, which in one sense may have been Christian but in another sense not. In the context of central and eastern Europe precisely this emphasis on a Christian Europe may aggravate nationalist tensions and strengthen antisemitic sentiment among those who see, as Robert Wistrich has put it, "their national and 'Christian' values being threatened by anonymous forces of modernity and change which they fear and hate."[20]

Much of the informed debate for and against the European Union and its extension has turned on whether or not it will be an open or an introspective and protectionist entity, a "fortress Europe." In the early days of integration, in the period of the original six—France, Germany, Italy, and Benelux—critics sometimes denounced it as a "Catholic Europe" and talked about "Rome rule." This was in many respects so much political knockabout, used by the East German Communist regime as well as Ulster Unionists. The consolidation of the European Union has quintessentially involved a reconciliation between France and Germany and centered on the Rhine corridor.

Contrary to this, the Roman Catholic vision of Christendom has focused on a greater Europe including Russia and the Ukraine.[21] In his "Europe and the Faith" of 1985 Pope John Paul II described it as follows: "Europe, in fact, as a geographical whole is, so to speak, the fruit of two currents of Christian tradition, to which are added two different, but at the same time complementary, forms of culture." It should be said that Protestant statements since 1989 have often been very explicit in their rejection of the idea of a Christian "reconquest of Europe." "There can be no question of reverting to a 'Christian Europe' where churches would wield some kind of power. The Church must place itself in the service of European society as it gropes towards unity," was the view expressed by the president of the Church of the Augsburg

Confession in Alsace-Lorraine in 1990. Here is a very different, plural-ist, emphasis. Answering the question "Was ist Christlich in Europa"? Professor Rudolf von Thadden at the Protestant Kirchentag in Dortmund in 1991 argued: "Europe has received both from Christian traditions and from the insights of the Enlightenment. Its future lies in the dialogue—possibly in the tension—between the Christian faith and secular society."[22] Stress here is laid not on the recreation of unity but on the plurality of the forces that have shaped Europe and the plurality of religious and philosophical traditions that make up the character of contemporary Europe.

Appeals to a common European cultural identity are also unreal-istic, not least because, as Edward Said put it: "Partly because of empire all cultures are involved in one another; none is single, pure; all are hybrid heterogeneous, extraordinarily differentiated and unmono-lithic." The dimension of openness is an internal one for Europe as well. The possibilities of dialogue between faiths and races are best envisaged in a Europe whose populations identify with pluralism, tol-erance, and civic political loyalty rather than exclusive ethnic loyalty.

In 1964 *Ecclesiam Suam* pointed to the imperative of dialogue in the following words: "Dialogue is demanded nowadays by the dynamic course of action which is changing the face of modern soci-ety. It is demanded by the pluralism of society...." The events in Europe since 1989 have, on the one hand, encouraged and, on the other, discouraged the possibilities of dialogue. In this negative bal-ance are included the surge of exclusivist nationalism, the close iden-tification of nationalism and Christianity (of which Poland presents a prominent example), and a concept of revived Christendom, which, in current circumstances, is more likely to hinder than to advance dia-logue, both in relations between Christian and Jew and between the Roman Catholic and Orthodox churches. In 1989 Paul van Buren wrote as follows: "The suspicion that 'Dialogue' is only the latest and most sophisticated form of Christian mission to convert Jews is diffi-cult to dispel, given the fact that some Christians in the Dialogue, and many not in it, cannot hide the fact that conversion is still their final hope for the Jewish people."[23] Any suggestion of a resurgent Christendom with all its historic connotations will make it more diffi-cult to dispel. The New Europe should offer genuinely new opportu-nities—above all a new openness.

NOTES

1. Jonathan Luxmoore and Jolanta Babiuch, *The Vatican and the Red Flag: The Struggle for the Soul of Eastern Europe* (London: Geoffrey Chapman, 1999), 315.

2. Robert Bideleux and Richard Taylor, eds., *European Integration and Disintegration: East and West* (London: Routledge, 1996), 221–22.

3. Simon Epstein, *Extreme Right Electoral Upsurges in Western Europe: The 1984–1995 Wave as Compared with the Previous Ones,* ACTA, no. 8 (Jerusalem: Vidal Sassoon International Centre for the Study of Antisemitism, 1996), 4.

4. Leon Volovici, *Antisemitism in Post-Communist Eastern Europe: A Marginal or Central Issue?* ACTA, no. 5 (Jerusalem: Vidal Sassoon International Centre for the Study of Antisemitism, 1994), 5.

5. Vladimir Tismaneanu, *Fantasies of Salvation: Democracy, Nationalism and Myth in Post-Communist Europe* (Princeton, NJ: Princeton University Press, 1998), 11.

6. Ibid., 89–90.

7. Ibid.

8. For an excellent historical survey, see Mark Mazower, *The Dark Continent* (London: Lane, 1998).

9. Jonathan Webber, ed., *Jewish Identities in the New Europe* (London: Littman Library of Jewish Civilisation, 1994), 72.

10. Ibid., 12–13.

11. Roger Brubaker, *Nationalism Reframed: Nationhood and the National Question in the New Europe* (Cambridge: Cambridge University Press, 1996), 105.

12. Translation taken from W. M. Abbott, SJ, ed., *The Documents of Vatican II, with Notes and Comments by Catholic, Protestant and Orthodox Authorities* (New York: America Press, 1966), 666–67.

13. Luxmoore and Babiuch, *Vatican and the Red Flag,* 303.

14. See William H. Swatos, Jr., ed., *Politics and Religion in Central and Eastern Europe: Transition and Traditions* (Westport, CT: Praeger, 1994).

15. Sabrina Petra Ramet, *Whose Democracy?: Nationalism, Religion and the Doctrine of Collective Rights in Post-1989 Eastern Europe* (Lanham, MD: Rowman and Littlefield Publishers, 1997), chapter 4.

16. Ibid.

17. Luxmoore and Babiuch, *Vatican and the Red Flag,* 303.

18. Christopher Dawson, *Understanding Europe* (London: Sheed and Ward, 1952), 26.

19. Ibid., 25.

20. Robert Wistrich, *Terms of Survival* (London: Routledge, 1995).

21. John Fulton and Peter Gee, *Religion in Contemporary Europe* (Lampeter, Wales: Edwin Mellen Press, 1994).

22. Ibid., 103.

23. Charles Wei-Hsun and Gerhard E. Spiegler, eds., *Religious Issues and Interreligious Dialogues: An Analysis in Developments since 1945* (Westport, CT: Greenwood Press, 1989), 416.

9
Israel within Jewish-Christian Relations

Andrew P. B. White

INTRODUCTION

In Jewish-Christian relations, Israel cannot be avoided—when Israel is in the picture so are politics. The political picture of the moment also has a major impact, as the state of the Middle East peace process will influence Jewish-Christian relations at even the most basic level. At the grass roots of our societies most people are not able to separate Israel from "the Jews," who are seen as being intimately tied up with the state whether they hold to a Zionist position or not. Moltmann sums up this dilemma by stating,

> with the name Israel, politics comes into the discussion: the politics of the state of Israel, of Zionism, of the PLO, of the Near East, politics of East and West, of oil interests, and much more about which the Church, in any case, is not competent. For the church is a non-political organisation; Israel in contrast, is a state.[1]

Moltmann's statement demonstrates one of the difficulties faced by those who are serious about Jewish-Christian relations; by necessity one also has to keep on top of the politics of the Middle East and attempt to compare religion and politics, which might seem to be incomparable. Christianity, though not without its own politics, is not

125

tied to any particular land or nation, with the possible exception of the Vatican City State. In contrast, since its beginnings, Judaism has looked to the promised land.

The birth of Zionism and the eventual establishment of the State of Israel in 1948 have had a major influence on the theology of all the Abrahamic faiths. From the Judeo-Christian position we are left with the challenge: Is this the return of the actions of God into space and time? The political opinion that one holds regarding Israel will profoundly affect one's theology. Likewise the theology that one holds regarding Israel will profoundly affect one's politics. It is extremely difficult to assess which comes first, the politics or the theology.

It has become clear to me in my research in this field over several years that there are three main Christian theologies of Israel, which I call the three R's: replacement theology, remnant theology, and recognition theology. It is fair to say that since the establishment of the State of Israel, there has been an increasing polarization of views between those who tend to be negative about Israel, even doubting its right to exist, and those who uncritically support Israel, seeing it as a vital part of their own eschatological hope. These two extremes have been the cause of much conflict, even within the church itself. The position that individual Christian denominations take vis-à-vis Israel is often influenced by the experiences of their own denomination within Israel itself. Once again this is in historical terms a fairly new phenomenon and one that is still developing. The whole emphasis on the coming of the third millennium of the Common Era has in itself been responsible for many churches taking a serious look at the role Israel plays in their own theology.

In order to examine more closely the present trends regarding the churches' response to Israel one needs to look more closely at these three dominant theologies.

REPLACEMENT THEOLOGY

The belief that the church has replaced Israel can be traced back to the beginnings of postbiblical Christian theology. Within the works of many of the church fathers there is a clear and systematic replacement position. Origen, who is often seen as the father of Christian doctrine, was a Platonic philosopher at the school of Alexandria. Much of his theology bears the distinctive mark of Neoplatonist and Stoic theories. His method of biblical interpretation corresponded to the tripartite nature of man as "bodily, psychical and pneumatic." The result was an allegorical and spiritualized interpretation of scripture. His conclusion regarding the people of Israel was that their favored role with God had been lost and that the Gentile majority of the church was now the "New Israel." This Origen saw as being the result of the way the Jews had treated "the Savior of the human race." In his words, "not only was Jerusalem destroyed and Israel sent into exile for crimes, but their divine election was revoked; they were destined to stand in perpetual opposition to God."[2]

Replacement theology has been the dominant response to the people and land of Israel through the centuries, contributing greatly to the development and maintenance of antisemitism. It can be seen throughout the ages in ecclesiastical art, the assigned biblical chapter headings, and, what's more, in how "Christian nations" formulated law regarding the Jews.

The establishment of the State of Israel probably would have had even greater opposition than it did from the Christian world if it were not for the growing realization of the extent of the tragedy of the Shoah. Despite this tragedy and the reassessment of Christian theology that grew out of it, there are sections of Christendom that still hold a strong theology of replacement. Only now the issue of *Eretz Yisrael* has to be addressed. The interpretation is consistent: the promised land is now the whole world that will hear the good news of Jesus and where the church will be established. Jerusalem is the heavenly city, which will eventually be the home of all Christians.

The development of a Palestinian theology of liberation has been one of the most significant evolvements of replacement theology since its inception in the church fathers. This particular strand of the theology has grown out of the everyday experiences of Palestinian Christians living in Israel since 1948. It has found support predominantly among the Western churches like the Latins, Anglicans, and Lutherans. Many of their clergy have received a Western theological education that has exposed them to Latin American liberation theologies. They in turn have greatly influenced the theology and politics of their own denominations around the world. It has also been noted that the Palestinians belonging to Western churches are in many respects the result of the

failed targeted missionary activity to the Jewish community in the last
century.

It is not too extreme to state that the Palestinian church has faced
a major theological crisis since the establishment of Israel. A considerable part of this crisis has been due to what they perceive as the use of
the Bible as a political Zionist text. Canon Naim Ateek stated:

> Before the creation of the state, the Old Testament was con-
> sidered an essential part of Christian Scripture, pointing and
> witnessing to Jesus. Since the creation of the State, some
> Jewish and Christian interpreters have read the Old
> Testament largely as a Zionist text to such an extent that it
> has become almost repugnant to Palestinian Christians. As a
> result, the Old Testament has generally fallen into disuse
> among both clergy and laity, and the Church has been
> unable to come to terms with its ambiguities, questions and
> paradoxes—especially with reference to the twentieth cen-
> tury events in Palestine.[3]

It is fair to say that a significant section of Christendom holds to a similar position. The theological stance of many churches has become so
intertwined with the politics of the "Palestinian problem" that politics
and theology are often difficult to differentiate. The message of several
of the Palestinian churches is that God is a God of the oppressed who
calls his people to fight for justice. The Palestinian people are
oppressed and without justice, and it is therefore the responsibility of
the church to fight for their rights and oppose their oppressor. Who is
their oppressor? The State of Israel. Who is Israel? The Jews.
Therefore, it is they who must be put under pressure so that the
oppressed may one day be set free to enter their promised land that is
being denied to them.

This may appear to be a rather simplified account of a highly
complex situation, but in reality the simplicity of the presentation has
been the reason for its success. It has influenced not only whole
denominations but also the majority of Christian pilgrimage companies
and many of the major mission and aid organizations. One such organization recently sent to every bishop in the United Kingdom a significant document outlining the extent of Israel's oppression of the
Palestinians and its failure to comply with the Oslo Accord. Emotive

language was used, accusing Israel of ethnically cleansing the Palestinians and systematically Judaizing Jerusalem. The desired purpose of the document was to call upon the churches to oppose Israel publicly in the millennium year.

After the establishment of Israel, many Christians who did not hold to a replacement theology hoped that the return of Jews to the land of their fathers would convince the churches of God's continued involvement in his people the Jews. In reality the existence of Israel has complicated Jewish-Christian relations because of the ambiguity of statehood and peoplehood. The fact that the supersessionist replacement theology can now be combined with the fight for justice for a minority Arab community has added to its weight and influence. It is difficult to pursue any Jewish-Christian dialogue without Israel continually being in the picture. As a Christian it is presumed that if you are involved in Jewish-Christian relations you support every action of the State of Israel. For the Jew there are often deeply offensive comments such as "Why, after all that you Jews have suffered in the Holocaust, are you now doing the same to the Palestinians?" This is a statement that I have heard on many occasions, coming not from the uneducated but from religious leaders, academics, and politicians.

REMNANT THEOLOGY

At the other end of the theological spectrum there are those who hold to a remnant theology. The proponents of this position would state that they held to a biblical theology that allowed for a consistency and continuity between the Hebrew Scriptures and the New Testament. The key passages quoted are from Paul's Letter to the Romans chs. 9–11. Here the church is presented with a picture of an olive tree. The roots of the tree are the people of Israel while the branches are a "faithful remnant" from Israel and the grafted gentile branches of the church who are reminded not to "boast over Israel, because you do not support it, it supports you."[4]

Although this theology, as all others, can claim biblical roots, remnant theology has been a much later development as a clearly defined entity. Many people have presumed that it is the result of the growth of the twentieth-century evangelical movement, while its origins can be traced at least as far back as the Puritans of the seventeenth century.

Within the developing theology of the Puritan movement there was a great desire to study scriptures in their original texts. While there was an abundance of Greek and Latin scholars, there were very few who had an in-depth understanding of the Hebrew Scriptures. It was, therefore, to Amsterdam that many of the Puritan scholars went to rectify this problem—not to the Calvinist scholars but to the rabbis. Under their guidance they not only mastered Hebrew but also began to develop a significantly new understanding of covenant. A theme dear to their hearts now had significance not only for them as Christians but also for the Jewish people. Rapidly they moved from a classical replacement theology to a position in which they believed that God's covenant with his people Israel was eternal. As this was a covenant of both land and people, they also reassessed their attitude regarding Palestine. They came to the conclusion not only that Palestine was the rightful home of the Jewish people but that God would eventually ensure that they returned to their homeland.

The political consequences of this were considerable. Immediate pressure was put on Cromwell to change the attitude of England toward the Jewish people. The Jews, having been expelled from England in 1290, were both invited and encouraged to return. The first Jews to seek refuge in England were those of Spanish and Portuguese origin who had fled to Holland escaping persecution in their own lands. The Bevis Marks Synagogue in the City of London bears witness to these first Jewish people to return to England.

The notion that God was still faithful to the Jewish people was not long lived, as there was soon a return to the classical anti-Judaic polemic that has been prominent in the church since its conception. The next demonstration of a positive Christian attitude to Israel (people and land) came in the nineteenth century. The mid-nineteenth century saw the development of the Catholic Apostolic movement, founded by the charismatic maverick Edward Irving. Irving, though dismissed by many because of his overemphasis on the prophetic, did have very considerable influence in the higher echelons of mid-Victorian London society. At the heart of his movement was the belief that God would restore his people Israel and return them to their promised land.

Similar views were held by the fathers of the Brethren movement such as J. N. Darby who worked for many years on a new translation of the scriptures. For the Brethren movement their understanding of Israel was determined by their dispensational eschatology. They believed that the rejection of Jesus by the majority of Judaism only postponed all God's promises for Israel until Christ's second coming. This parousia would bring in the millennial reign of Christ during which time all God's plans for Israel, which were thwarted at Christ's first coming, would be restored and come to full fruition. One of their key texts was 2 Samuel 7 in which God states that the covenant with David is ever-lasting.

It was not just those on the fringe who were beginning to recon-sider God's purposes for Israel. The Anglican cleric William Hechler had a major influence on the young Theodore Herzl, continually encouraging him in his quest to reestablish the homeland of the Jewish people in Palestine. The 1870s saw the establishment of the Mildmay Mission to the Jews by John Wilkinson, and in 1889 he published his influential book *Israel My Glory*. It is in this book that we see one of the earliest articulations of a remnant theology. In the conclusion of the book he writes:

> [The] Jewish portion of the Church is called "a remnant according to the election of grace"; and the Gentile portion, "a people taken out for His name"; both one in Christ, who is the head of his body the church.
>
> We have also gathered that a future restoration to Palestine, in unbelief, is assured to the entire nation of Israel; that the time of Jacob's troubles will culminate after restoration in the attempt of Antichrist to crush the nation out of existence, in order to produce universal atheism; and that in Israel's extremity the Lord Jesus Christ will appear in person on Mount Olivet...to destroy Antichrist and estab-lish universal peace.[5]

Although this position held by Wilkinson may appear to be extreme, we know that it was influential among many politicians at the begin-ning of the last century and almost certainly influenced Balfour to make his declaration regarding the support of His Majesty's govern-ment for the establishment of a homeland for the Jewish people in Palestine.

Today there are many modern manifestations of this position, par-ticularly among the evangelical and charismatic sections of the church. The proponents of remnant theology are technically known as Christian

Zionists, a movement that is believed to have over 100 million supporters. A recent survey showed that the majority of evangelicals in the
United States considered themselves to be Christian Zionists. The
movement has, however, spread much farther than the United States
with supporters throughout the world, including some unlikely countries such as Japan.

While it may appear to be a fairly clear-cut and unified theology,
there are indeed many subdivisions, one of the major ones being the
position that proponents take regarding the conversion of the Jewish
people. While influential groups such as the International Christian
Embassy in Jerusalem publicly speak out against all evangelistic activity among Jews,[6] others, such as the Anglican mission agency CMJ,[7]
actively seek to encourage Jews to acknowledge Jesus as their
Messiah. This second group tends to work more closely with the various "Messianic Jewish" groups. These are Jewish people who, though
accepting the major tenets of the Christian faith, do not call themselves
Christians but rather identify themselves as Messianic Jews.

All of these groups would agree that the modern State of Israel is
intrinsically related to the Israel of prophecy and is a direct fulfillment
of it. They will often support Israel politically, usually siding with the
more religious and right-wing political parties. However, although
Christian Zionism has developed considerably in recent years, it has
failed to have a major influence on the Anglican Church. This is almost
certainly due to the fact that a Palestinian bishop has for many years
now led the Anglican Church in Israel, and most of its members are
Arabs.

RECOGNITION THEOLOGY

This third theology is the newest of the three positions. In reality
it is a post-Holocaust development, and its genesis can be traced to the
influential meeting of church leaders in Seelisberg in 1947. This gathering eventually gave birth to the International Council of Christians
and Jews. The meeting was called at a time when the enormity of the
Shoah was just coming into realization. Religious leaders, particularly
from the nations where the genocide of six million Jews had taken
place, asked themselves some serious questions in the light of what was
beginning to emerge. How could six million Jews be killed in the heart

of Christian Europe? How had Christian theology contributed to this atrocity? In the deliberations of Seelisberg it became clear that supersessionism, which had given birth to replacement theology, had played a major role in creating an antisemitic culture that denied the Jewishness of Jesus and thus the Jewish roots of Christianity.

While this theology was developing in the European mainland, two British visionaries, James Parkes, an Anglican priest and scholar from Oxford, and W. W. Simpson, a Methodist minister, had already laid the foundations. Well before World War II both men had been calling for a reassessment of Christian theology regarding its attitude toward the Jewish people. Key to the whole development of this theology is the understanding of the nature of covenant. Rather than starting from the point of salvation being for and through the church, it begins with the acknowledgment that God's covenant with his people Israel is everlasting. Thus the question is: How does the Gentile church also share in salvation history and its fulfillment?

The fundamental point of this position is that God has not forsaken his people Israel. His covenant of people and land remains. The establishment of the State of Israel is seen as a profound vindication of the truth of Hebrew Scripture without accepting that this has great apocalyptic and eschatological implications for Christians. Thus this theology differs from remnant theology in the respect that it allows far greater self-definition for the people and land of Israel. This position has had particular influence in the Dutch Reformed Church, where it has sat well with their Calvinistic understanding of adoption. In 1970 the churches' synod adopted a document, which stated that the return of the Jewish people to the land "is a sign for us that it is God's will to be on earth together with man. Therefore we rejoice in this reunion of people and land."[8]

This theology continues to remain a position predominantly held by the theologically articulate, and, unlike the other two theologies, has never had a major popular following. It has failed to gain support by many as it is perceived to be too liberal by both evangelical Protestant Christians and Catholics. Often it is simplistically seen as justifying salvation by "works" rather than by "grace."

CONCLUSION

With the increasingly polarized views of Christians regarding Israel, we are seeing that there is a potential crisis looming in Jewish-Christian relations as it is becoming increasingly difficult to discuss the subject without Israel being the dominant theme. Those who are involved in an ongoing dialogue are often criticized for their Zionist position, despite the fact that Israel is not even being discussed. There is also an increased ghettoization between the proponents of each theology, with one camp refusing to talk to the other. The State of Israel is itself caught up in this Christian confusion and has concentrated on showing public support and appreciation for the Christian Zionists, who with their remnant theology provide a great amount of support for Israel.

The continuing problems faced by the Palestinian people have added to the crisis in Jewish-Christian relations. Replacement theology has been revitalized by the development and success of Palestinian liberation theology, a theology that attempts to provide hope for the sufferings of all Palestinians. There is a great deal of frustration among many Arab Christians that they have had to pay the price of Western Christian antisemitism. Until 1948 Jews and Christians lived in harmony together in many Arab nations as *Dhimmi*. Unlike the Western church, the church of the Orient never developed an anti-Judaic polemic. In the writings of many of the desert fathers one is presented with a theology of great respect and admiration for God's ancient people, the Jews.

It has to be acknowledged that the world of Jewish-Christian relations has failed the Christians of Israel and Palestine by failing to be involved in a dialogue with Arab Christians. At the other end of the spectrum it is also true that little substantive dialogue has taken place between the proponents of a recognition theology and the Christian Zionists. This is often because there is a very real fear among Jewish parties involved in dialogue that those who hold to a remnant theology have a hidden missionary agenda. There is also a real fear of bringing Messianic Jews into any dialogue between Christians and Jews. Several councils of Christians and Jews around the world have specifically said that it is inappropriate for Messianic Jews to be involved in the dialogue process at any level. While I can accept the reasons for this stance, it may add to the division between Christians on the issue of Israel.

Interestingly, in recent years there has been the beginning of a dialogue process between Messianic Jews and Palestinian Christians in Israel. Both groups have been discriminated against and have found reconciliation when they have been able to share what they have in common.

If there is to be any consensus or reconciliation between the proponents of each of these three theologies they must begin to be in dialogue with one another. Sadly this division is perpetuated by so much of the Christian pilgrimage industry. Most companies that take people to Israel and Palestine have their own political line that they seek to promote. Thus pilgrims can go through their entire ten or twelve days in Israel without meeting a Messianic Jew, a Palestinian Christian, or a member of an ancient church. If Israel is to become a means of reconciliation between Jews and Christians the whole pilgrimage industry needs to be challenged. Risks must be taken by bringing together those who strongly disagree with one another. They need to hear the story of the other and begin to understand their pain.

Christianity also needs to examine the role of *Eretz Yisrael* in its own theology. Why has Christianity been so attached to the land? Why like the other two great monotheistic faiths has it also fought over this real estate, which is called holy? These and many other questions need to be asked if the church is to have any role in trying to bring healing and wholeness to the divisions of Israel and Palestine. When the right questions are asked and people begin to listen to one another, they may well discover that Israel can indeed be an instrument of both unity and spiritual growth.

NOTES

1. Jürgen Moltmann, *Church and Israel: A Common Way of Hope?* (London: SCM Press, 1989).

2. Origen, *Against Celsus* 4.22f., in *Ante-Nicene Christian Library,* ed. A. Roberts and J. Donaldson (Edinburgh: T&T Clark, 1867–72), 24:506.

3. Naim Ateek, *Justice and Only Justice: A Palestinian Theology of Liberation* (Maryknoll, NY: Orbis Books, 1989), ch. 4 "The Bible and Liberation."

4. A simplified interpretation of Romans 11.

5. John Wilkinson, *Israel My Glory* (London: Mildmay Mission, 1889).

6. They believe that Paul's statement in Romans 11 that all Jews will be saved will be an apocalyptic event that will happen before the *parousia* as a miraculous act.

7. The Church's Ministry among Jewish People. In Israel it is known as the Israel Trust of the Anglican Church (ITAC).

8. *Israel: People, Land and State. Suggestions for a Theological Evaluation* (1970), quoted by Petra Heldt and Malcolm Lowe in "Theological Significance of the State of Israel," *Immanuel* 22/23 (1989).

10
The Effect of the Holocaust on Jewish-Christian Relations

Stephen D. Smith

Written in Pencil in the Sealed Railway-Car

> here in this carload
> i am eve
> with abel my son
> if you see my other son
> cain son of man
> tell him that i

> by Dan Pagis

Cain and Abel. The archetypal story of jealousy, competition, and murder between brothers. Cain slew Abel and then attempted to absolve himself of responsibility of the crime that he had committed. "Am I my brother's keeper?" he responds to God's inquiry about the whereabouts of his younger brother. William Jay Peck complains that God unfairly forgave Cain, leaving the future open to a history full of fratricides.[1] This was not the first disruption in the short narrative "history" of humankind in biblical sources, but it was a disturbing one. Envy, murder, guilt, and denial became precedents of the human experience, and thereafter fratricide and, by extension, genocide and mass death became possible. Since the conclusion of the Second World War a new and more recent disruption has confronted the human experience. Among a foray of unanswered and perhaps unanswerable questions, one in particular challenges a

137

reassessment of the state of relations between the church and the Jews: "Your brother's blood is crying out to me from the ground" (Gen 4:10).

Like it or not, there is a connection between current developments in the Jewish-Christian relationship and this demanding question. The Holocaust has become the prism through which the relationship is viewed, tested, and judged. But underlying the question is a more serious accusation, that of culpability. Cain's answer was not to answer. The question here remains though, How has the Christian church answered the same question in the light of the Holocaust?

"The common future of Jews and Christians demands that we remember, for 'there is no future without memory.' History itself is *memoria futuri.*"[2] The question to emerge from this is a simple one: What exactly do we mean, "to remember" in the context of the Jewish-Christian relationship? Could it not be construed that the Christian answer in the form of inculcating memory is the answer of Cain—that is, *no* answer, as it avoids the real issue of culpability. Does not the cliché of remembrance cloud the fact that when Jews and Christians fulfill their duty to remember it is not a common one at all? Jews and Christians look back on the Holocaust in very different ways, and the Holocaust demands very different responses of them. The absolute victimization of all Jews without exception within the context of a passive, or even actively engaged, Christian church creates a different set of mnemonic parameters for Jews and Christians. Moreover, these memories, taken in their fullness, are not memories to unite but to divide, as the Holocaust demonstrates the quintessentially destructive nature of the relationship between Jews and Christians.

Johann Baptist Metz's concept of a "dangerous memory" would suggest that there are memories in which earlier experiences break through to the center point of our lives and reveal new and dangerous insights for the present.[3] If these are memories "which we have to take into account," then surely they fit into the Metzian concept of a memory of suffering that impacts on present and future. However, what those memories mean and how they impact on the identity of Jews as Jews and Christians as Christians may be entirely different to their impact on the Jewish-Christian relationship. The impact of the Holocaust on this relationship and its future role in the independent and shared memories of Jews and Christians is not, therefore, a passive memory instigated by the respective parties out of deference or reverence for the victims of the Holocaust. It is a memory that demands of the identity of the parties, a memory that accuses on the one hand and confuses and disrupts on the other. It is a memory of disturbing consequences that indicts individuals clearly not directly involved and suggests that the context as well as the perpetrators themselves are in some way culpable. How Jews and Christians then bridge the divided memory of the Holocaust and face the consequence of its disruptive nature is the context in which the Jewish-Christian relationship works in the present and on which the Holocaust imposes itself.

In this regard a full and proper reevaluation of the relationship between Jews and Christians could be either too late or too early. Too late, because such an encounter with the historical crisis of the relationship prior to the Holocaust might have precluded it. Too early, because Jews and Christians cannot surely enter into a meaningful dialogue until the nature of the crisis is clearly understood.

Before attempting to evaluate how that crisis may be further confronted in the future, a number of observations on the role that it has come to play up to the present will be instructive. I hope that the continuum of thought to date will in some way help assess the trajectory of reaction hereafter or will observe what more may be added.

The history of Jewish-Christian relations is of course as old as the point at which the two streams of religious tradition were identifiably bifurcated, which in itself is a matter for scholarship to continue to grapple with. That most of the relationship has been spent either competing to predominate or in outright domination of one by the other leaves it in a tangibly poor state.

The development of the possibility of a more congenial relationship is identified as the point at which it was perceived by a number of Christian individuals that such enmity and contempt was not a Christian virtue—this of course predated the Holocaust. For any individual to demonstrate that Christian contempt of the Jews, accompanied by the appellant social, political, and personal violence, was a negative trait of the Christian tradition was a brave undertaking for any sufficiently enlightened so to do. James Parkes is an obvious example of an individual theologian prepared to admit that "a good theology cannot be built on a bad history," as is needed in any revolution of Christianity after the Holocaust.[4] He in turn makes reference to other lonely individuals such as Conrad Moehlman[5] of Colgate-Rochester Divinity School and Erik Peterson,[6] both of whom began to realize in their publications as early as 1933 that all was not well in Christendom.

The list of individuals obviously thinking around this issue could also be extended to the likes of Paul Tillich, Reinhold Niebuhr, and Jacques Maritain, who all reflected on the issue of antisemitism and the Christian response. However, it appears that much of their reaction was a response to the early stages of the Nazi regime's unfolding policies toward the Jews, so I would argue that they were actually formulating some of the first reactions to the Holocaust itself rather than creating precursors.

So too, Dietrich Bonhoeffer and Martin Niemoeller were providing early Christian responses to the destruction of European Jewry. Bonhoeffer reasserts that, "The Church of Christ has never lost sight of the thought that the 'Chosen People' who nailed the redeemer of the world to the cross must bear the curse for its action through a long history of suffering."[7] While Bonhoeffer went on to suppress these sentiments during his own struggle against Nazism, his response to the crisis demonstrates the poor development of theological understanding even among the opponents of Nazism. Niemoeller's confirmation that "the Jewish people must go its way under the burden which Jesus' decree has laid upon it"[8] also signifies the dire straits the Jews were in.

Even though the first National Conference of Christians and Jews had been established in America in 1927,[9] and the Council of Christians and Jews in Britain in 1942 during the war period, in the aftermath of the Second World War Christians realized that the tragedy of mass death visited on the Jewish communities of Europe was not without consequence. Geoffrey Wigoder notes that the first international gathering of Christians and Jews in Oxford in 1946 was lacking what he identifies as:

> the two issues which were to become paramount in Jewish-Christian relations in the post war world: the role of Christian teaching in creating an atmosphere in which the Holocaust was possible—this realization had not yet dawned—and the struggle for the Jewish state then in full swing....[10]

While these two agenda items might well have been missing, what Wigoder does concede at this point was the significance of this gathering in the immediate postwar period. Whether or not the consequences of mass death were on the agenda, the fact that German clergy and

Jewish survivors could commingle so soon after the events at all was a first act of considerable courage. By 1948, when the First Assembly of the World Council of Churches met in Amsterdam, committee IV reported on "The Christian Approach to the Jews." The report opens in solemn recognition of the fact that "No people in [this] world have suffered more bitterly from the disorder of man than the Jewish people," and observes that "[we cannot] forget that we meet only five years after the extermination of six million Jews." After this fine preamble, in the next paragraph it restates its conviction that "Go ye into all the world and preach the gospel to every creature,"[11] including the Jews. The underscoring of mission to the Jews as a part of the Christian duty clearly fails to understand anything of the causal nature of evangelism in the genesis and perpetuation of antisemitism and the resultant conditions in which mass death could occur.

More positively, it is important to highlight the fact that the previous year in Seelisberg the International Council of Christians and Jews met for their second conference and were more honest in their confrontation of the Holocaust. As Christians and Jews working together, honesty had to be a part of their relationship. The fact that any Christians at this point were in a position to note that Christian affirmation of the un-Christian nature of antisemitism had "not sufficed to prevent the manifestation among Christians...of an undiscriminating racial hatred of the Jews as people"[12] was progress in the right direction. This honesty led to the "Ten Points" of Seelisberg, which set out the stall for the development of a more understanding relationship, particularly on the part of Christians toward Jews and Judaism. At the heart of this statement was the realization that "we have recently witnessed an outburst of antisemitism which has led to the persecution and extermination of millions of Jews."[13]

While in neither case do the authors of the reports go so far as to blame Christianity for the Holocaust, the history of antisemitism is seen as being causal, if only in providing the context in which Nazism could operate. Clearly at this point the Holocaust is demanding a reaction, particularly from the Christian churches in reconsidering its relationship with the Jews.

The apparent need of the churches to react seems to be predicated on a number of emotions, guilt among them. In a bid to address that feeling of guilt, Christians had to perform theological contortions in order to repent, without giving up any of their previously held supersessionist convictions. At the Second Assembly of the World Council of Churches, in 1954, a breakaway group of twenty-four delegates issued a statement on the "Hope of Israel." In their brief statement they managed to conclude that: "In view of the grievous guilt of Christian people towards the Jews throughout the history of the Church, we are certain that: The Church cannot rest until the title of Christ to the kingdom is recognized by his own people...."[14] This remarkable statement clearly demonstrated the dilemma the churches had found themselves in. There was the conviction that something must be done in reaction to the Holocaust but that whatever it was it would not constitute sufficiently demanding criteria as to force a rethinking of Christian theology.

Hereafter, the World Council of Churches became more concerned with the Middle East than with Christian culpability in either the Holocaust or its precursory history. In fact by the sitting of the Sixth Assembly at Vancouver in 1983, the WCC had sufficiently moved its focus to state that churches should undertake to:

> remind Christians in the Western world to recognize that their guilt over the fate of the Jews in their countries may have influenced their views of the conflict in the Middle East and has often led to uncritical support of the policies of the State of Israel, thereby ignoring the plight of the Palestinian people and their rights.[15]

Whatever the rights and wrongs of that situation, it is now possible to consider Jews as perpetrators in their own right. The church had a convenient route to shed some of its own guilt about the Holocaust and to refocus minds away from the necessity of dealing with antisemitism as a problem specific to the Christian church. In this new political context, Jews as the perpetrators of ethnic hatred against the Palestinians provided the perfect balance to antisemitism. If Jews could discriminate against Palestinians, Christians no longer need to repent to Jews for discriminating against them.

For the Catholic Church to reaffirm in 1965 that the cross of "Christ Our Peace reconciled Jews and Gentiles, making both one in himself" may have felt like a quantum leap forward. That *Nostra Aetate* undertook to absolve all Jews everywhere of Christ's death was no noble action but simply an admission of the state the church had allowed itself to fall into. However, where clarity is required, for example on the status of the covenant, *Nostra Aetate* remains muted. Similarly, on the status of Hebrew Scriptures the document is ambiguous, as it is about mission to the Jews and the State of Israel. Perhaps the success of *Nostra Aetate* can be summed up in the opportunity it gave for change. While criticizing the document's weaknesses, Geoffrey Wigoder notes that "a complete new vocabulary was now employed in referring to the Jews and this contributed to the creation of a fresh atmosphere conducive to mutual understanding and dialogue."[16]

Nostra Aetate was followed ten years later by a set of guidelines for its implementation, and again in 1985 a further set of "Notes."[17] These expanded "Notes" address topics such as dialogue, liturgy, teaching and education, and joint social action. While they show a growing awareness of the need for developing stronger links, the "Notes" still fail to address the fundamental theological issues at stake. Wigoder in a strongly worded reply to the "Notes" comments, "I can only read [here] an affirmation that the road to salvation is through Jesus and the Church. Here, too, the deepest level of Jewish self-understanding is being negated and the Jews are being denied their own validity."[18] The sometimes confused messages coming from the highest Vatican authorities must also be noted. In 1985 the pope commented that the Jews are "the People of God of the Old Covenant which has not been revoked"; but in a series of sermons in 1986 he referred to the promise of a new covenant for his chosen people, "ratified with the blood of His own son, Jesus on the cross."[19]

While on one level the churches were trying to formulate their response, which was, at least in part, political, theologians had their own (also sometimes political) responses. In 1967 theologians Karl Rahner, Johann Baptist Metz, and the Czech philosopher Milan Machovec were in conversation in Munich. Metz relays part of the content of this conversation in a 1984 article published in *Concilium*.[20] Machovec referred to Theodor Adorno's dictum that "after Auschwitz poetry is obscene," and asked whether the same applied to the prayers of Christians after Auschwitz. Metz reports that he replied, "We can pray after Auschwitz, because there were prayers in Auschwitz" (although he omits that these were mainly prayers on the lips of dying Jews). He then goes on to say: "We Christians can no longer go back behind Auschwitz, but neither can we go on beyond Auschwitz except together with the victims of Auschwitz. This, in my eyes, is the root of Jewish-Christian ecumenism." Ecumenism is not quite what he means, as ecumenism does not demand the theological shift of individuals, but Metz does. He develops a radical approach to a new Christian theology after the Holocaust and identifies three principle theses, which refer to fundamental reworkings of Christian theology rather than an improved Jewish-Christian relationship through dialogue. His theses, also outlined in the same *Concilium* article, encompass the *formation* of Christian identity in the face of the Jews, the *comprehension* of their identity in the face of the Jews and the importance of stressing the *Jewish dimension* in Christian beliefs.

It is instructive to compare the example of Metz's response to the Holocaust to that of James Parkes, whose interest and expertise in the problematic of the Jewish-Christian relationship went back well before the Holocaust. In contrast to Metz, in the post-Holocaust period Parkes sees Christianity and Judaism as twin foci of a single revelation addressed to humanity in the individual and social dimensions of life, making the distinction that Judaism is directed to humans as social beings, while Christianity is directed to humans as personal beings.[21]

Colin Richmond, a medievalist, questions whether Parkes went far enough in realizing and alerting to the danger of antisemitism and the teaching of contempt within Christian tradition:

> I do not think he saw just how corrosive such contempt has
> to be. From the Twelfth Century European culture becomes
> a persecuting, a victimizing culture. What I call a culture of
> contempt was born: it was Christian and classical and a dis-
> aster for us one and all.[22]

If even Parkes, the pioneer of Jewish-Christian dialogue, was insufficiently aware of the dangers of contempt, how can more conservative defenders of the tradition hope to admit the role of Christian theology in creating and perpetuating it, even in light of the destruction of European Jewry? There is little doubt that Parkes had broken new ground. The four fundamental changes he proposed were:

I. recognition that the New Testament is incorrect in its teaching about Jesus;
II. the Church's need to qualify its claims to religious truths;

III. a shift of emphasis from being christocentric to theo-
centric;
IV. a new relationship with Judaism based on a theology of
equality.[23]

As hard-hitting as these must have been for many Christians to take,
Parkes remained a staunch defender of the Christian faith and did not
advocate the Judaization of Christian theology.

Parkes's response to the Holocaust, therefore, avoids a radical
revision of Christianity, and yet placed against Metz's theses we find
little to fault him on. He recognizes his identity in the face of the Jews,
he protects his own Christian identity together with the history and
belief of the Jews, and makes no attempt to block out the Jewish heritage within Christianity.

A final example of the struggle of theologians to rethink their
position in the post-Holocaust world is drawn from Franklin Littell,
who indicates that, for Christians, antisemitism (and by extension its
ultimate manifestation in the Holocaust) is not just a form of racial
prejudice, but both blasphemy and apostasy. Littell's condemnation
states that Christians betrayed all people and their own faith in their
betrayal of the Jews and that this was not salvaged by the good repute
of the few that he considers acted in a way befitting the desirable standards of Christianity.

> Those comparatively few Christians who maintained their
> integrity during the Holocaust did in fact challenge the dom-
> inant culture, and some thousands perished…But that does
> not excuse the rest of us, who wittingly or unwittingly
> accommodated; certainly it does not cover the apostasy of
> the millions who collaborated.[24]

To talk of the apostasy of Christians indicates that the Christianity of
those Christians who supported or allowed National Socialism's
assault on the Jews was in some way lacking the true merits and convictions of the Christian faith. Actually, Littell points out that at the
time the teaching of contempt was not considered heretical and therefore did not result in apostasy but that Nazi doctrine clearly was heretical and adherence to it therefore was a form of apostasy. To balance this
apostasy Littell also observes that Christians:

must begin [their] agonizing self assessment and re-appraisal
with the fact that in a season of betrayal and faithfulness the
vast majority of martyrs for the Lord of history were Jews.
The Jewish people carried history while the Christians fled
headlong from their professed vocation.[25]

The response he suggests should in itself be an act of faith. Indeed,
even Littell's chosen book title, *The Crucifixion of the Jews,* is itself
indicative of a neochristological position that he and others take, in
which the suffering of the Jews at the hands of Christians calls into
question, or at least makes relative, the suffering of Christ. Such reactions look for a theology to bridge the disruptive nature of the
Holocaust and to find a means to a future Christian reality through the
continuity of faith in spite of the irreconcilable contradictions. Littell is
under no illusion that Christians have to address this as a Christian
issue:

...so far as Christian thinkers are concerned, the words that
hit like hammers and burn like fire (Jeremiah 23:29) must
be addressed first and singly in this generation to our own
condition; our task is not the condition of "the Jews," but the
condition of "the Christians."[26]

Observing these few perspectives on the impact of the Holocaust on the
Jewish-Christian relationship to date provides a context for discussing
its future impact, which remains moot. The dialogue between Jews and
Christians cannot and will not exist without the presence of the
Holocaust impacting upon it in some way. What kind of impact
depends on the willingness of Christians to continue to confront it.

To talk about the future of the Holocaust on Jews and Christians it
appears necessary to formulate several preliminary questions. First,
what is the future of Jewish-Christian relations on our understanding of
the Holocaust? Second, and more fundamentally, what is the future of
either Judaism or Christianity as religious traditions in the light of the
Holocaust? Finally, how can the Holocaust conceivably be linked to a
constructive future in the Jewish-Christian relationship when its quin-
tessential nature is the ultimate demonstration of the rupture of that
relationship? These preliminary questions predicate discussion around
the two traditions and their respective confrontation with the reality of

the Holocaust to date, and an evaluation of how their two distinct reactions may impact the future of a shared relationship.

To better evaluate the future of the Holocaust in the Jewish-Christian relationship it first appears necessary to observe the nature of the relationship between Jews and Christians. At this time the relationship is still largely a cultural exchange in response to religious crisis. The crisis predates the Holocaust experience but is significantly magnified through it. At the same time it is the crisis that has come to act as the catalyst to the development of the (largely cultural) relationship in the post-Holocaust era.

For Jews the personal impact of the Holocaust on Jewish identity is virtually inescapable and is somewhat exacerbated in the presence of the Jewish-Christian relationship. Christian theological and cultural identity on the other hand is not shaped or even distinctly molded by the Holocaust experience. To suggest that Christian identity should change in the light of the Holocaust to most Christians would imply some form of guilt. In turn this would imply some form of wrongdoing or negligence, a charge that, on the whole, the churches still fail to recognize, as such an admission of guilt would clearly indicate serious theological implications and their attendant corrective actions.

While theologians such as those listed above have been outspoken in their theological analysis, their audience has clearly been a Christian one. The need for Christians to talk to Christians and Jews to Jews, remains necessary. But just because Christians are talking about the fault lines in their own Christianity, a new relationship with the Jewish community does not necessarily follow. While the cultural exchange is good, and indeed necessary, there are still fundamental issues vis-à-vis the impact of the Holocaust on Christianity that Christians have yet to face or at least to reconcile. I believe these are fundamental, prior to there even being talk of the possibility of a Jewish-Christian relationship, but I still think that Jewish-Christian relations are perfectly feasible, if problematic. For the sake of clarity these issues will best be divided into three: memory, justice, and continuity.

On Memory: Jews and Christians experienced the Holocaust in different ways and therefore remember it differently. For Christians to enter into the memory of the Holocaust as Jews might, they must face the Holocaust, complete with its overwhelming, identity molding, faith destroying threat. In order to do so, sympathy from the Christian will not do, and neither is empathy sufficient. Shared memory of the past can only be found in a sense of common experience in that past and a shared destiny in the future. While a shared destiny is not impossible to imagine, the common experience is found only in the ultimately destructive nature of the relationship in the past. In this sense whenever Jews and Christians remember the Holocaust they can do so only as diametrically opposed opposites. Therefore, any declared Christian intent to "remember" the past requires careful examination. For Christians, to "remember" as self-identified professing Christians, should be to remember that the Christian was absent in all but a few courageous cases. This is not to create the conditions for guilt but to recognize the historical reality. Without this historical reality Christians will remember the dead and forget their own past; and if Christians want to remember, memory should not be that selective.

On Justice: Abel is dead. Is it now enough just to show concern for his surviving "brother"? If Christianity is admitting some form of culpability as acting as an accessory to murder, then surely punishment is the only course of action. Is the self-granted amnesty of a Christian world that has found its conscience appropriate under the circumstances? Christians may not need to feel or express guilt, but Christianity is at least in part guilty, if only by that which it did not do.

In some respects the issue is whether the reevaluation of the Jewish-Christian relationship in the light of the Holocaust has anything to do with justice at all. Perhaps it is actually the *avoidance* of justice through the tenuous creation of social, cultural, and religious intercourse at a somewhat superficial level. It is important to remember that at stake is: the nature of God, of people, and of religious belief and conviction; the murder of millions of innocent souls; and the theological foundation of what is still just about the world's largest religion.

Herein lies the problem: Does a theological response to the Holocaust, by necessity, have to be a compromise of some form? Is the discourse surrounding the failure of Christian theology to be reduced to a process in which the theological implications are spelled out, the severity of the culpability explained, and a thorough review of what happened made public? Then, once everything has been said that can be said, will theological amnesty be granted, provided a more conciliatory tone is struck in the future? More like a Truth and Reconciliation

Commission in nature, honesty about the past gives the best chance of securing a relatively stable and shared future.

Do not be too heartened by the suggestion that such an encounter is easy or even possible or that the resulting compromise is the most desirable outcome. If "truth" and "reconciliation" are to work, there still may be the necessity of reworking certain Christian "truths," which are fundamental to Christianity's own integrity as well as the relationship with Judaism in the post-Holocaust environment. This leads to the issue of Christian continuity.

On Continuity: The nature of the discussion in various Jewish theosophical debates is predicated on the assumption of either the continuity or the discontinuity of theological thought prior to, during, and after the Holocaust. If continuity is assumed, then the accepted traditional theological conclusions and norms can be applied to the Holocaust and its interpretation. If, on the other hand, the Holocaust is seen to disrupt the tradition and its assumptions, a reworking of the theosophical tradition may be necessary. In the Christian environment, the Holocaust has yet to be evaluated in such terms, and, it might be argued, not even the most convinced theologians have presented the absolutely disruptive nature of the Holocaust on Christian theological continuity.

You might tell me that Christianity has made great strides and broken from its past since the Holocaust, that things have changed. Christians do now recognize that all Jews everywhere are not Christ-killers, that Judaism is a valid religious tradition in its own right, that it is possible to talk to Jews rather than about them or to drive them from their homes, that Hebrew Scripture remains valid to Jews, that Christians should recognize the Jewish identity of Jesus, and that anti-semitism is wrong. So what? This does not present the challenge of possible disruption to the Christian church. More simply, the Holocaust has forced Christianity to become more rational and more civil to their Jewish neighbors; but Christians do not struggle with the nature, omnipotence, omnipresence, or revelatory power of God in the context of their relationship with the Jews. Christians struggle with Christianity. In so doing they avoid the real disruption, the caesura of discontinuity. What if the meaning of the Holocaust is that Christians can no longer claim to have justification to go into all the world and preach the message of salvation? What if the message of the Holocaust is that the "crucifixion of the Jews" was an antisalvific event and that, in participating, if only tangentially, Christian institutions have removed the right to claim salvation through Christ's death? What if this means that forgiveness in the Christian tradition is called into question? Christianity will now always carry the historic burden for that for which forgiveness may not be possible. How then can you preach a message of forgiveness? What happens if, like Cain, Christianity is accursed for its murder of its brother and sent out of the presence of God? Are we asking these questions? Are we prepared to? Why should the Jews have to face the possibility of a change to the perception of covenant and election, or face the possibility of an abusing God who hides his face, or change the understanding of the power and presence of God and all because they were abandoned by the Christian world?

In fact, I would suggest that much of the discourse around Jewish-Christian relations engaged by Christians to date is about the defense of Christian continuity rather than a challenge to it. The problem is that all Christians are Christian by conviction. Jews are Jews, like it or not. To profess Christianity is to keep it, to justify it, and to defend it, even when the ultimate disruption of Christian continuity says you cannot, because at such a point you either cease to believe or believe something else. Even Metz, as he does theology "in the face of Auschwitz," seeks to keep and to redefine Christianity, but the reality of the Holocaust is that you must question that and be prepared, if necessary, to let it go.

Until Christians are prepared to face the possibility of discontinuity and by extension the demise or reformation of Christianity in the light of the Holocaust, I believe there can be no meaningful Jewish-Christian relationship, as Jews and Christians will be unequal partners—the Jews making concessions, conceding to the Christian majority once again. For a meaningful relationship to exist, discussion around historical and theological similarities and differences is clearly not enough. Nor is the establishment of interreligious respect out of deference to the other. If there is to be a real relationship, Christians must struggle with their own identity and memory and be confronted with the possibility of nothingness. This sounds harsh, but in the light of the oblivion of Shoah, theological oblivion is spiritual paradise.

If one understands discontinuity to be a break with the past, during that moment of breaking, however brief, there is no theology, no God, no relationship, and no faith. For Jews faced with the possibility of discontinuity, Jewish identity still exists even in the temporary void of nonfaith, the terror of victimization, or the confusion of religious and spiritual identity. That is, even at the point of caesura, Jews remain Jews. For the Christian, the moment theology, dogma, doctrine, revelation, and history are suspended or redefined, the identity of the individual is suspended with it. In other words, the Christian has to undergo a further conversion process — another act of faith, which may even terminate the belief structure itself.

I conclude by daring to say that, to date, there is no Jewish-Christian relationship. Dialogue does now exist, but dialogue can take place between any two individuals or groups, even between adversaries. But a relationship is something that is formed not in words but in common understanding, shared experiences, and aspirations. Talk, by all means talk — we need to talk with one another. But never talk of a Jewish-Christian relationship after the Holocaust until you know what it means to face the consequence of the ultimate disruption of oblivion.

NOTES

1. In A. L. Eckardt and A. R. Eckardt, *Long Night's Journey into Day: A Revised Retrospective on the Holocaust* (Oxford: Pergamon Press; Detroit: Wayne State University Press, 1982), 193.

2. *We Remember: A Reflection on the Shoah* (Commission for Religious Relations with the Jews, Vatican City, March 16, 1998).

3. J. B. Metz, *Faith in History and Society,* trans. David Smith (London: Burns and Oates, 1980), 109.

4. J. Parkes, *Prelude to Dialogue* (London: Valentine Mitchell, 1969), 7.

5. C. Moehlman, *The Christian-Jewish Tragedy: A Study in Religious Prejudice,* as quoted in G. Wigoder, *Jewish-Christian Relations since the Second World War* (Manchester: Manchester University Press, 1988), 2.

6. Peterson published *Die Kirche aus Juden und Heiden* in 1933. Quoted in Wigoder, *Jewish-Christian Relations,* 2.

7. In E. Fleischner, *Judaism in German Christian Theology* (Metuchen, NJ: Scarecrow Press, 1975), 24.

8. In A. T. Davies, ed., *Anti-semitism and the Christian Mind* (New York: Herder and Herder, 1969), 110.

9. Wigoder, *Jewish-Christian Relations,* 3.

10. Ibid., 4.

11. From *Man's Disorder and God's Design: World Council of Churches* (1st Assembly: 1948: Amsterdam) (New York: Harper, 1948), 160.

12. Conference of the International Council of Christians and Jews, "An Address to the Churches," Seeligsberg (Switzerland) 1947. See http://www.jcrelations.net/stmnts/10points.

13. Ibid.

14. *The Evanston Report: The Second Assembly of the World Council of Churches 1954* (London: SCM Press, 1955), 327.

15. D. Gill, ed., *Gathered for Life* (Geneva: WCC, 1983), 147–51.

16. Wigoder, *Jewish-Christian Relations,* 80.

17. Known more fully as, "Notes on the Correct Way to Present the Jews and Judaism in Preaching and Catechesis of the Catholic Church."

18. Wigoder, *Jewish-Christian Relations,* 94.

19. Quoted in ibid., 95.

20. J. B. Metz, "Facing the Jews: Christian Theology after Auschwitz," in *The Holocaust as Interruption,* ed. Elisabeth Schüssler Fiorenza and David Tracy, *Concilium* 175 (Edinburgh: T&T Clark, 1984), 26–33.

21. Wigoder, *Jewish-Christian Relations,* 21.

22. C. Richmond, "Parkes and I," *The Parkes Lectures* 1994, University of Southampton, 12.

23. Quoted in Wigoder, *Jewish-Christian Relations,* 40–41.

24. F. Littell, *The Crucifixion of the Jews* (Macon, GA: University of Mercer Press, 1986), 4.

25. Ibid., 79–80.

26. Ibid., 3.

11

A Third Epoch: The Future of Discourse in Jewish-Christian Relations

Peter Ochs and David F. Ford

INTRODUCTION

Peter Ochs

Baruch…shecheyanu, v'kiyamanu, v'higiyanu lazman hazeh. "Blessed are you…Who has kept us alive, sustained us and brought us to this special time." The establishment of the Centre for the Study of Jewish-Christian Relations in Cambridge is indeed an occasion for blessings. But even more, it may prove to be part of a vital turn in modern Western society more generally. There is an urgent cultural need today for profound Jewish-Christian dialogue of a kind that has not yet happened with the level of energy and on the level of sophistication that is truly needed today. We would hope and pray that the Centre could provide a setting for such a level of dialogue.

PROLOGUE

We say, in the spirit of Ecclesiastes, *"eyn chadash tachat hashemesh,"* "there is nothing new under the sun." But, in the traditional rabbinic prayers, we also declare each morning, *"hu mechadesh b'khol yom maaseh breshit,"* "Each day he renews—makes new—the order of creation."

Jewish-Christian dialogue is defined in part by what will never change until the end of days: that, for Jews, the God of Israel separates us from other nations to fulfill the Torah, and that, for Christians, the God of Israel is incarnate in Jesus of Nazareth who was crucified and resurrected and whose church comes to the Father by way of his Son joined to him by the Holy Spirit. The divine source of our scriptures is, however, demonstrated in part by the inherent mystery of the scriptural words: that their meaning cannot on any one occasion be fully clarified to our finite minds once and for all. That is why we are called to renew the meanings of scripture in every generation. Some generations are called to more radical renewal than others, and ours is one of these generations.

From the perspective of our generation, there have been two previous epochs in Jewish-Christian relations, each of which retains its persistent representatives today. One is the epoch of communal self-definition over against the other. The early church defined itself, to a great extent, by its differences from rabbinic and Israelite Judaisms. Jews living in what became Christian lands later returned the favor: often defining their theological identities by being not-Christian. In the second epoch, both Jews and Christians found themselves assimilated, to varying degrees, to the far greater power of modern, secular Europe. The new aspect of Jewish-Christian dialogue in this epoch was the effort to locate a neutral ground to which Jewish and Christian beliefs could be leveled: the effort to overcome difference by affirming some least common denominator.

The Shoah marks the end of this second epoch. Did most Jews lose their faith in God during and after the horrors of Shoah? The Jewish theologian Eugene Borowitz argues forcefully that most Jews had already lost *that* faith long before the Shoah, through the power of modern secularism alone. What we lost in the Shoah, he says, is our faith in humanity. The question is: Will this tempt us to seek a way back to the beliefs of the first epoch? For the Christian theologian Paul van Buren, of blessed memory, the memory of Shoah prohibits any return to the first epoch. For him, and a growing number of peers in the Christian community, Christianity was defined in that epoch as a religion that superseded Judaism, and the Shoah demonstrates the horrible potential of beliefs in supersessionism. For Jews, the choice between tradition and modernity remains confusing, but a new generation now begins to envision an alternative.

The Jewish-Christian dialogue in which David Ford and I participate belongs to the beginnings of a third epoch, in which Jews and Christians reaffirm their separate religious identities but not through the device of mutual exclusion. This epoch is still "aborning," so we cannot yet try to sketch out its tendencies conceptually. Instead, we will try to illustrate some of its tendencies through the way we respond to each other's theological movements into "the third epoch."

DIAGNOSIS OF OUR SITUATION

David F. Ford

Peter Ochs said that he and I have been involved in Jewish-Christian dialogue of a certain sort for some years. What we want to do now is to think together about the discourse of that dialogue and its possibilities for the future. I will comment largely on Ochs's approach; and Ochs, on mine.

Our first task is to try to describe the situation as we see it. What is the context of our discourse? Ochs has already begun to answer this with a rudimentary typology of three epochs in Jewish-Christian relations. I will now draw further on his work in order to sketch what I consider to be some key features of the context for contemporary Jewish-Christian dialogue.

At the heart of Ochs's conception of our time is that many things have gone drastically wrong in recent centuries, culminating in the Shoah, but that this has not only exposed the problems of what is called modernity,[1] it also has led us to examine the inadequacies of what gave rise to modernity and allowed it to develop as it did. For Christians and Jews, this means a critique of their premodern forms (what Ochs has just described as "the epoch of communal self-definition over against the other") and of their modern forms (prone to assimilation by secular Europe). So there is a threefold but interrelated diagnosis needed, probing the pathologies and inadequacies of our own communities as well as of Western civilization in the modern period. The primary concern of this diagnosis is not scoring intellectual points about, for example, the inadequacies of Cartesianism (though a critique of that is involved) or of Christian supersessionism (though that too requires critique). Rather, the concern is to face the terrible evils, sufferings, and breakdowns of our world, and to try to contribute to healing them, to repairing them.

So the concern for healing and mending is primary. There is no despair about modernity, Judaism or Christianity; there is a commitment to drawing on each of them in order to help repair each of them. The basic attitude is one of compassion for our world and our religious communities. This leads to prayer, work, thought, and dialogue oriented toward *the compassionate redemption of modernity*. That is very different from many critiques of modernity, which tend either to recommend a return to the premodern or to intensify the suspiciousness of modernity by heading toward relativistic or even nihilistic postmodernism.

In line with the concern for mending is a discernment of the present as a time not only of crisis but of opportunity. Critiques by postmodernists, feminists, postcolonialists, and many others have shaken much of the confident certainty of modernity, as have multiple crises, injustices, genocides, and wars. Traditionalist religious alternatives have appeared as mirror images of modernist confidence, imperialist certainty, and have led to or threatened comparable evils and suffering. The opportunity is for something that avoids the fruitless alternatives and enables healing.

One of Ochs's symbols for such a time of opportunity in time of crisis is "the burnt Temple." Jewish discourse was transformed in different ways through the destruction of the First Temple and the Babylonian Exile, through the Roman destruction of the Second Temple in 70 CE, and through the expulsion from Spain in the fifteenth century. The Shoah is the latest destruction, and it calls for a comparable creativity in terms of interpretation, practices, institutions, and intellectual life. I will explore some of his own creative suggestions later in this session. But I want to conclude my contribution to this diagnostic section by asking whether it is possible to see contemporary Christianity in analogous terms.

My answer in brief is that there is a comparable pattern of crisis accompanied by opportunity. The crisis can be described in many ways, not necessarily mutually exclusive. Viewed globally, the threat to Christianity is not through destruction or reduced numbers (at an estimated one and a half billion and growing there is every likelihood that, numerically, the next century will be a "successful" one). I see the main threats correlative to Ochs's first two epochs of Jewish-Christian relations: a traditionalist, fundamentalist Christianity aggressively confronting and trying to dominate the world; and a Christianity marginalized, domesticated, or eviscerated by its involvement in a powerful late modern culture. Perhaps the most potent threat of all to the quality of Christianity comes from the uniting of the two: an alliance of fundamentalisms with elements of late modern capitalism. The opportunity offered by this has analogous elements to those found by Ochs in Judaism: the possibility to work simultaneously for the healing of Christianity and modernity by attempting a renewal that is both inspired by previous renewals and reformations while also being a specific creative response to the current situation.

Peter Ochs

In the third epoch of Jewish thought, Jewish-Christian dialogue is a theological event. This means it is not a mere instance of some generally good thing—like human dialogue or friendship among peoples. David Ford is a profoundly hospitable person, and his Christianity is a profoundly hospitable religion, but even the mutual sharing of religious hospitality is not a sufficient condition for Jewish-Christian dialogue. Beyond care for the other, this dialogue requires a NEED of the other. Today's dialogue is led by the discoveries that something is very wrong with the modern society that Jews and Christians share, *and* that Jews and Christians will need each other's help in repairing what is wrong. The problem is, moreover, not merely outside us, in the social environment of our religions; it also affects our religious communities and practices themselves. There is something wrong with our mainstream religions, and Jewish-Christian dialogue may actually contribute to the repair of each religion on its own terms. That is why this dialogue is a theological event, and an event that is specific to the needs of our own age.

David Ford's broad corpus of theological writings offers a cultural, philosophic, and theological diagnosis of what is wrong with the society Jews and Christians share. On the level of symptoms, he observes human beings being overwhelmed by a surfeit of words, visual stimuli, sounds, news, data, objects of desire, commodities, obligations, beliefs, and opinions they cannot possibly attend to, reflect on, respond to with care and discrimination. This kind of overwhelming diminishes rather than augments the human being's comprehension of what he or she is supposed to do in life, what responsibilities there are to undertake; it diminishes face-to-face relations among human beings and the virtues that serve relationship; and it diminishes human self-worth. In sum, there is a reduction and thinning out of the abundance of what we were created to enjoy and generate and share, and a diminution of justice—

since, with less capacity to understand other human beings and their needs, we have less capacity, as well, to serve and to protect them.

Ford observes that, paradoxically, this diminishment of the individual's enjoyment of creation corresponds to the growth of a program of cultural education that focuses increasingly on the individual self and its supposed material wants, alone, independently of its participation in relations, in social groups, in traditions of belief and value, and in the broader ecosystem that sustains its life. Ford's diagnosis is that this educational program emerges not from modernity alone—not from humanism itself nor from the flourishing of experimental, natural science—but from the gradual separation of the modern arts and sciences from the religious, scriptural, and theological traditions that, through much of the Renaissance, still situated science and humanism in the broader ecology of Jewish, Christian, and Muslim communities and faiths.

THE SIGNIFICANCE OF SCRIPTURE AND PHILOSOPHY FOR THE RENEWAL OF JEWISH-CHRISTIAN DISCOURSE

David F. Ford

In this section I want to focus mainly on Ochs's major work to date, *Peirce, Pragmatism and the Logic of Scripture.*[2] I will begin by drawing on it to make two basic points about Jewish-Christian dialogue.

First, it is not an easy book, and I have a long way to go before adequately understanding it. But its very difficulty says something important about it as a contribution to Jewish-Christian dialogue. If that dialogue avoids the most difficult issues and the complex discourses that their difficulty necessarily requires, then it can still do some good, but it cannot claim to offer thorough diagnosis or healing. The issues raised are as large as the naming of God, creation in relation to revelation and redemption, the interpretation and assessment of major philosophical, religious, and scientific thinkers, the understanding of modernity in relation to both the premodern and whatever it is we are part of now, the interpretation of scripture, the shaping of communities and institutions, and so on. We cannot hope to do justice to such matters if we resist the demand for hard conceptual work. Both Judaism and Christianity have for many centuries been grappling with the most sophisticated available thought and have been coping with huge intellectual as well as other challenges. So one lesson for the future of Jewish-Christian discourse is that, somewhere in the ecology (which has, of course, plenty of other important niches as well), there should be ways (preferably several ways in dialogue with each other) of conceiving the issues that are as philosophically sophisticated as Ochs's interpretation of Peirce. Without that, it is likely that shortcuts are being taken and the dialogue is being shortchanged.

Second, as the title suggests, it brings together philosophy and scripture. I consider that one of Ochs's main contributions to the third epoch of Jewish-Christian relations, in which "Jews and Christians reaffirm their separate religious identities, but not through the device of mutual exclusion," is his insistence that each community within itself and in dialogue with the other should bring together philosophy and scripture. (These should be understood in broad terms to embrace, under *philosophy,* those philosophers, theologians, ethicists, social, economic, and political theorists, and others who engage in rational discourse in their fields; and, under *scripture,* scholars of scripture and of its traditions of interpretation, together with a range of historical and literary disciplines.) This core dialogue, called *textual reasoning* or *scriptural reasoning,* embodies a triple commitment: first, to ever-renewed engagement with scripture; second, to engaging scriptural interpretation with a range of intellectual discourses, past and present; third, to each community doing its textual/scriptural reasoning not only "at home" but also in thorough dialogue with each other in the interests of mending our terrible history. At root these commitments are not an instrumental method: they spring from the heart of faith in a God who communicates in history; who invites our participation in a compassionate healing of our world, which begins with ourselves and our communities being corrected, repaired, mended; and whose creation invites rational understanding and explanation, with human intelligence at full stretch.

Now I want to look at some aspects of the book and reflect on their significance for the discourse of Jewish-Christian dialogue. Given very limited time, this is just a sampling of what I think most fruitful.

Peirce

The choice of Peirce is worth noting. Ochs, a Jewish thinker, spends many years of his life intensively studying a Christian philosopher. In fact, he even recovers the Christian dimensions of Peirce's thought that have been largely ignored and makes them available as a contemporary resource to Christians as well as to others. There are, happily, increasing numbers of analogous enterprises in current academic life, as Jews and Christians study each others' traditions in depth and in the process often help to rethink and to reapply them.

But apart from that general lesson, there is specific significance in the choice of Peirce. He is not only a Christian whose thought has special resonances with St. Augustine; he is also a mediating figure between classical philosophy, medieval scholastic philosophy and theology, the Cartesian-Kantian tradition in modern philosophy, modern inquiries into language, logic, semiotics, and pragmatics, and an Anglo-American tradition of empirical natural science allied closely with mathematics. At a time when many Christian and Jewish thinkers find their most exciting dialogue partners among contemporary continental European philosophers who are deeply suspicious of most of the schools of thought just listed, this Peircean voice needs to be heard. Even where American pragmatism is drawn on, it is rarely Peirce who is primary, and even more rarely is it Peirce as understood and developed by Ochs. To put it in historical terms, the common engagement by Jews and Christians with Platonic, Aristotelian, and Kantian philosophy has been of considerable benefit in allowing what worthwhile dialogue has occurred under often adverse historical circumstances; there would seem to be wisdom in adding to the repertoire of available, appropriated thinkers someone with Peirce's range and rational rigor.

Compassionately Correcting the Cartesian-Kantian Tradition

At the heart of the book is Ochs's interpretation of Peirce's critical appropriation of the Cartesian-Kantian philosophical tradition. This might act as a paradigm for how to treat not only the legacy of "modernity" but also our own religious traditions.[3]

The main thrust of Ochs is to show how Peirce offers a "pragmatic reading" of Cartesian-Kantian philosophy, paying particular attention to the problems that have emerged over time, so as to correct and redefine it, especially through engagement with logic, semiotics, mathematics, and the experimental methods of the natural sciences.

One key feature of Peirce's correction is to show how that tradition's claims to discontinuity with the past were part of a misconstrual of its own nature and significance. In fact, Peirce and Ochs claim, the Cartesian-Kantian tradition is better seen as a correction of features of the tradition of medieval scholastic (and earlier) philosophy, and both traditions are to be understood in relation to "common sense." The common sense of any community needs to be open to correction, but it also contains many "indubitable beliefs" on which people act and which it is wiser to trust rather than indulge in a Cartesian principle of radical doubt. Efforts at correction should be stimulated by "real doubts"—avoiding, for example, a foundationalist attempt to meet every "paper doubt."

Failing to do justice to the tradition or community of which they are part is one aspect of a broader Cartesian-Kantian failing. This is the tendency to describe judgments, statements of fact, and propositions in dyadic, subject-predicate terms rather than in a triadic logic of relations.[4] An important implication of this is that there is a "third grade of clearness" in the meaning of a conception, beyond Cartesian "clarity" and "distinctness." The third grade considers "the practical effects which the object of a conception would have,"[5] (what Peirce calls the conception's "interpretant") and includes attending to when, where, how, and by whom it is received. There is here no rejection of clarity and distinctness but a correction and supplementing of them in a way that especially insists on the significance of discourse, symbolic action, and dialogue, as well as community, tradition, and common sense. Many key concepts cannot be clarified in the abstract: they await further determination as they are applied or communicated in a specific context.

This leads to the helpful idea of *vagueness,* which refers to a meaning that is neither determinately specific nor indeterminately general but rather only discloses its meaning by way of some interpretant.[6] Since "vague entities define one another dialogically"[7] and some concepts are "irremediably vague" (including indubitable beliefs and many other concepts concerning metaphysics, values, and theology),[8] there can be no undergirding foundationalism: "a logic of vagueness is at the same time a logic of dialogue."[9]

Part of that dialogue in a tradition is its constant attempt to deal with its own problems, sufferings, contradictions, "burdensome" elements, doubts, and incompletenesses. "Pragmatic reading" responds to problems in the plain sense of the texts of a tradition by drawing on the resources of the tradition itself in order to correct or redefine it for particular readers in particular situations, taking their common sense both seriously and critically. Ochs describes how Peirce himself did this as he corrected and redefined his earlier *pragmatism* in his later *pragmaticism.* He also shows how the logic of dialogue can (and, where the issues at stake are as embracing as those in philosophy and theology, should) lead beyond the boundaries of one tradition and bring different communities of readers into conversation.

So the recipe is: to see how the innovations of a tradition can be read as a correction of what it inherited; to take seriously that need for correction in the parent tradition but at the same time to consider how the child may be in need of comparable correction, revealed by the burdensome elements that have emerged; to explore first the resources of the tradition itself for self-correction by moving beyond a plain sense reading to a pragmatic (in Jewish terms, *midrashic*), contextual reading of it; and to follow the pragmatic, triadic logic of relations into further relevant dialogues with other traditions.

It is worth noting in the process a range of key Peirce/Ochs terms that offer themselves as concepts worth trying out more widely in Jewish-Christian dialogue. My own list includes: triadic logic of relations; pragmatic reading with reference to interpretants; common sense and indubitable beliefs; vagueness; and compassionate correction or redemption. The latter indicates the spirit of the whole enterprise, and it is especially instructive to see it principally applied to the Cartesian-Kantian tradition, which is currently so much out of fashion in many quarters as representing (whether to traditionalists or postmodernists) the essence of a rejected modernity.

Dialogue of Communities

The final long chapter of the book is a development of Peircean pragmatism in dialogue with a series of "communities" (some of which overlap): pragmatists; commonsense pragmatists; pragmatic logicians; theosemioticians (those pragmatic logicians who relate their logic to belief in God); scriptural pragmatists; rabbinic pragmatists; and Christian pragmatists. This is where the book has most direct relevance to the discourse of Jewish-Christian dialogue, though it is condensed almost to the point of being aphoristic. But the main lines are clear, and I have already summarized them in what I have written.

Ochs names some of those Jews and Christians whose thinking is in harmony with the wisdom distilled from Peirce. He himself is mainly in the rabbinic pragmatist tradition, and is concerned with articulating, in ways that moderns might be able to appreciate, the moves the rabbis make in their interpretation of scripture. Pragmatism helps him do this; and it also gives the concepts for a rationale to describe how communities can go deeply, appreciatively, and self-critically into their own heritage, while at the same time being both rational and dialogical within themselves and in relation to other communities. Overall, it is a threefold intensification—of engagement with scripture and the traditions of its interpretation, of philosophical and theological thought, and of dialogue within and between traditions. The challenge it poses to those of us concerned for Jewish-Christian dialogue in the future is whether those three can be sustained simultaneously, long-term, and with compassion, in the interests of the healing of modernity and of our own communities.

That is as radical and unimaginable as many other things that Jews and Christians believe about God's involvement in history.

Peter Ochs

For those who may not know David Ford's work, I want to tell you that he is a discerning and recondite Christian philosophical theologian, writing on Karl Barth, on scriptural, liturgical, and trinitarian theology. Yet, through all his professional life he has pondered the work of the Jewish philosopher Emmanuel Levinas. The most important thinker for Jewish philosophic circles today, Levinas was both France's most celebrated philosopher—known for his work in phenomenology—and head of a high school for Talmudic studies in Paris. Phenomenology is a field of philosophy that, beyond all differences of theory, belief, and ideology, seeks to examine general patterns that may show up in the raw field of appearances that fill our everyday consciousnesses. The most powerful image in Levinas's phenomenological work is that of the Face, appearing in this raw field as an image of the Other we can never fully understand or assimilate to any other collection of appearances: the Face that pierces the circle of our private selfhood as if to say "even deep within your isolation I break in and demand your attention!" While Levinas is careful to separate his philosophic from his biblical and Talmudic studies, this image of the Face represents the irrepressible contribution of these studies to his analysis of human experience: a Jewish claim that, like Jonah, who is unable to hide from God's presence, the self cannot hide itself from the face of the human other. This claim visits many of Ford's writings and becomes the dominant trope of his latest book, *Self and Salvation: Being Transformed.*[10] In this book, not only Ford's words but also his performance as writer offer a prototype of how Jewish-Christian dialogue would most successfully be articulated in the coming decades. He does not claim this of his book, but I do. Expressing my own reading of his work, I will, then, proceed to outline this prototype for you, offering illustrations drawn from Ford's book.

The first step in preparing Jewish Christian dialogue is to look at the face of suffering but to bring to it the face of healing.

Our epoch is marked by the Shoah and by the exhaustion of modern secularism both leading up to and in response to the Shoah. These two faces of suffering are both conditions for Jewish-Christian dialogue in our age. For the Jews, the Shoah would seem to mark the end of Europe's hospitality, a sign that our home must be elsewhere than in the West. The land of Israel also remains partly in the West, however; and besides that, we as a people have apparently chosen not to end this Diaspora fully. A third epoch for Judaism suggests that our home is, in part, in a different time of the West rather than merely a different space. The time of modern assimilation failed us, as did the time of communal self-enclosure before it. We seek a third time. For Christians, the Shoah would seem to mark a final proof that supersessionism and Constantinian imperialism bear more evil than good: Christianity will have to find a way to serve Christ without making the Jews into ghosts and to proclaim the gospel without lording over the rest of the world. But modern Christian secularism has proved itself to be comparably dangerous: incapable of protecting its flock from the temptations of anti-Christian totalitarianism or, for that matter, of a degradingly untempered capitalism.

In *Self and Salvation,* Ford illustrates how Christians may turn a healing face to each of these four sad faces of modernity. As illustrated in the facing of Dietrich Bonhoeffer, Ford summons Christians to face up to the people Israel's oppressors and, thereby, to face Jewish suffering as an object of Christian concern and care. But as illustrated in the Holy Face at which St. Therese gazed, Ford summons Christians to see the face of the Jew as also a face of the Jew Jesus Christ. It is at once the face of Jesus as a boy—a face in which to rejoice—and the face of Jesus Christ dead on the cross—a face for which to care and to give thanks—and the face of Christ risen—a face in which to hope and through which to bring healing. One miracle of Ford's text is the way that his facing the Jew as Jesus affirms the particular mission of the church without compromising recognition of

Israel's enduring covenant. One vehicle of this miracle is the way Ford faces Jewish secularism as well.

The second step in preparing Jewish Christian dialogue is to locate a place of both shared suffering and mutual need.

With respect to the Shoah, Christian and Jewish suffering is asymmetrical. But with respect to modern secularism, their suffering is overlapping. Both Jews and Christians are overwhelmed negatively by the materialisms and alienations of the modern West and both inherit those evils from overlapping political, economic, and educational processes. In *Self and Salvation,* Ford selectively examines the alienation of selfhood in modernity. He cites the writings of Eberhard Jüngel and Paul Ricoeur as Christian witnesses to this alienation. He cites the writings of Emmanuel Levinas and also Franz Rosenzweig as Jewish witnesses. Carefully examining each writer's responses to this alienation, Ford then uncovers what is at once the burden and wonder of his book. The Jews and Christians — Jüngel and Levinas prototypically — have different responses, *and each response fails in precisely the points at which the other succeeds.* In other words, in order for there to be a successful response to the alienated self, Jüngel and Levinas need both to help and to learn from each other; to recover from the burdens of modernity, Jew and Christian need each other.

The third step in preparing Jewish Christian dialogue is to locate the face of healing behind the very face that suffers, remembering that this is now a dialogic process.

This is the central work of Ford's book and a primary rule for salvific work in the third epoch of Jewish-Christian relations. The books of religious philosophy from which I have learned most are all written from out of the very tradition of modern thought that they come to redeem. Charles Peirce's Christian pragmatism and Franz Rosenzweig's Jewish speech thinking are each fruits of their author's recovering, from within and behind some practice of Cartesian-Kantian philosophy, the scriptural and theological sources for redeeming that philosophy's secularizing tendencies. *Self and Salvation* is written in terms of Continental practices of phenomenology that have this same Cartesian-Kantian pedigree. Ford locates within that pedigree sources of *both* the alienation of the modern self *and* its reclamation. Showing us only the work of reclamation, Ford reveals only indirectly his analysis of the alienation.

From the perspective of Levinas, the Jewish philosopher, we see that, even in its pure form as transcendental unity of apperception, the Cartesian-Kantian ego is trapped in a circle of self-reference, its Law of Identity, and its educational model of mimesis or identical repetition. Levinas's cure is to disclose the Face of the Other that rests irreplaceably and irreducibly among the field of appearances that defines the ego's consciousness. The face cannot be reduced to the Same, cannot be transported into the self's system of knowing the world, cannot be reproduced or effaced. The cure for the self-enclosed self is thus simply to accept responsibility for the Other that already appears within its own consciousness. One arrives at adult consciousness already utterly bound to that Other, because the Other demands attention and response but one has in oneself absolutely no prior knowledge of what the Other means or what to do: one can only wait for its command. We are hostage to the needs of the Other. This is Levinas's philosophical version of what the rabbis call the bindingness of the *halachah* and the demand of the biblical word. The word demands attention, the way the Israelites declared at Mt. Sinai, *naaseh vnishmah,* "we will do (your word first, before we can) understand it."

For the Christian Jüngel, however, the modern self is alienated by its inability to enjoy the fullness that God makes available to it: it does not realize that it is loved by the other and cared for by the other, that God has already lent it God's word. The Cartesian-Kantian self is diminished by its presumption of being alone and being fully responsible, alone, to complete a work that is too great for it. The cure for this depleted self is to recover its capacity to *enjoy* its existence, to *allow* itself to be loved and cared for by those who already love it, and simply to trust that God is also there for it in a way it has forgotten. The biblical word brings grace.

For Ford, both Levinas's and Jüngel's cures for the modern self come by reclaiming assumptions that are ultimately implicit in, but occluded under the history of, the Cartesian-Kantian project for repairing the world through critical reasoning alone. The fact that their cures appear mutually exclusive is a mark that their efforts at reclamation remain incomplete. For self-contradiction is itself a lingering feature of the separation of the self from its place in an indefinitely encompassing ecology. By affirming itself, alone, the self affirms also what it is not. Ford's response is to offer Levinas's and Jüngel's self to each other so that, in their sharing in a greater community and communion, each of their contributions can be seen to be one vital part of a salvific activity that requires both of their voices as well as the third one that joins them. This is the voice of the community in which the self always already finds itself. As Ford draws from the work of Paul Ricoeur, it is the mediating presence of the community of biblical interpreters, with respect to which the biblical word *both* commands and discloses something that is already most intimate to the self. This corresponds, in turn, to the hermeneutic of the talmudic sages, for whom the written word commands absolutely but only as clarified in the Oral Torah, as it is itself disclosed by and for the community that hears those commands.

The modern Jew and Christian need each other's help to overcome the burdens of their shared modernity.

The fourth step is to share in the taste of performing the healing, and not just talking about it.

Shorn of grace and miracle, the modern self wins sobriety, but in the same act it also robs itself of the object of its desire. Levinas calls this "la tentation de la tentation," the phenomenon of always seeking what one cannot have. As a case in point, he cites the modern academic's discipline of speaking only through third person, descriptive sentences, even though these sentences cannot deliver the final answer to any modern question: which must be to *illustrate* precisely how one is to act in response to something wholly new. Illustrating Levinas's cure, Ford devotes the second part of his book to illustrating how the self actually acts in the world, at once, to care for the Other *and* to rejoice in the Other. These illustrations unfold naturally from the range of traditional religious narratives and rituals that Cartesians and Kantians have left aside *for no good reason:* for no good reason, since they provide the modern self with the sustenance it lacks, without conflicting with the modern ideals of scientific rationality and human rights. Ford's illustrations are of what he calls the worshipping self, the singing self, the eucharistic self, the loving self, the self that faces God and faces Christ, and the feasting self.

The fifth step in preparing Jewish Christian dialogue, as illustrated in Ford's book, is for the dialogue partners to feast as well as work together, but also for them to remember to return home after a time, bringing both a healing face and a feasting heart back to their own, different, communities.

THE UNIVERSITY AS A SETTING FOR
JEWISH-CHRISTIAN DIALOGUE

David F. Ford

Dialogue between Jews and Christians of course needs to go on in many places, but I want to draw attention to ways in which the contemporary university is one perhaps surprisingly favorable setting for such dialogue. The university is a key institution of modern society, and it is probably becoming more significant as our economy and culture becomes more knowledge- and information-based.

I begin from the fact that Jews and Christians actually do come together in our universities in many settings and now increasingly in theology and religious studies departments. The university is, at its best, a place of disciplined conversations. A disciplined conversation between Jews and Christians, which is also open to bringing in other partners (Muslims, secularists, and so on) and which engages in scriptural study and philosophy in the ways I have described, has the possibility of enriching all the partners and offering resources that none can provide by itself.

It is quite radical for the university to recognize Jews as Jews and Christians as Christians (just as it has been radical for it to begin to recognize women as women): its tendency has been to homogenize everyone and eliminate such differences. But for all sorts of reasons that has been changing, and the late modern or postmodern university may well be far more hospitable to dialogues of differences that are committed to being disciplined in the academic sense. It seems to me that this is crucial to the quality of education it offers, one that enables people to try to do justice to various traditions and to respond collaboratively to the massive transformations and problems that our world and its religious communities face.

There is even the possibility (and certainly there is the ethical and theological imperative) of a civility that moves beyond neutrality and tolerance into mutual hospitality in depth, each being both guest and host. This is the context in which the richest dialogue can happen, together with the most agonizing differences—but also, as we acknowledge our God of peace, compassion, and faithfulness, the deepest friendships.

TEXTUAL REASONING AND THE SOCIETY FOR SCRIPTURAL REASONING

Peter Ochs

A few years ago, David Ford and I joined with Daniel Hardy of Cambridge and the Jewish scholar Elliot Wolfson of New York University to form the Society for Scriptural Reasoning (SSR). The goal of the society is to draw Jewish, Christian, and Muslim scholars together for shared study of our several scriptures and of the reasonings that emerge from our readings of these scriptures, both separately and together. We believe our three subgroups represent the three constituencies of the university as it emerged from its medieval sources and as it may be made pluralistic through the experiences of modernity. A group of about fifty of us has met together four times now, at the annual meetings of the American Academy of Religion. We share together a worshipful space for shared religious study, for academically disciplined argument, and for unexpected events and kinds of reasoning. On the sabbath, Jews taste for a day what it will be like to enjoy life in the end of days in the world to come. In the society meetings, we are seeking to taste for a few hours what it might be like, in some end of days, when faithful members of the three Abrahamite religions can come together to a university that, without exclusion, enables them to study both our sciences and our religious, scriptural, and theological traditions.

While coming to the university for such a common space, we must also return home, of course, to our particular communities. A few years before the SSR, several of us Jewish philosophers and text scholars, including Robert Gibbs, joined together to form the Society for Textual Reasoning. This is a society to foster the kind of Jewish text study that would both prepare Jewish scholars to join the SSR and also provide a vehicle through which they might share some of the lessons of Jewish-Christian and Muslim dialogue with members of their Jewish congregations.

EPILOGUE

David F. Ford and Peter Ochs

The third epoch that we have been discussing has already seen something unprecedented in Jewish-Christian relations and holds the promise of more to come. We see it as a movement that has the capacity to draw together the deepest religious and academic commitments in the interests of the healing and flourishing of our religious, educational, and political communities.

Yet there is, of course, no inevitability about that. It needs to inspire more contributions and conversations, to develop its discourse and networks, and also to find more of the sort of institutional space and support that the Cambridge Centre for the Study of Jewish-Christian Relations is providing.

> Wisdom has built her house,
> she has hewn her seven pillars...
>
> 'Come, eat of my bread
> and drink of the wine I have mixed.
>
> Lay aside immaturity, and live,
> And walk in the way of insight.'
>   (Proverbs 9:1, 5–6)

NOTES

1. *Modernity* is used as shorthand for the complex of changes in politics, war, economics, philosophy, science, technology, religion, and other areas, which originated largely in western Europe and has had global consequences. The timeline between premodern and modern is drawn variously in different fields and regions, some going back to the Middle Ages, others to the nineteenth century.

2. Peter Ochs, *Pierce, Pragmatism and the Logic of Scripture* (Cambridge: Cambridge University Press, 1998).

3. The account below repeats a good deal of my discussion of the same issue in "A Messiah for the Third Millennium," *Modern Theology* 16, no. 1 (2000): 75–90.

4. Ochs, *Peirce,* 254ff.

5. Ibid., 36; Ochs quoting Peirce.

6. Ibid., 37.

7. Ibid., 211.

8. Ibid., 226.

9. Ibid.

10. David F. Ford, *Self and Salvation: Being Transformed* (Cambridge: Cambridge University Press, 1999).

12
Women's Voices in Jewish-Christian Relations

Christine Trevett

INTRODUCTION

It has been a tenet of feminism that *experience* is to be treated seriously and is a valid category for analysis. The subject of this study is late twentieth-century Jewish and Christian women's responses to their experiences within their religions.[1] Some of those responses have emerged through scholarly writings. Others have emerged in innovative liturgical, spiritual, and women-centered practices and women-focused study. However, neither Judaism nor Christianity is monolithic in character. Responses to the changing (secular and religious) status of women and to their self-awareness vary. They vary from group to group *within* the religions concerned. Hence the future of women's voices in the respective religions, as well as in Jewish-Christian relations, is a topic inextricably linked with competing understandings of authority and tradition in those religions, as well as with questions of whether and in what way we are seeking, men and women alike, to change the world. These are big subjects. They can only be touched on in this paper, and what follows is a personal view.[2]

THE WRITER AND CHRISTIAN-JEWISH ENCOUNTER

I write as a Christian who has had contact with Jews and Judaism through my whole working life. For twenty years I have

171

been a Quaker, which in terms of my location within the Christian tradition makes me not of the mainstream but rather of a group that has been open to positive interfaith encounter,[3] even in its proselytizing beginnings.[4] It is also a group in which, from the outset, *women* have enjoyed greater equality in ministry and in religiously motivated action in public than was true elsewhere in Christianity. Such egalitarianism has been aided by the fact that Quakers in Britain have continued to have no clergy.[5]

This places me on a radical Protestant, nonconformist point on the Christian spectrum, in a group that deems scripture and tradition secondary to continuous revelation (and thus is unlike much of "classical" Protestantism). Long ago it abandoned not just clergy but other things generally seen as definitive of Christianity, such as creeds, sacraments, and liturgy. Some Jews may recognize certain parallels within the spectrum of Jewish communities. They will understand when I say that Quakerism is sometimes defined by people in other churches as being not Christian at all.

Despite this "handicap," I have been much involved in Christian ecumenism. In the past I would not infrequently be the *only* female, even the only nonclergy person, sent by churches to an ecumenical committee. Yet what was once an anomalous activity for a woman has become more common. And while it remains the case that as a woman I could *not* be ordained were I within the majority (Catholic and Orthodox) traditions or within some minority Christian traditions too, nevertheless, layperson and female as I am, part of my job involves me in the academic training of Christian clergy. This is by virtue of what I am supposed to *know*.

Such shifts are due, of course, to the democratization of knowledge both secular and (slowly) religious and to the changing roles of women within religious groups, as well as outside of them. It also indicates changes in perceptions of what authority entails:

> I permit no woman to teach or to have authority over a man; she is to keep silent. For Adam was formed first, then Eve; and Adam was not deceived, but the woman was deceived and became a transgressor. Yet she will be saved through childbearing, provided they continue in faith and love and holiness, with modesty. ("St. Paul" in 1 Tim 2:11-15)

In my own case, then, I am neither clergy nor in Christian terms even "orthodox"[6] yet still, in some respects at least, I am not (dangerously borrowing an analogy from Judaism for the Christian sphere) among the *'am ha'arets*.[7]

My own experience within Christianity speaks of some directions in which change has occurred, when looking at the recent history of women's relation to institutionalized religion. It is a more complex relationship than it was, multifaceted and less transparent and categorizable. One important development, however, is that there are many more women than in the past who would deny that their lives were in any way touched by the tentacles of religion and who would say that they prefer it that way.

Continuing the theme of where I am coming from, I would add that I am also Welsh. In the mining valleys of South Wales in the 1950s, beyond the conurbation of Cardiff or of Newport, Jewish people were regarded as exotic. We met few of them. Roman Catholics, on the other hand, were seen by some as both exotic and dangerous. Everyone "knew" that they (namely, the local Italian café owners and the Polish doctor) would impose Vatican control at the drop of a hat![8] Those were not days of school visits to synagogues or of itemizing the festivals of other people's faiths. We now have a much-liberalized, if imperfect, school religious education system. Consequently circumstances determined that my own knowledge of Jews came from chapel study of the New Testament, which was never intended to be a textbook on Judaism and does not make a good one.

My direct encounters with Jews, rather than just with real textbooks on Judaism, came because of research. To recount the first such meeting is to say much about other changes that have come about in the last thirty years or so. I was at home in South Wales during a vacation and was failing to track down a tradition that (I had heard) originated in early *Midrash*. In need of a footnote for my research master's thesis, I telephoned the local-ish Orthodox rabbi. This was the 1960s. I was twenty-two years old. He seemed surprised but invited me around. He listened quietly while I outlined the problem—which really amounted to the fact that what I knew about *Midrashim* went on a pinhead. There was a pause and he looked at me quizzically. "Why are you interested?" he asked. I held forth with Tigger-ish enthusiasm about the wealth of Jewish tradition and what readers and interpreters of early Christian texts might gather from it. There was a long pause. He sighed. Then he said kindly, "Tell me, is there some boy in my congregation you are hoping to marry?"

Female scholarship is not an oxymoron in Judaism or Christianity nowadays. Knowledge of each about the other, being interested, and sharing insights is encouraged to a greater extent. I never did find the *Midrash* but now I find myself from time to time sharing university classrooms with the local Orthodox and/or Reform rabbis.

Subsequent studies brought me into the shades-of-gray world of early "Jewish Christianity"[9] and of those Christians who were thought too "Judaizing" for other Christians' comfort. Those studies taught me more about ancient Judaism, at least, and that it was not to be seen as synonymous with the Old Testament. Thereafter other things fed my interest in Jewish-Christian relations: there was Jewish humor, which spoke to my tendency to be argumentative and wary of conformism, and there was also the notion of bilingualism.[10]

To a limited extent at least, interfaith dialogue has things in common with bilingualism. Let me explain by quoting David Lochhead:

> When one becomes bi-lingual, one learns to operate within the categories that are appropriate to each particular language. Each language is considered to have its own integrity. A category of one is not applied to the other...the bilingual person does not usually have equal facility in both languages. One of the languages remains the "mother-tongue"...at the same time one comes to understand one's own language in a more profound way.[11]

We remain, Lochhead observed, no less committed to our own traditions. I recognize that the analogy is an imperfect one. It was disconcerting to read, for example, that "Bilinguals often find it difficult to remember which language was used during particular speech exchange"![12] Nevertheless given the troubled history of Christian-Jewish relations and the fact of borrowed words and ideas, bilingualism seems an honorable ideal, for there are dangers both of assuming that we cannot readily come to understand one another's language and that because Christians and Jews use many of the same words we mean the same thing by them.[13]

"SISTERS UNDER THEIR SKINS"

The preceding observations have been about women, religion, and change, and also about personal encounter. Before turning to some ways in which Jewish and Christian women have furthered the cause of mutual understanding it is necessary to acknowledge the general disempowerment of women within religions. In Christianity, for example, maleness has been normative in the creation and interpretation of tradition so that a woman starts from the position of being other.[14] In Christianity, but not there alone, women have been legislated *for* but not legislating, they have filled the places of worship but not stood at the altar. They have been party (sometimes willing, sometimes not) to a separation of spheres based on the philosophy of "equal but different." Above all, until recent decades, Christian women (and Jewish women too, to judge from their complaints) have been kept in ignorance of all but the most basic knowledge of their own religion and of the texts and the interpretation of those texts that have determined their place *as women*.[15]

Christians, both conservative and liberal, should not be fooled. The recent spate of ordinations of women in Anglicanism and then in the (disestablished) Church in Wales, the slightly longer history of women's ordination in various Nonconformist churches, and our own western European perspective should not blind us to the fact that in numerical and chronological terms such Protestantism is a pimple on an elephant's head. Women in Christianity continue to have neither "the knowledge" (which frees one both for questioning and for greater depth of observance)[16] nor the power base that brings the right of decision making in a religion. The decline in church attendance in Britain is related in part to the alienation of women—for it was always women who made the majority in the pews. The concern of the chief rabbi of the United Kingdom, Dr. Jonathan Sacks, to have a "Decade of Renewal" for Judaism and the consequent analysis of data about Jewish women suggests awareness of something similar in Judaism.[17]

Christians and Jews alike are in the process of dealing with, or staving off, change from the position I have described. They are having to plan for the future of the religious past,[18] especially with regard to the use of text and tradition. Some women, and some men who feel themselves marginalized or oppressed in their communities of faith,[19] have maintained that scripture, tradition, traditional interpretation, and legitimized ways of reading continue to be used (as they see it) to hold them and others in thrall. At the same time in those same communities other people fear that challenges to these *precious* things are part of the onslaught of secularization. They foresee decline into "New-Ageism" and a lack of rootedness[20] and that if the challenges are not another passing fad they may threaten religious survival. These kinds of complaints and fears have emerged in Christian and Jewish circles alike. From time to time they surface even in interfaith settings where there is trust.

In the Christian sphere, however (and I would expect it to be so in the Jewish one too), secularization is far from the agenda of women who, nevertheless, are on the side of change. Indeed they may well be suffering the disapproval of their disaffiliated or lifelong secular sisters. The strongest disapproval I have encountered, both to my own claim to be a feminist and to my remaining part of a worshiping community, has come not from my co-religionists but from secular feminists, some of whom not only would point to religion as a major root of "the problem" but would shed no tears at its demise.

It is important to stress, then, that the questionings of some Christian and Jewish women have not been simply synonymous with a disaffected or negative kind of feminism. They often have gone hand in hand with expressions of love for the history and insights of their community of faith and with telling of what has sustained them there despite their reservations or feelings of marginalization. A "sisterhood under the skin"[21] exists between Jewish and Christian women who know the same emotional attachment and feelings of frustration where their religions are concerned and who welcome an agenda for change. The idea of such sisterhood has to be treated with caution, of course. It has nothing to do with the specter of biological determinism or with a whimsical "they're all the same/believe the same things really" approach to interfaith relations. No, they are not and do not. But in recent decades *some* Jewish and Christian women in Europe and the United States have recognized in each other a commonality of experience and it has borne fruit in publications. It stems from being *religious women* with (as they see it) knowledge of failures and oppressions within religions where, ironically, liberation from bondage has been an important peg onto which a lot of theological baggage has been hung.

Christian and Jewish writers alike have made use of a range of critical apparatuses common to feminist, postmodern, and other kinds of analysis, as well as making use of interpretive skills honed in their particular religions. New ways exist of seeing women's experience reflected, and not reflected, in a variety of media and at different times in history. Both Christian and Jewish writers have been exploiting them, aware that there has been no *single* consistent transhistorical phenomenon named *woman*.

On the liberal wings sisterhood has sometimes been explored through local groups that have included Christians and Jews together. Aimed at furthering understanding, and rich in humor, they have been mutually supportive—religious women for religious women.[22] I discovered through such meetings and (more so) through reading the sameness in some of our questioning. Thus when Marcia Falk wrote of her teenage self that,

> I could not really believe that a genius like God would not get bored with all the praise in the prayerbook: did he really need so much positive feedback?—always in the same language.[23]

I recalled that as a teenager I had asked precisely the same thing. While my response was eventually to ally myself with a group without liturgy hers had been to work on a feminist Jewish reconstruction of prayer.

Jewish and Christian women, then, have been learning about and from each other, in some places through direct contact, but often without even meeting except through the printed page. The burgeoning of writings on spirituality, ecological concern, and the like has provided further points of contact. Insofar as analysis of the position of women in religion was concerned, if Christian women writers of feminist persuasion were first off the starting blocks, their Jewish counterparts soon followed. They took from the accessible store of feminist analysis and from new and not so new modes of religious study to provide antiphony for what Christians had written. In turn they facilitated borrowings by Christians. Christian women encountered treatments of tradition that were wholly unexpected and mind expanding and in their women's groups or alternative worship circles they tried them for themselves. Some people may not agree, but in my view Christian women's attempts have not yet matched what Melissa Raphael has called "the hermeneutical *chutzpah*" of Jewish feminist *Midrashim*.[24]

DEMOCRATIZING KNOWLEDGE AND
FINDING A VOICE

An important way in which women's voices have indeed been heard in Jewish-Christian relations in recent decades is through that *challenge* to aspects of the status quo in both Christianity and Judaism that has brought "the woman question" into higher relief.

In the second half of the twentieth century women were negotiating and renegotiating their space and their roles in the secular as in the religious spheres.[25] In the West, at least, some things were common to women in that task because of changes from which they all benefited. Education was a notable example. No longer did women take for granted what had always been taken for granted and that included exclusion from cultural life.[26]

As they had greater access to a range of knowledge, so too some women came to a range of *religious* knowledge as well and began to challenge the bases of their exclusion in religion. Some of them were priests at last.[27] Orthodox Jewish women with PhDs were teaching Talmud, even perhaps with the patronage and teaching of a sympathetic male rabbi and with talk of private ordination in the air (I have encountered such women in Israel in recent years). In other branches of Judaism women were indeed rabbis. Whether they were religiously observant, disaffected, disaffiliated, or wholly secularized, women were not just better informed but, to aid their reassessments, had access to modes of analysis and criticism that were particularly applicable to their history and condition as women (which can enlighten those of men, too). Such things were not even invented in their grandmothers' day.[28]

The most learned among them used their skill to rediscover, examine, and proclaim the place of women within religion past and present. Matters have moved on since the simple reclaiming of women's stories from the marginalia and interlinearities of the text (important though that has been). They have moved on since apologists for tradition could point to the same female precedents as the reclaimers were pointing to—Mary Magdalene or Priscilla, medieval abbesses and mystics, Deborah, Esther, Beruriah. There has been deeper and wider investigation of the social and economic roles that Christian and Jewish women have played through the ages,[29] thereby challenging the way in which people have had to read the female voice "as a palimpsest through the script of the dominant narrative" (that is, through the script of the male-devised narrative and male concerns).[30]

The titles of books by Christian and Jewish writers tell of a mood of increased hermeneutical and scholarly female confidence in study of the Bible: *Has the Lord Indeed Spoken Only through Moses?* reflective of Miriam's question,[31] *Texts of Terror,*[32] and books with the words *unconventional* or *subversive* or *countertraditions* in their titles.[33] Schüssler Fiorenza's *In Memory of Her* was a reminder of the marginalizing of women and the patriarchalization of the church, taking as its starting point that woman whose memory would live, Jesus declared, by virtue of her loving act of anointing him (Matt 26:13; Mark 14:9). It did not, for she was not recalled in the Christian liturgy and her name was not recorded in the text. *When Women Were Priests,* with its long subtitle about scandal and subordination, made clear the agenda of a sober historian of late antique Christianity.[34]

Many fresh insights have emerged as critical-historical study has been joined by consideration of the *reader* and of the reception of texts. Women of Bible and tradition in art, in film, and in literature are now subjects of study. In parallel with such study, ideological, ethical, and other critiques of the Bible have emerged.[35] As for what God had *really* been saying, the liberation theological perspective has borne fruit among Asian, African, African American, Mujerista, and also European and American white Christians, stressing justice, the finding of a voice, and God's bias to the oppressed. Jewish women writers have recognized its power and its relation to their own biblical tradition.

"The political effects were immediate," as one writer observed of this explosion of analysis.[36] Men and gender, hierarchy and tradition, power, politics, ideology, civilization itself were in the frame, ripe for review.[37] The writers concerned have not pretended to neutrality. Nevertheless they have become increasingly self-critical and conscious of their own lack of sensitivity. Interaction between Jewish and Christian women helped in that process.

For example, the first generation of Christian women writers was challenged by its Jewish counterpart. This was because the "feminist Jesus" and the alleged golden age of early Christian egalitarianism that had been "rediscovered" by Christian feminist writers stood, by contrast, with a misleading picture of Judaism. The latter was monochrome, made no acknowledgment of the diversity of Judaism in the first Christian century or of the problem of sources. The liberated early

Christian woman who had been rediscovered was being predicated upon an image of downtrodden Jewish women eager for liberation.[38] Jewish feminist critics pointed out these things. More than this, critics have also come to realize that in analysis of women the experience of white, first-world, middle-class women was being privileged and elevated above that of the others, and Ashkenazi Jewish women over the rest. There had been marginalization, even racism, in the process that was meant to give women a voice.[39]

Little of academic debate normally trickles down. Feminist theology *did,* however, to a limited extent trickle down, notably through the work of influential writers such as Ruether, Schüssler Fiorenza, and Plaskow. In the late 1970s, 1980s, and 1990s books were passed from hand to hand in the women's study groups of churches and synagogues or where women were meeting in alternative venues or were being passed over the garden fence. On the fringes of religious communities or still firmly within them, women who felt spiritually bereft and who were looking for alternative or modified forms of worship and for a greater sharing of responsibility started to acknowledge their unfulfilled religious needs. The result has been women's innovative worship groups, fresh liturgies and rituals, interest in more inclusive language, and also the reclaiming of old rituals for new circumstances. Such things, it should be said, have not been the preserve of the liberal fringes alone. In some settings an ethos has been created that is more conducive to women's wider participation. It has been touching even congregations not notable for female activism.

THE CHALLENGE OF CHANGE

Many Christian and Jewish people may not be fully apprised of what has been happening. Some will not approve of what they *think* has been happening. Nevertheless it is impossible to disguise the fact that something has been happening. On the one hand there have been diminishing numbers of women at worship in the late twentieth century while on the other expectations have changed among some of the women who are still there. There was nothing new in Jewish and Christian religious scholars interacting, informing, and challenging each other. That had been happening for almost two millennia and it continues. To cite two recent examples, Hyam Maccoby's *Paul and*

Hellenism followed decades of non-Jewish scholarship on Paul and Judaism,[40] and Matthew Fox, emerging from the Christian fold and doyen of late twentieth-century eco-conscious spirituality, writes for *Tikkun*.[41] But what *has* been new in recent decades is that several generations of *women*—educated, articulate, analytical—have been speaking out of their own and their mothers' and grandmothers' experience as well as recovering through scholarship the insights and experiences of hitherto silent foremothers.

The desire of such women is usually not for abandonment of their religion but for its healing and for the healing of the world as well. Indeed the female voices raised in questioning and criticism may also be the same voices to be found at other times in prayer and praise. For my own part I have recognized in the statements of some Jewish women that same "bloody-mindedness factor" that has informed my own refusal to label myself *post* anything where religion is concerned. Certainly there are women, Christian and Jewish, who have come to regard their former religions as irredeemable and, with the spiritual quest still alive in them, such post-Jewish, post-Christian women have turned to neopaganism, goddess cults, or one of myriad other alternatives.[42] They are more exception than norm, however. For a greater number, on the fringes or still within the family, other factors are often in play. Beyond the deep emotional attachment to a religion and a community, beyond the knowledge of "alternative" or special interest groups *within* the fold, and beyond the inability to think of somewhere else to flee, the bloody-mindedness factor goes like this: "It is *my* church, *my* community, *my* sacred text—and *they* are not having the monopoly of it."[43]

Self-fulfillment is the kind of topic aired constantly through television. We hear and read of the alleged current powerlessness or demise of religion, of its restrictions and unacceptable modes of authority in an age of individualism and of women with "choice." Such things are grist for the mill of women's magazines and women (and men too) now have a language in which to discuss such things. They do so over the garden fence, in the office, over coffee at the playgroup, at the gym. In those settings women (and men) who are post-Christian/post-Jewish or marginally Jewish/marginally Christian communicate, as do the religiously unaffiliated (but opinionated about religion). It's another kind of Jewish-Christian relations!

The challenge for those *within* the community of faith who want to reclaim the disaffiliated for whom (a) increasingly *spirituality* is a more meaningful term than religion and (b) fundamentalism would be no answer is to find ways of communicating to them the existence and energy of new things *within* religions. Some of those who continue to shun the community of faith are doing so because they believe (and say so) that *all* worshippers remain untouched by the questions that have helped to form them as late twentieth-century women. They are wrong, though responses to such things vary, from church to church, synagogue to synagogue.

PROPHECY AND MENDING

Conservatives fear that the boat might sink if rocked too much. How can change with regard to women in Christianity and Judaism be achieved without jeopardizing what are (as some see it) essential truths of those traditions? In place of the sinking boat I turn to the ebbing bathwater. Bathwater and babies are familiar things. The one, we remind ourselves, is not to be thrown out with the other. The challenge of course is to recognize it for what it is, the *life* that is at the center, and to not jeopardize it, while negotiating change in (and indeed abandonment of) what is peripheral to it. The challenge, as not a few Christian and Jewish women have discovered, is to get everyone else to agree about what the baby—the really important thing—looks like, as well as about abandoning the bathwater. This debate is not a new one, but in Christianity and Judaism of recent decades women's voices have been part of this debate about metaphorical babies and bathwater. That is new. Moreover the debate involves women's place as never before.

Being, for the first time in millennia, party to such a debate and to the forming of faith for a new age is not a painless process nor is the process a very rapid one. In 1981, so Judith Plaskow reported, the women in the Jewish feminist spirituality collective *B'not Esh,* with which she was involved, found it hard to talk of spirituality and their futures.[44] In the early 1990s, when I was chairing the CYTÛN ecumenical group *Christian Women together in Wales* the conflicting understandings of and hopes for women in the church were at first very apparent. Nevertheless there has been emerging among women an agenda for the future that has moved beyond those of institutions. It certainly concerns their religious communities but beyond them it concerns their societies and their planet as well. To end this paper I shall touch on just two elements that play a part in it.

The first element is keeping alive the prophetic ideal and the prophetic challenge, which is a role not only for women. Whether, on the one hand, it is in reminding people not to throw out babies with bathwater or, on the other, in challenging traditionalists with the fact that there are many kinds of idolatry to beware of, women's voices can be akin to prophetic ones. Biblical prophecy has been an important inspiration for a wide variety of Christian theological feminist writings[45] and prophetic women function as important foremothers in both religions. In Christianity, women's demand to be taken seriously *as prophets* continued for centuries.[46] So while Judith Plaskow wrote of "contradictions" in biblical prophecy and told of the prophets' call for justice being partial and unchallenging of *in*justice to women, nevertheless, she said, "feminists can affirm our debt to, and continuity with prophetic insistence on connecting faith and justice," though *going beyond what they envisaged.*[47]

Second, as women have been *menders*—closing the breaches in breeches and applying the balm that soothes and mends hurts—so too they have become acutely conscious of spoiled relationships. These exist in terms of disharmony between the sexes and this is exacerbated by claims to power, domination, and exploitation in religion as elsewhere. Similar spoiling exists between peoples and also between ourselves and the rest of creation, so that Christian, Jewish, and eco-feminist awareness of our obligations to our planet have come to the fore in recent years.[48] "The second wave of religious feminism," wrote Melissa Raphael, "has been a prophetic call for the renewal of a loving sense of connection between the sexes and between humans and nature, both of which are profoundly damaged...."[49] Jews have a good phrase for what some Christian and Jewish women hope the future must hold. It is participating in *tikkun 'olam*—the mending of a broken world. The words of Inge Lederer Gibel, quoted in the front of the book *Women of Faith in Dialogue* seem subdued and rather unoptimistic some years after their writing. But "the few" are no longer so few and the goals are recognized as good ones by a greater range of people, even when they encompass the mending of religion too:

> And what can we do, a few women whom the world listens
> to less than it should? Continue talking to each other, and
> others; continue learning and caring about each other's sto-
> ries…keep building bridges, overcoming barriers, turning
> the other into the human.

Such tasks are not just for women who have been the other for so much
of history. They are tasks related to the mending of the world. In
Christian-Jewish relations turning the other into the human is exactly
the point.

NOTES

1. This short study will refer to many matters that deserve more explanation, defense, or discussion than is possible. The much-debated issue of
experience and feminist interpretation is one of them: Linda Hogan, *From
Women's Experience to Feminist Theology* (Sheffield: Sheffield Academic
Press, 1995).

2. Thanks are due to Dr. Piet van Boxel, librarian of Leo Baeck
College, for access to some of the material in the following notes.

3. Quakerism was born (in the 1640s) at a time when England was rife
with hope for "the conversion of the Jews." At the end of the twentieth-century
ultraliberal Quakerism had triumphed in Britain, and it eschews evangelism.
See B. P. Dandelion, *A Sociological Analysis of the Theology of Quakers: The
Silent Revolution* (Lampeter, Wales: Edwin Mellen, 1993); Christine Trevett,
Previous Convictions and End of the Millennium Quakerism (London: Quaker
Home Service, 1997).

4. In late summer of 1657 Mary Fisher, an ill-educated unmarried servant, ignorant of Islam and a Quaker, was en route alone to convert the Grand
Turk Sultan Muhammad IV, who was encamped at Adrianople. The Muslims
were surprised that such a one "should come to them as far as from England
with a message from the Lord God" and they treated her kindly. "They are
nearer the truth than many nations," she wrote on her return. "There is a love
begot in me towards them which is endless." Margaret Fell, "mother of
Quakerism," composed an open letter and a tract directed to the conversion of
the Jews, at a time of some millenarian fervor (there were Hebrew translations): "For Rabbi Manasseth-ben-Israel" (1656) and "A Loving Salutation to
the Seed of Abraham" (1656). On these things: Christine Trevett, *Women and
Quakerism in the Seventeenth Century* (York: Sessions, 1991); Phyllis Mack,
Visionary Women: Ecstatic Prophecy in Seventeenth Century England
(Berkeley/Oxford: University of California Press, 1992); Bonnelyn Young

Kunze, *Margaret Fell and the Rise of Quakerism* (London: Macmillan, 1994); Stefano Villani, "I primi Quaccheri e gli Ebrei," *Archivio italiano per la storia della pietà,* vol. 10 (Rome: Edizioni di storia e letteratura, 1997), 43–113.

5. *Quaker* was a hostile epithet applied to the seventeenth-century sectarians. Quakerism began in England. In the United States and elsewhere it has become fragmented, and some forms of it have paid ministers.

6. "What is the responsibility of a theologian when she no longer believes what she taught to others as Torah?" asked Rachel Adler, charting her own change from Orthodox to Reform Judaism (*Tikkun* 8 [1993], 38–41, p. 38). British universities are secular institutions, and staff may not be subject to "religious tests."

7. A lot of Jewish and Christian scholars' ink has been spilled over the precise definition of the "people of the land"—suffice it to say that the term encompasses those who were insufficiently religiously educated and/or sensitive about observance for the liking of those who were more so.

8. David Lochhead, *The Dialogical Imperative: A Christian Reflection on Interfaith Encounter* (London: SCM Press, 1988), ch. 11, deals with changing perspectives on memories.

9. This phrase was often ill defined and might mean "the early Christianity practiced by those who were converts from Judaism" (rather than paganism) through "the early Christianity derived from traditions traceable to the Jerusalem mother church" to "early Christianity expressing itself in categories derived from Judaism"—this last being so all-embracing as to render the term effectively redundant. For relevant literature, see Jack T. Sanders, *Schismatics, Sectarians, Dissidents, Deviants: The First One Hundred Years of Jewish-Christian Relations* (London: SCM Press, 1993); and M. D. Nanos, *The Mystery of Romans: The Jewish Context of Paul's Letter* (Minneapolis: Fortress Press, 1996).

10. Wales provides education through the medium of Welsh, an option chosen by many English-speaking families for their children.

11. Lochhead, *Dialogical Imperative,* 69.

12. Suzanne Romaine, *Bilingualism* (Oxford: Blackwell, 1989), 258.

13. On Christianity's influence on aspects of Jewish practice, see Michael Hilton, *The Christian Effect on Jewish Life* (London: SCM Press, 1994). Jewish "influence" in Christianity's early phase is surely a misnomer. *Christianity* was a Jewish phenomenon.

14. Jewish feminist writers say the same thing. Like Christians they cite the seminal analyses of feminists such as Simone de Beauvoir and Mary Daly. See, e.g., Alexandra Wright, "An Approach to Jewish Feminist Theology," in *Hear Our Voice: Women Rabbis Tell Their Stories,* ed. Sibyl Sheridan (London: SCM Press, 1994), 152–61.

15. See E. M. Umansky, "Women in Judaism: from the Reform Movement to Contemporary Jewish Religious Feminism," in *Women of Spirit: Female Leadership in the Jewish and Christian Traditions,* ed. Rosemary R. Ruether and Eleanor McLaughlin (New York: Simon and Schuster, 1979), 334–54.

16. This is also true for many Christian men, of course.

17. See, e.g., S. Miller et al., eds., *Women in the Jewish Community: Survey Report* (London: Office of the Chief Rabbi, 1994); and J. Goodkin and J. Citron, eds., *Women in the Jewish Community: Review and Recommendations* (London: Office of the Chief Rabbi, 1994).

18. "The Past: Does It Hold a Future for Women?" is the title of one of the major divisions of Judith Plaskow and Carol Christ, eds., *Womanspirit Rising: A Feminist Reader in Religion* (San Francisco: Harper and Row, 1979).

19. Some gay men, for example.

20. It was a fear expressed in 1976 by the rabbi's wife Blu Greenberg in "Judaism and Feminism," in *The Jewish Woman: New Perspectives,* ed. E. Koltun (New York: Schocken, 1976), 179–92. But compare her later article "Confrontation and Change: Women and the Jewish Tradition," in *Women of Faith in Dialogue,* ed. Virginia Ramey Mollenkott (New York: Crossroad, 1987), 17–25. "It's feminist: but is it Jewish?" ran the question in Judith Plaskow's introduction to *Standing Again at Sinai: Judaism from a Feminist Perspective* (New York: HarperCollins, 1991). On spiritual nurture within a traditional Jewish framework, see Blu Greenberg, *On Women and Judaism: A View from Tradition* (Philadelphia: Jewish Publication Society, 1981); Jody Myers and Rachel Litman, "The Secret of Jewish Femininity: Hiddenness, Power and Physicality in the Theology of Orthodox Women in the Contemporary World," in *Gender and Judaism: The Transformation of Tradition,* ed. T. M. Rudavsky (New York: New York University Press, 1995), 51–77; Tamar Frankiel, *The Voice of Sarah: Feminine Spirituality and Traditional Judaism* (San Francisco: Harper, 1991). In Britain, Elaine Storkey's *What's Right with Feminism* (London: SPCK, 1985) was a measured contribution from an evangelical Christian.

21. "The colonel's lady and Judy O'Grady are sisters under their skins." R. Kipling, "The Ladies," *Complete Verse* (London: Kyle Cathie, 1990).

22. For example, I used to belong to a Women in Ministry group in South Wales, which included clergy and laypeople, a range of Christian denominations and Jewish membership.

23. Marcia Falk, "Notes on Composing New Blessings: Toward a Feminist-Jewish Reconstruction of Prayer," *Journal of Feminist Studies in Religion* 3 (1987): 39–56, quote at 40.

24. Melissa Raphael, "Cover Not Our Blood with Thy Silence: Sadism, Eschatological Justice and Female Images of the Divine," *Feminist Theology* 8 (1995): 85–105, 97. For a recent attempt around the Great Banquet narrative of Luke 17, see Zoe Bennett Moore and her male students, "A Midrash," *Feminist Theology* 18 (1998): 29–30.

25. See, e.g., Barbara Borts, "On Trespassing the Boundaries: a Reflection on Men, Women and Jewish Space," in *Hear Our Voice: Women Rabbis Tell Their Stories,* ed. Sibyl Sheridan (London: SCM Press, 1994), 169–79; Judith Plaskow, "We Are Also Your Sisters: The Development of Women's Studies in Religion," *Women's Studies Quarterly* 21 (1993): 9–21.

26. Such past exclusion becomes a subject for critical analysis. See Nancy Jay, "Sacrifice as Remedy for Having Been Born a Woman," in *Immaculate and Powerful: The Female in Sacred Image and Social Reality,* ed. Clarissa W. Atkinson et al. (Boston: Crucible, 1985), 283–310, 283.

27. See, however, Mark Chaves, *Ordaining Women: Culture and Conflict in Religious Organisations* (Cambridge, MA/London: Harvard University Press, 1997).

28. Elisabeth Schüssler Fiorenza's seminal study *In Memory of Her: A Feminist Theological Reconstruction of Christian Origins,* 2nd ed. (1983; London: SCM Press, 1994) was important in reclaiming women's contribution and explaining their marginalization. Nowadays critical and cultural theory, the insights of anthropology, and varieties of feminist literary criticism play a part in laying bare assumptions and analyzing gender roles. Headings such as cultural-anthropological, socio-historical, rhetorical-critical, Womanist, Mujerista, Asian feminist theological, phenomenological, literary/textual, post-structuralist, process metaphysics, and others figure in the indexes of approaches to the subject. See, e.g., "women's experience" in the index of Rebecca S. Chopp and Sheila Greeve Davaney, eds., *Horizons in Feminist Theology: Identity, Tradition and Norms* (Minneapolis: Fortress Press, 1997), 165–78, 168.

29. Paula Hyman in "The Other Half: Women in the Jewish Tradition" (in *The Jewish Woman,* ed. E. Koltun [New York: Schocken, 1976], 105–13, 108) called for such study of Jewish women's history. Since that time it has been happening in respect to both Jewish and Christian women.

30. Alice Bach, introduction to *The Pleasure of Her Text: Feminist Readings of Biblical and Historical Texts,* ed. Alice Bach (Philadelphia: Trinity Press International, 1990), xi. Bach cites the dictum of Harold Bloom in his study of *kabbalah* and criticism: "That which you are, that only can you read."

31. R. J. Burns, *Has the Lord Indeed Spoken Only through Moses? A Study of the Biblical Portrait of Miriam,* SBLDS 84 (Atlanta: Scholars Press, 1987).

32. Phyllis Trible, *Texts of Terror: Literary Feminist Readings of Biblical Narratives* (Philadelphia: Fortress Press, 1984). See also Y. Sherwood, *The Prostitute and the Prophet: Hosea's Marriage in Literary Theoretical Perspective* (Sheffield: Sheffield Academic Press, 1996); C. Camp and C. R. Fontaine, *Women, War and Metaphor: Language and Society in the Study of the Hebrew Bible* (Minneapolis: Fortress Press, 1993).

33. Ilana Pardes, *Countertraditions in the Bible: A Feminist Approach* (Cambridge, MA: Harvard University Press, 1992); A. LaCocque, *The Feminine Unconventional: Four Subversive Figures in Israel's Tradition* (Minneapolis: Fortress Press, 1990); Cheryl Exum, *Fragmented Women: Feminist (Sub)versions of Biblical Narratives,* JSOTSS 163 (Sheffield: Sheffield Academic Press, 1993).

34. Schüssler Fiorenza, *In Memory of Her;* Karen-Jo Torjeson, *When Women Were Priests: Women's Leadership in the Early Church and the Scandal of Their Subordination in the Rise of Christianity* (San Francisco: Harper Collins, 1993). See too Anne Jensen, *God's Self-Confident Daughters: Early Christianity and the Liberation of Women* (Kampen: Kok Pharos, 1992). The following two works consider both Christian and Jewish women: Deborah R. Sawyer, *Women and Religion in the First Christian Centuries* (London: Routledge, 1996); and Ross S. Kraemer and Mary Rose D'Angelo, eds., *Women and Christian Origins* (Oxford: Oxford University Press, 1999).

35. Dorothée Sölle, Joe H. Kirchberger, and Herbert Haag, *Great Women of the Bible in Art and Literature* (Grand Rapids: Eerdmans, 1993); Cheryl Exum, *Plotted, Shot and Painted: Cultural Representations of Biblical Women,* JSOTSS 215 (Sheffield: Sheffield Academic Press, 1996). See also Cheryl Exum and Stephen D. Moore, *Biblical Studies/Cultural Studies* (Sheffield: Sheffield Academic Press, 1998). For methodologies, see Schüssler Fiorenza, ed., *Searching the Scriptures,* vol. 1, *A Feminist Introduction* (London: SCM Press, 1993).

36. Sheila Briggs, "A History of Our Own: What Would a Feminist History of Theology Look Like?" in *Horizons in Feminist Theology: Identity, Tradition and Norms,* ed. Rebecca S. Chopp and Sheila Greeve Davaney (Minneapolis: Fortress Press, 1997), 165–78, 168.

37. See, e.g., Judith Plaskow, "Transforming the Nature of Community: Toward a Feminist People of Israel," and Paula M. Cooey, "The Redemption of the Body: Post-Patriarchal Reconstruction of Inherited Christian Doctrine," both in *After Patriarchy: Feminist Transformations of the World Religions,* ed. P. M. Cooey et al. (Maryknoll, NY: Orbis Books, 1992), 87–105, 106–30.

38. Contrast Léonie Archer, *Her Price Is Beyond Rubies: The Jewish Woman in Greco-Roman Palestine,* JSOTSS 60 (Sheffield: Sheffield Academic Press, 1990); Bernadette J. Brooten, *Women Leaders of the Ancient Synagogue*

(Chico, CA.: Scholars Press, 1982); Amy-Jill Levine, ed., *"Women like This":
New Perspectives on Jewish Women in the Greco-Roman World,* SBL Early
Judaism and Its Literature (Atlanta: Scholars Press, 1991); Ross Shepard
Kraemer, ed., *Maenads, Martyrs, Matrons, Monastics: A Sourcebook on
Women's Religions in the Greco-Roman World* (Philadelphia: Fortress Press,
1988); Eadem, *Her Share of the Blessings: Women's Religions among Pagans,
Jews and Christians in the Greco-Roman World* (Oxford: Oxford University
Press, 1992); Tal Ilan, *Jewish Women in Greco-Roman Palestine* (Peabody, MA:
Hendrickson, 1996). See too some of the studies in Judith R. Baskin, ed., *Jewish
Women in Historical Perspective* (Detroit: Wayne State University Press, 1991).

    39. See, e.g., Sheila Greeve Davaney, "Continuing the Story, but
Departing the Text: A Historicist Interpretation of Feminist Norms in
Theology," in *Horizons in Feminist Theology: Identity, Tradition and Norms,*
ed. Rebecca S. Chopp and Sheila Greeve Davaney (Minneapolis: Fortress
Press, 1997), 198–214; Kwok Pui-lan, "Racism and ethnocentrism in
Feminist Biblical Interpretation," in *Searching the Scriptures,* ed. Elisabeth
Schüssler Fiorenza, 101–13, and in the same volume, Judith Plaskow, "Anti-
Judaism in Feminist Christian Interpretation," 117–29; Glenna Jackson,
"Jesus as a First-Century Feminist: Christian Anti-Judaism?" *Feminist
Theology* 19 (1998): 85–98; and Susannah Heschel, "Jesus as Theological
Transvestite," in *Judaism since Gender,* ed. Miriam Peskowitz and Laura
Levitt (New York: Routledge and Kegan Paul, 1997). On intergenerational
tensions between scholars, see Regula Grünenfelder, Emily R. Neill, Marla
Brettschneider (who discusses Ashkenazic scholarship), Grace Ji-Sun Kim et
al., "Roundtable Discussion: From Generation to Generation," *Journal of
Feminist Studies in Religion* 15 (1999): 102–38. See too Maurie Sacks, "An
Anthropological and Post-Modern Critique of Jewish Feminist Theory," in
Gender and Judaism: The Transformation of Tradition, ed. T. M. Rudavsky
(New York: New York University Press, 1995), 295–305.

    40. Hyam Maccoby, *Paul and Hellenism* (London: SCM Press, 1991).

    41. *Tikkun* 13, no. 3 (1998) marked his first appearance as columnist.

    42. In Britain, Daphne Hampson is the best-known post-Christian femi-
nist writer: *Theology and Feminism* (Oxford: Blackwell, 1990), and *After
Christianity* (London: SCM Press, 1996). See too Judith Plaskow, "The Jewish
Feminist: Conflict in Identities," in *The Jewish Woman: New Perspectives,* ed. E.
Koltun (New York: Schocken, 1976), 3–10. See also Naomi Goldenberg,
Changing of the Gods: Feminism and the End of Traditional Religions (Boston:
Beacon Press, 1979); Pamm Lunn, "Do Women Need the Goddess: Some
Phenomenological and Sociological Reflections," *Feminist Theology* 4 (1993):
17–38; Asphodel Long, "The Goddess Movement in Britain Today," *Feminist
Theology* 5 (1994): 11–39; A. Pirani, ed., *The Absent Mother: Restoring the
Goddess to Judaism and Christianity* (London: Mandala, 1991); and Carol

Christ, *Rebirth of the Goddess: Finding Meaning in Feminist Spirituality* (London: Routledge, 1997).

43. "You are not driving me out": see Dorothea McEwan's interview with a Benedictine sister and scholar, "Joan on Joan: 'Clearly Confrontational and Boldly Orthodox.' An Interview with Joan Chittester OSB," *Feminist Theology* 16 (1997): 100–117.

44. Plaskow, *Standing Again at Sinai,* 212.

45. See Sheila Shulman, "Some Thoughts on Biblical Prophecy and Feminist Vision," in *Hear Our Voice: Women Rabbis Tell Their Stories,* ed. Sibyl Sheridan (London: SCM Press, 1994), 55–63.

46. See, e.g., Mary Rose d'Angelo, "Remembering Women: Prophecy and Resistance in the Memory of the Early Churches," *Horizons* 19 (1992): 199–218; Christine Trevett, *Montanism: Gender, Authority and the New Prophecy* (Cambridge: Cambridge University Press, 1996); eadem, *Quaker Women Prophets in England and Wales 1650–1700* (Lampeter, Wales: Edwin Mellen, 2000); Mack, *Visionary Women*; Beverly Mayne Kienzle and Pamela J. Walker, eds., *Women Preachers and Prophets through Two Millennia of Christianity* (Berkeley: University of California Press, 1998).

47. Plaskow, *Standing Again at Sinai,* 216–17.

48. Rosemary Ruether, *Gaia and God: An Eco-Feminist Theology of Earth-Healing* (London: SCM Press, 1993); Anne Primavesi, *From Apocalypse to Genesis: Ecology, Feminism and Christianity* (Tunbridge Wells: Burns and Oates, 1991); Karen Baker-Fletcher, *Sisters of Dust, Sisters of Spirit: Womanist Wordings on God and Creation* (Minneapolis: Fortress Press, 1998); Lynn Gottlieb, in *She Who Dwells Within: A Feminist Vision of a Renewed Judaism* (San Francisco: Harper, 1995), writes about "eco-kashrut."

49. Raphael, "Cover Not Our Blood," 85.

13
Considering a Jewish Statement on Christianity

Edward Kessler and James K. Aitken

DABRU EMET

A JEWISH STATEMENT ON CHRISTIANS AND CHRISTIANITY

In recent years, there has been a dramatic and unprecedented shift in Jewish and Christian relations. Throughout the nearly two millennia of Jewish exile, Christians have tended to characterize Judaism as a failed religion or, at best, a religion that prepared the way for, and is completed in, Christianity. In the decades since the Holocaust, however, Christianity has changed dramatically. An increasing number of official church bodies, both Roman Catholic and Protestant, have made public statements of their remorse about Christian mistreatment of Jews and Judaism. These statements have declared, furthermore, that Christian teaching and preaching can and must be reformed so that they acknowledge God's enduring covenant with the Jewish people and celebrate the contribution of Judaism to world civilization and to the Christian faith itself.

We believe these changes merit a thoughtful Jewish response. Speaking only for ourselves—an interdenominational group of Jewish scholars—we believe it is time for Jews to learn about the efforts of Christians to honor Judaism. We believe it is time for Jews to reflect on what Judaism may now say about Christianity. As a first step, we offer eight brief statements about how Jews and Christians may relate to one another.

1. Jews and Christians worship the same God. Before the rise of Christianity, Jews were the only worshipers of the God of Israel. But Christians also worship the God of Abraham, Isaac, and Jacob, creator of heaven and earth. While Christian worship is not a viable religious choice for Jews, as Jewish theologians, we rejoice that, through Christianity, hundreds of millions of people have entered into relationship with the God of Israel.

2. Jews and Christians seek authority from the same book — the Bible (what Jews call *Tanakh* and Christians call the Old Testament). Turning to it for religious orientation, spiritual enrichment, and communal education, we each take away similar lessons: God created and sustains the universe; God established a covenant with the people Israel; God's revealed word guides Israel to a life of righteousness; and God will ultimately redeem Israel and the whole world. Yet, Jews and Christians interpret the Bible differently on many points. Such differences must always be respected.

3. Christians can respect the claim of the Jewish people upon the land of Israel. The most important event for Jews since the Holocaust has been the reestablishment of a Jewish state in the promised land. As members of a biblically based religion, Christians appreciate that Israel was promised — and given — to Jews as the physical center of the covenant between them and God. Many Christians support the State of Israel for reasons far more profound than mere politics. As Jews, we applaud this support. We also recognize that Jewish tradition mandates justice for all non-Jews who reside in a Jewish state.

4. Jews and Christians accept the moral principles of Torah. Central to the moral principles of Torah is the inalienable sanctity and dignity of every human being. All of us were created in the image of God. This shared moral emphasis can be the basis of an improved relationship between our two communities. It can also be the basis of a powerful witness to all humanity for improving the lives of our fellow human beings and for standing against the immoralities and idolatries that harm and degrade us. Such witness is especially needed after the unprecedented horrors of the past century.

5. Nazism was not a Christian phenomenon. Without the long history of Christian anti-Judaism and Christian violence against Jews, Nazi ideology could not have taken hold nor could it have been carried out. Too many Christians participated in, or were sympathetic to, Nazi atrocities against Jews. Other Christians did not protest sufficiently against these atrocities. But Nazism itself was not an inevitable outcome of Christianity. If the Nazi extermination of the Jews had been fully successful, it would have turned its murderous rage more directly to Christians. We recognize with gratitude those Christians who risked or sacrificed their lives to save Jews during the Nazi regime. With that in mind, we encourage the continuation of recent efforts in Christian theology to repudiate unequivocally contempt of Judaism and the Jewish people. We applaud those Christians who reject this teaching of contempt, and we do not blame them for the sins committed by their ancestors.

6. The humanly irreconcilable difference between Jews and Christians will not be settled until God redeems the entire world as promised in scripture. Christians know and serve God through Jesus Christ and the Christian tradition. Jews know and serve God through Torah and the Jewish tradition. That difference will be settled not by one community insisting that it has interpreted scripture more accurately than the other, nor by exercising political power over the other. Jews can respect Christians' faithfulness to their revelation just as we expect Christians to respect our faithfulness to our revelation. Neither Jew nor Christian should be pressed into affirming the teaching of the other community.

7. A new relationship between Jews and Christians will not weaken Jewish practice. An improved relationship will not accelerate the cultural and religious assimilation that Jews rightly fear. It will not change traditional Jewish forms of worship, nor increase intermarriage between Jews and non-Jews, nor persuade more Jews to convert to Christianity, nor create a false blending of Judaism and Christianity. We respect Christianity as a faith that originated within Judaism and that still has significant contacts with it. We do not see it as an extension of Judaism. Only if we cherish our own traditions can we pursue this relationship with integrity.

8. Jews and Christians must work together for justice and peace. Jews and Christians, each in their own way, recognize the unredeemed state of the world as reflected in the persistence of persecution, poverty, and human degradation and misery. Although justice and peace are finally God's, our joint efforts, together with those of other faith communities, will help bring the kingdom of God for which we hope and long. Separately and together, we must work to bring justice and peace to our world. In this enterprise, we are guided by the vision of the prophets of Israel:

It shall come to pass in the end of days that the mountain of the Lord's house shall be established at the top of the mountains and be exalted above the hills, and the nations shall flow unto it…and many peoples shall go and say, "Come ye and let us go up to the mountain of the Lord to the house of the God of Jacob and He will teach us of His ways and we will walk in his paths." (Isa 2:2–3)

Tikva Frymer-Kensky, University of Chicago
David Novak, University of Toronto
Peter Ochs, University of Virginia
Michael Signer, University of Notre Dame

DABRU EMET AND ITS SIGNIFICANCE

Edward Kessler

September 10, 2000, may be remembered as one of the most important dates in modern Jewish-Christian relations, perhaps the most important since October 28, 1965, which marked the beginning of the sea change in the Catholic understanding of Jews and Judaism. In 1965 the Catholic Church published a hugely significant document called *Nostra Aetate* (In Our Age), which called for a reevaluation of Christian attitudes. On September 10, 2000, another document, *Dabru Emet* (Speak Truth), was published[1] — this time consisting of a Jewish reassessment of Christians and Christianity.

Like *Nostra Aetate,* the text of *Dabru Emet* is short and seemingly simple, but each carefully crafted phrase carries meaning and significance. Although the statement is addressed to the Jewish community, it has been produced with an awareness that another community is, as it were, looking over the Jewish shoulder to see whether it has been validly portrayed. Over 150 Jewish scholars, teachers, and rabbis signed this declaration, and the broad range of signatories, including Orthodox and Progressive Jews, underlines its importance. It is the first detailed modern cross-denominational statement published in the name of Jews and Judaism. The document stressed that it was time for Jews to learn about the efforts of Christians to honor Judaism and to reflect on what Judaism may now say about Christianity.

The significance of *Dabru Emet* is also highlighted by the lack of official Jewish statements about the Jewish understanding of Christianity. Jewish-Christian relations rarely feature in institutional statements. Those statements that consider the subject are generally published by one particular Jewish organization or another. None succeeds in crossing denominational boundaries.[2]

The importance of *Dabru Emet* is increased still further when one considers that there is a major imbalance between the number of writings that consider Christian views of Judaism and those that consider Jewish views of Christianity. Much more has been published on the former than the latter. One thinks immediately of Christian theologians such as Hans Küng or Roy and Alice Eckardt who made significant contributions to a Christian theology of Judaism as well as a large number of Christian institutional statements that discuss relations with Judaism.[3]

As far as Jewish authors are concerned the names of David Novak and Eugene Borowitz come to mind, but although all have touched on the subject of a Jewish theology of Christianity none has offered a detailed study.[4] Claude Montefiore's call for the creation of a Jewish theology of Christianity has remained unanswered for over seventy-five years.[5] Montefiore, who died in 1938, was a pioneer in Jewish-Christian relations. Although his writings on Christianity caused great controversy among his Jewish and Christian contemporaries, even Montefiore did not attempt to create a Jewish theology of Christianity but limited himself to a number of important studies on the New Testament as well as a few short essays on Jewish attitudes toward Christianity.

Dabru Emet therefore represents a new stage in the Jewish-Christian relationship. The declaration reflects on the place of Christianity in Jewish thought and considers questions such as:

- What was the purpose behind the creation of Christianity?
- Does the fact that Jesus was a Jew have any implications for Jews?
- What are the implications of the fact that the followers of Jesus the Jew today number almost two billion people?

Until now, the stimulus for Jewish-Christian dialogue has arisen, inevitably, from the Christian side—to be more accurate, from the Protestant churches and from the Roman Catholic Church. After the Second World War Christians reawoke to the fact that Christianity arose out of Judaism and, at the same time, began to appreciate that Christian teaching made a significant contribution to Jewish suffering. Although a number of Christian scholars, most notably James Parkes, acknowledged the existence of anti-Jewish teaching earlier, it was only at the Seelisberg Conference in 1947 that the process of tackling the anti-Jewish heritage, which is deeply ingrained in Christianity, began to take place in a meaningful way.

Most Jews responded to the new Christian interest with suspicion—a legacy of the consequences of the "teaching of contempt." For the most part, there was little desire among Jews to engage in dialogue with Christians and Christianity.[6]

The Christian teaching of contempt arose out of the Jewish rejection of Jesus as their long-awaited Messiah. Christian theology responded to the Jewish "no" with polemic. For example, Christianity portrayed Jews as arrogant by their experience of being the chosen people, as spiritually blind, and as religiously decadent. Jews were blind to the new teaching and instead lived a life of legalism and empty rituals and deeds. Over the years, as we know only too well, Jews were portrayed as Christ-killers, a people guilty of deicide, children of the devil who practiced ritual child murders, and so on. This Christian stereotype of the Jew was the primary cause of forced conversions, expulsions, and pogroms. Eventually, it was assumed Jews would repent and turn to Christ.[7]

It should be realized that Judaism also reciprocated the teaching of contempt. Although there is little evidence of an *Adversus Christianos,* Christianity was dismissed as a religion practiced by morally and culturally inferior gentiles—a religion that was based on unbelievable claims, such as God-in-the-flesh, and that had degenerated into idolatry.[8]

Three factors were necessary before attitudes could begin to change:

- The consequences of the Enlightenment
- The Shoah
- The creation of the State of Israel

The first factor, which might be described as modern culture, disseminated the principles of equality and dignity of all people. It became harder to preach contempt for another people and to treat its religion as inherently inferior without losing one's own credibility in a culture of universal human dignity. At the same time, there was the growing power of secularism, which was eroding all religious claims. Some spiritual leaders concluded that it was more important to form religious alliances to battle secularism and materialism than to fight and kill one another.

The second factor arose out of the Second World War and the murder of six million Jews and five million non-Jews. The Shoah resulted in a general awareness of the immensity of the burden of guilt that the church carried not only for its general silence, with some noble exceptions during 1933–45, but also because of the teaching of contempt toward Jews and Judaism that it carried out for so many centuries. As Jules Isaac showed immediately after the war, it was this that sowed the seeds of hatred and made it so easy for Hitler to use anti-semitism as a political weapon.[9] Although no one would deny that Nazism was opposed to Christianity, it is well known that Hitler often justified his antisemitism with reference to the church and to Christian attitudes toward Judaism.

The third factor is the establishment of the State of Israel in 1948. Israel is the only state in which Jews form the majority; as a result, Jews have had more confidence in their dealings with Christians. All the Christian holy places are now in Israel or in Israeli controlled territory, which means that the entire Christian world takes a close interest in developments. This has led to strong reactions—both of a favorable and of an unfavorable nature—but the very existence of this spotlight shining so strongly on Israel, and especially on Jerusalem, gives particular importance to any attempt at mutual understanding between Christians and Jews inside Israel.

Of the three factors that I have identified, many Christians involved in dialogue (particularly in the West) point to the Shoah as the major cause of change. In their view, before a genuine dialogue could begin Christianity had to publicly acknowledge the history of the church and its attitude toward the Jews. This involved a proper appraisal of Christian antisemitism, anti-Judaism, and the significance of the Shoah. As a result of the soul-searching that took place after 1945, many Christians began the painful process of reexamining the sources of the teaching of contempt and repudiating them. Christian institutions, most notably the Vatican, the World Council of Churches, and many Protestant denominations have, since then, issued declarations against the perpetuation of this teaching.[10]

Recent Christian institutional statements have consistently condemned antisemitism, and documents such as the recent Vatican statement *We Remember* (1998) illustrate a willingness to tackle this subject. Most Christian theologians involved in Jewish-Christian dialogue have now acknowledged that the slaughter of six million Jews in the Shoah would not have been possible were the roots of antisemitism not deep within the Christian tradition. Such views are nearly always mentioned in the forewords and introductions of modern Christian writings on Jews and Judaism, many of which begin with a personal reflection on this reality.

It is therefore interesting to note the statement in *Dabru Emet* that comments on the Shoah, assessing Christian guilt while separating Christianity from Nazism. This statement has caused some controversy within both the Jewish and the Christian communities. The need to tackle such issues as the Shoah in Jewish-Christian dialogue is self-evident but there are dangers if they are not conducted in perspective. Fackenheim's proclamation that the Shoah resulted in a new commandment, the 614th, that stressed that it was incumbent upon Jews to survive as Jews is a case in point. According to Fackenheim one remained a Jew so as not to provide Hitler a posthumous victory. However, as a result, Jewish identity became Shoah-centered and, at the same time, Jewish-Christian dialogue became Shoah-centered. The danger is that by focusing solely on the Holocaust, Jews and Christians will gain a distorted view. For example, a young Jew will construct a negative Jewish identity, which without the positive side of Judaism, will not be a value to be handed down over the generations. A young Christian will come away with an exclusive picture of the Jew as victim without an awareness of the positive aspects of Jewish culture. If the Jew disappears from the horizons from the end of the biblical period and only reappears again in 1933, where is the Jew and what is Jewish-Christian dialogue?

It is a result of the emphasis on Shoah and antisemitism that Jewish-Christian dialogue often appears to consist of an attempt to educate Christians about Judaism in order to prevent or, at the very least, to reduce Christian antisemitism. Thus, Jews and Christians have become involved in dialogue on account of defensive factors, in other words, to stop the possibility of antisemitism from breaking out in churches in the future. Although Jewish-Christian dialogue has proceeded at many levels, one should realize that while reaction to the Shoah is an important driving force, a theology of dialogue cannot be built solely on responses to antisemitism and Christian feelings of guilt. Indeed, no healthy and enduring relationship between people is built on guilt.

There is a danger, therefore, if Christian documents on Jews and Judaism focus solely or even primarily on issues associated with guilt. The statement *Building Bridges of Hope,* issued by the Methodist Church in 1996, places great stress on "acknowledgment of complicity and responsibility, repentance," which can make some of those involved in the dialogue uneasy.

If recent Christian soul-searching in the aftermath of the destruction of European Jewry leads to a new approach and a revision of traditional anti-Jewish teaching, so much the better. However, the future relationship cannot be built on the foundations of guilt. The sense of guilt is transient and does not pass to the next generation; moreover, it is unstable, inherently prone to sudden and drastic reversal.

The section in *Dabru Emet* on the Shoah is probably the most controversial. Some have criticized it for going too far. These people are convinced that any move toward reconciliation with those Christians who have rethought their theology of Judaism is foolish. They remain convinced that most Christians have not forsworn their triumphalism and point to the targeted proselytism of Jews by the American Southern Baptists and missionary Christian groups such as Jews for Jesus. Within the Christian community, it is new and troubling to some to learn that many Jews do view Nazism as the logical outcome of European Christian culture; others express concern that Christians might feel completely exonerated by the Jewish statement.

Another factor, often expressed as the key to dialogue in recent times, has been Israel. There is little doubt that while the church has for many years been grappling with issues related to Christian antisemitism, attitudes toward the land and State of Israel have, from the theological perspective, proved more difficult to tackle. Theological difficulties have made a Christian reorientation to Israel problematic. Simply put, it has been easier for Christians to condemn antisemitism as a misunderstanding of Christian teaching than to come to terms with the reestablishment of the Jewish state.

Nevertheless, many Christian denominations have in very recent years reexamined the place of the Land and State of Israel in Christian thought.[11] While their statements unsurprisingly exhibit extreme sensitivity to Palestinian concerns, they do acknowledge the centrality of Israel to Jews and Judaism. Thus, the pope stated in 1984 that, "for the Jewish people who live in the State of Israel, and who preserve in that land such precious testimonies to their history and their faith we must ask for the desired security and the due tranquility that is the prerogative of every nation and condition of life and of progress for every society." The exchange of ambassadors between the Vatican and the State of Israel in 1994 and the moving visit of the pope in March 2000 are symbolic of the change in attitude among Christians.

It is therefore of little surprise to read in *Dabru Emet* that "Christians can respect the claim of the Jewish people upon the land of Israel." However, there are a number of dangers with basing a theology of Jewish-Christian dialogue primarily on Israel. One is the fact that dialogue becomes linked to certain stages of achievement, which give an impression of a direct line of progress. Valuable as the stages of achievement are, they are often far from the complexities of the reality itself. For example, there is great danger in arguing that what was once an interpretation about the nature of the biblical word and promise is now, in the situation of Israel, concretized in a contemporary event. The challenge to Jewish-Christian dialogue as a result of an emphasis on fulfillment of biblical prophecy can be seen in the writings of some evangelical Christians as well as fundamentalist Jews.

However, there are also dangers to Israel-based dialogue as illustrated by those who, in the name of dialogue, move from a position of commitment to the well-being of Israel to one of almost "Israel can do no wrong." This is not conducive to dialogue for it is not an honest and sober conversation firmly related to present realities.

This makes the breadth of the recent publication of *Dabru Emet* most welcome. The document does not solely focus on Christian anti-semitism and Shoah and/or the creation of the State of Israel. It examines the relationship as a whole between Judaism and Christianity, beginning with Christianity's historic attitude toward Judaism: "Christians have tended to characterize Judaism as a failed religion or, at best, a religion that prepared the way for, and is completed in, Christianity." It acknowl-edges that in recent years many Christian denominations have reassessed their stance regarding Judaism and have renounced their historical posi-tions; in light of this the statement declares: "We believe these changes merit a thoughtful Jewish response."

The statement goes on to assert eight points:

- Jews and Christians worship the same God;
- Jews and Christians seek authority from the same book (the Bible);
- Christians can respect the claim of the Jewish people upon the land of Israel;
- Jewish and Christians accept the moral principles of Torah;
- Nazism was not a Christian phenomenon;
- The humanly irreconcilable difference between Jews and Christians will not be settled until God redeems the entire world as promised in scripture;
- A new relationship between Jews and Christians will not weaken Jewish practice;
- Jews and Christians must work together for justice and peace.

Dabru Emet is the most positive affirmation of Christianity ever made by a committed Jewish group. It states unequivocally that

Christians worship the God of Israel and legitimately draw on the Hebrew Bible—our contradictions notwithstanding. This statement is problematic for some Jews as a result of doctrines such as the Trinity and incarnation that can be seen as compromising the integrity of Jewish monotheism. In response, some Christians are shocked to discover that Christianity can be seen by some Jews as idolatrous.

The authors and signatories have also had the courage to reject the assumption that dialogue results in increased assimilation, intermarriage, and Christian missionary activity. It is likely that some Jews who oppose theological dialogue will simply resist or ignore the declaration. Others, whose residual Jewish memory triggers a knee-jerk reaction of fear and anger at Christianity, will also refuse to go along with its findings. Both these groups carry the unhealed wounds of the past two millennia.

It is also possible that *Dabru Emet* will be abused by some Christian fundamentalists in order to advance their missionary efforts. Hopefully, however, the declaration's emphasis on a pluralist affirmation of Judaism's eternal covenant will be respected by even the more extreme Christian groups. Ironically, this affirmation of Christianity shows that Judaism's vitality is undiminished; it too can self-correct.

Dabru Emet does not claim to answer the divine purpose behind the creation of Christianity but does explore the question in its suggestion that "The humanly irreconcilable difference between Jews and Christians will not be settled until God redeems the entire world as promised in scripture." One of the main achievements of *Dabru Emet* is that it puts into practice what I would describe as the foundational principle of dialogue: Dialogue involves a respect that takes the other as seriously as one demands to be taken oneself. *Dabru Emet* makes a contribution to the bold claim that peace itself and the future of humankind hang on the success of the interfaith exercise.

WHAT DOES CHRISTIANITY IN JEWISH TERMS MEAN?

James K. Aitken

The publication of "A Jewish Statement on Christians and Christianity" by Jewish scholars in the *New York Times* is a surprising event but indicates the significance that Jewish-Christian relations holds for the signatories. What is also surprising is the unified acclaim with which the statement has been received in the Christian world, even if some Jewish activists have been critical of parts.[12] It has been seen as "an unsolicited gift,"[13] "a noble-minded response,"[14] and a "landmark in the relations between Jews and Christians."[15] It has been praised for "its scope and eloquence"[16] and commended to congregations so that they might "read it with care and loving respect."[17] There are, of course, controversial aspects and it is almost impossible to produce a brief statement to which all Christians can give assent, but even those who might question sections of it emphasize the importance of the statement. The National Council of Churches of Christ in the United States, for example, admits that, "While we may not agree with all that is affirmed in the document, there is much in it that many among us will readily embrace."[18] The one note of disdain has come from the evangelical side, as is to be expected. Southern Baptists in the United States have pointed to the paragraph stating that "Jews and Christians worship the same God," and have objected that it should have been made clear that the Christian God is triune: Father, Son, and Holy Spirit. Such criticism notwithstanding, the universal acceptance on the part of Christians, even including expressions from Christians that they are hardly worthy of such an honor, is in marked contrast to Jewish reactions to Christian declarations. What does this indicate about the present state of Jewish-Christian relations? Do Christians not expect anything from Jews? How much has been sacrificed by Jewish scholars in issuing it? Is the declaration an ultimate gift of charity? Or, is it a sign of a new generation of dialogue? Is it a bold undertaking by all concerned? Will Jewish-Christian relations now be on an even footing?

The statement *Dabru Emet*[19] itself is necessarily brief and is aimed at a nonscholarly audience. It must abbreviate complex theological questions, avoid technical language, and minimize problems in order to be coherent. It is, therefore, churlish to dwell too long on the wording of the individual paragraphs, but some consideration of the implications is necessary, and it would not be to give the statement respect if we did not debate it. The statement is also, however, a reflection of a wider agenda of considering *Christianity in Jewish Terms,* inaugurated by a book with that title that was published to coincide with the issue of the statement.[20] The consequences of such a concept are far-reaching and potentially challenging for Jewish-Christian relations, but progress in relations in these terms must be undertaken with care if it is not to become a hindrance to real dialogue. It remains to be seen whether Christianity in Jewish terms is a new concept in the dialogue or a development of an older tradition of understanding, and also whether this concept will be the lasting benefit of *Dabru Emet* rather than the debatable issues contained within the statement. The real meaning of Christianity in Jewish terms is awaiting an explanation, and the affect it will have on Christians (or Christianity) and dialogue with them will be known only in time. In the meantime we may infer some indications of the possible directions that it will take.

The Road to Dabru Emet

The four authors of *Dabru Emet,* Tikva Frymer-Kensky, David Novak, Peter Ochs, and Michael Signer, who, together with David Sandmel of the Institute for Christian and Jewish Studies in Baltimore, edited the book *Christianity in Jewish Terms,* represent a North American Jewish scholarly tradition. Their concerns arise from a North American context, but the principles from which they speak are applicable to the wider situation of Jewish-Christian relations in many countries. Most of the 170 initial signatories are from the United States and Canada, but some Jewish scholars or rabbis from Great Britain, Israel, and other parts of Europe have also signed it. The social standing of Judaism in the United States has no doubt contributed to the ability of the authors to frame the document, and their own academic positions, employed in universities and working with Christian colleagues,[21] distinguish them from rabbis working in communities or teachers in seminaries. Their own scholarly work, even when discussing Judaism, is informed by methods employed by both Christian and Jewish scholars, and they are open to learning from Christians and Christian modes of exegesis. They emphasize that in their work they enhance the power of Jewish sources to heal the divisions from which we suffer today— "between human reason and Jewish faith, as well as between Judaism and Christianity."[22] It is an enlightened reading of religious tradition.

No less is to be expected from a modern academic, but it in part accounts for the origins of the statement with them. Arising from their experience they are able to offer to Jews a balanced approach to the relationship of Judaism to Christianity.

They are not the first to take a religious interest in Christianity, as Edward Kessler has noted. In 1967 Samuel Sandmel, a historian of ancient Judaism and Christianity, called for a declaration on "The Synagogue and the Christian People."[23] His proposal was for a statement that would have been similar to *Dabru Emet* in its aim. It would note the regrettable history of enmity and would recognize the change in Christianity that had been recently witnessed with the condemnation of Christian persecution (this was the time of Vatican II). He emphasized that Christianity was not to abandon its belief but hoped that all humanity would keep their own distinctive elements while joining in a spiritual bond toward a greater transcendence. It has taken some time for Sandmel's hopes to be realized for such a declaration, but it is perhaps no surprise that it was a historian of antiquity who first proposed it.

Jewish interest in Christianity has often centered on the figure of Jesus, the Jewish sage whom Jews can respect for his piety and observance. The first book to be written in Hebrew on Jesus, without polemical or missionary aims, was Joseph Klausner's *Jesus of Nazareth: His Life, Times, and Teaching*.[24] He felt that he was able to write about Jesus because of Jesus' "Hebrew cultural outlook," based on a life whose spiritual center lay in Palestine. His book emphasizes the Jewishness of Jesus, born and brought up in Palestine and observing a Jewish lifestyle. Together with a later work, *From Jesus to Paul*,[25] it traces, with the assistance of Jewish sources, the Jewish origins of Christianity and presents it as a part of the Jewish climate in the first century. In such a thesis the early Christian messianic expectation is seen as a continuation of the already existing Jewish belief. At that time Klausner felt that the historian living in Palestine was safe, freed from the fears and hostility of the Diaspora, to study the origins of Christianity, accepting it as part of his nation's whole life. That Jewish scholars nowadays can study Christianity outside of Israel is a sign of the change that has taken place both in Christianity itself and in the social position of the religions. Jesus has remained a prime source of interest for Jewish scholars,[26] but it is important to note that his interest has been as a historical Jewish figure, not as he is understood in Christology. Much of the research, therefore, on Jesus the Jew, even if it can be seen as a bold enterprise by writers such as Klausner, has not really been an appreciation of Christianity as such. If anything, it could be argued that it has been a denial of the most central tenet of Christianity, namely, the divinity of Jesus. Klausner did note the connections between early Christian messianic expectations and Jewish expectations, but he understandably did not consider the truth-claims of such expectations.

Undoubtedly, the recognition of Jewish aspects of Jesus' life has contributed to a better appreciation of Christianity by Jews, but it is not a whole-hearted appreciation as such. Klausner is important because he progresses beyond Jesus to consider Paul too, a recognition not always given. Martin Buber did give consideration to Paul, but distinguished the faith of Jesus (which he tendentiously translated by the Hebrew *emunah*) as the biblical pattern of faith belonging to the people of Israel too, from the faith (translated by the Greek *pistis*) of Paul, a Greek propositional faith.[27] This approach again places emphasis on Jesus as part of the Jewish/Israelite tradition, using an idea, perhaps alien to Jesus, of the religious significance of the Hebrew language. It furthermore draws a distinction between Jewish and Greek thought that is not appropriate to first-century Judaism or to Christian tradition.[28] It is ironic that the early apostles, who were also Jewish, are often ignored, perhaps because they believed after the resurrection event in the divinity of Christ. The divinity of Christ is the central doctrine of Christianity; while that is not discussed it will remain a problem to Jewish appreciation of Christianity. It is noteworthy that despite the continued appreciation of Jesus the Jew in Jewish circles it is omitted from *Dabru Emet,* either because it would still be too controversial for some Jews to read about Jesus in such positive terms, or because of the recognition that the presentation of Jesus as a Jew is a historical matter (albeit important for Christology) and not one of religious sentiment that would be appropriate for the statement.[29]

A more fruitful approach than concentrating on the historical figure of Jesus has been the appreciation of the religious contribution of Christianity, and its religious sentiments shared with Judaism.[30] Probably the most famous exponent of such a position has been Franz Rosenzweig, who, drawing on the philosophy of Hegel, saw the living vitality of Christianity as one branch and Judaism as another branch of the one tree. This has laid the grounds for a Jewish view of a double covenant, Christianity being the covenant for Gentiles. Such a view had already been implied in writers as old as Rambam (for example, *Mishneh Torah, Melakhim* 8.11) and has also been adopted by Christian thinkers involved in Jewish-Christian dialogue.[31] Rosenzweig was influential on his pupil Ignaz Maybaum,[32] and in more recent times on David Novak, one of the authors of *Dabru Emet*.[33] Rosenzweig and Maybaum also were both interested in Islam, although more disparaging of it than of Christianity, and the context from which they were writing is informative. Rosenzweig served in the army in Macedonia, where he would have encountered both Sephardi Jews and Muslims, as well as Orthodox Christians, and he finally completed the *Star of Redemption* in 1918 while in hospital in Leipzig and Belgrade. Maybaum, coming from Vienna, may have been aware of that city's long history of Turkish occupation and relations. In his time it was an important international city, the center of an empire during his youth, and on the crossroads between eastern and western Europe. Both Rosenzweig and Maybaum had experience of multiethnic countries, and both came into contact with other religions. It is this experience of a multicultural environment that has contributed to their understanding and appreciation of Christianity, and it is probably similar circumstances that have initiated the renewed appreciation of Christianity.

The explicit reasons given for the appearance at this time of a "Jewish view of Christianity" are twofold. First, according to the prologue of *Dabru Emet,* it is because there has been a dramatic change in Christianity since the Holocaust, seen in the efforts of Christians to reform Christian teaching and preaching and in an attempt to acknowledge God's enduring covenant with the Jewish people and the contribution of Judaism to civilization. These are aspects that are of course familiar to anyone involved in Jewish-Christian dialogue, but it is clear that they are unfamiliar to many Jews, and therefore the authors declare that, "we believe it is time for Jews to learn about the efforts of Christians to honor Judaism." The statement is presented as a response to the change in Christianity, and it is correct to say that Christianity had to change first before Jews could speak so publicly about it. Nevertheless, it does raise the question as to why, if many Christians have changed so much, and there is such commonality between the two faiths, there are in many countries so few Jews involved in dialogue. In some countries there are indeed many organizations with a large proportion of Jews, often with social issues at the forefront, but in others, even given the smaller number of Jews in the particular country, there are few Jews wishing to participate in dialogue. Such a situation the statement aims to address. It could have been stated, therefore, all the more strongly that it is a necessity for there to be a Jewish response, and not merely in the belief of the authors. Without a thoughtful Jewish response to Christian changes, there is always the danger of Judaism once again being misrepresented by Christians if they do not have contact with Jews. Probably the most obvious impression that Christians have of Jews is the reaction by Jewish organizations to church statements, which communicates a message of hostility. It is also imperative that Jews grapple with the realities of Christianity and the depths of its theology, something not even achieved in much of Jewish-Christian dialogue, in order that they may see both the good and the bad within the tradition. A better appreciation of the complexity of another religion will enable better appreciation of the problems involved in dealing with it and of the potentiality for harm in any religion.

The second stated need for a "Jewish response to Christians and Christianity" is that "living as a minority in a still largely Christian America—and Christian West—Jews need to learn the languages and beliefs of their neighbors."[34] In this regard emphasis is placed on the position of Judaism in society. Thus, Jews need to understand what Christians are saying about "what modern society should become, and about the place of the Jewish people itself in that society." This will enable Jews to explain better their own "goals and ideals for society in terms that their Christian neighbors will understand."[35] To the role of society we will return below. What is of interest here is the declared place of Judaism as a minority in a Christian majority. While this is the case, especially in many countries of central and eastern Europe, it is not the whole story. The election of George W. Bush as president of the United States, who stood on a religious platform and was supported by a vocal Christian minority in some issues, does indicate the power of Christianity still to influence affairs. In many countries too we can see a revival of Christian influence in public affairs. But the situation has changed in the course of the century. One might now speak of post-Christian countries, where the country, its decision-making processes, values, and citizens are no longer Christian as such, although where the influence of Christianity is still to be felt.[36] Indeed, the very decrease in influence of Christianity may be one reason why it has had to change and adapt. If there is still one dominant discourse it is Christianity, but the power of that discourse has been considerably weakened. Hence, a further unstated reason why Christianity in Jewish terms is so important at the moment is the need for these two religions that are so close to each other to cooperate when neither is anymore in the majority. Other forces are at work in society, and the ethical ground shared by Judaism and Christianity is under threat. If Jews can understand Christianity better they might appreciate its values and recognize them as Jewish values also, not least in terms of the Noahide commandments, and thereby join forces to promote those values. That is perhaps why the role of society is emphasized in the preface to *Christianity in Jewish Terms.*

The Understanding of Judaism

Dabru Emet has been compared to *Nostra Aetate* in the hope that it will change attitudes among Jews in the way that *Nostra Aetate* did in the Catholic Church.[37] The two declarations are, of course, of a different order. *Nostra Aetate* arose out of a need for change following the destructive lengths that Christian teaching could be put to, and it involved a radical change in the way Christianity expresses much of its core doctrine and a realignment in much of its teaching, particularly relating to salvation. It did not discuss everything that some of its instigators had wished, but it was an important contribution to the church's rethinking on many matters. *Dabru Emet* cannot claim to have the status of a conciliar document, since such authoritative bodies do not exist in Judaism, but the nature of its list of signatories, being both international (increasingly signatories are being sought outside of North America) and representing all shades of denomination (Orthodox, Conservative, Reform, and Reconstructionist), is an indication of its broad recognition within Jewish circles. Judaism has never had a history like Christianity's, and therefore has never had to have such a radical rethinking of its tradition. *Dabru Emet* could never be like *Nostra Aetate* in the extent to which the latter has had a profound effect on the way Christianity thinks about itself, and not just about others. It is, nevertheless, appropriate to ask whether Christianity in Jewish terms does represent a change in the ways Jews conceive of Judaism, and how it presents both Judaism and Christianity.

As already indicated, the framers of *Christianity in Jewish Terms* conceive of their task as healing a division that has arisen in Judaism (one might add, in many religions) over the past two hundred years, separating the realms of science and faith from those of faith and tradition.

It is a revival of Judaism, based on the classical texts (Bible, Talmud, and other classical sources) as well as on human reason, since the sources themselves present a partnership of humanity and God. This reunderstanding of Judaism is twofold: to heal the division between reason and faith, and the division between Judaism and Christianity. It is therefore a natural outcome of the healing of inner Jewish division, and this is a new contribution to the understanding of Judaism and of the Jewish-Christian relationship. No longer is it correct, as I have all too frequently heard (and always believed, mistakenly), that Jewish-Christian relations is for Christians and not for Jews. If Judaism is so important for Christian understanding, as some would have it, and if the divide has been so inimical to Judaism, as it certainly has been, then Judaism is affected by or even dependent on Christianity. The healing of the division is not only a matter of self-protection for Jews, it is a matter for the preservation of Judaism as a religious tradition.

The statement is not intended to be an explication of Judaism and so should not be taken as defining Judaism. The Judaism that it does, nonetheless, present to its readers is primarily biblical and humanitarian. Biblical language appears throughout the statement, indicated by the very name *Dabru Emet,* "Speak Truth" (an allusion to Zech 8:16), its closing with a quotation from Isaiah 2, the use of terms such as "Promised Land" and "created in the image of God," and the paragraph that states that "Jews and Christians seek authority from the same book—the Bible." This last point has obviously been shaped by Christianity being more of a Bible-based religion, but there are still rightly a reference to Jewish tradition and ambiguous uses of the word *Torah* (the Pentateuch or Oral Torah?). But the Bible still remains the center of focus and even after the mention of Jewish tradition, attention is drawn to disputes over the interpretation of *scripture,* and it is declared that the difference will not be resolved until God "redeems the entire world as promised in Scripture."[38] It seems that the Bible, or more accurately the Hebrew Bible, is a source for uniting Jews and Christians, and therefore Jewish tradition is given second place.

The humanitarian concerns are revealed in a number of places. The full quotation of Zechariah 8:16 is, "Speak the truth to one another, render in your gates judgments that are true and make for peace," which presents the twin roles required of establishing justice and of promoting peace. Justice comes to the fore in the passing allusion to the Palestinian question that, "Jewish tradition mandates justice for all non-Jews who reside in a Jewish state." This particular reference is directed to the issue of the State of Israel, and does not have wider consequences for social justice since its stipulation is restricted to those residing in a Jewish state. However, the next tenet recognizes the "inalienable sanctity and dignity of every human being." It expresses the desire, especially after the horrors of the past century, for both faiths to be a witness for improving the lives of fellow humans and for countenancing immorality. Even the controversial statement on Nazism can be seen as an encouragement to those Christians who have begun this work to continue it. But the final tenet of the statement, with its closing quotation of Isaiah 2:2–3, is the strongest declaration that "Jews and Christians must work together for justice and peace." The benefits of a Jewish understanding of Christianity is that the two can trust each other enough to work in harmony for a better world. It is a socially minded Judaism that is presented, something that is brought out in the preface to *Christianity in Jewish Terms*. Ultimately what is called for is a Judaism that contributes to wider society, that is able to work with Christianity for that contribution, and is able to understand what Christianity means by social justice in order to share with it. It is a Judaism that is aware of its responsibility to the wider world, its responsibility both to appreciate what Christianity has achieved and to bring justice to its fellow human beings.

The Presentation of Christianity

Once more we begin with what the statement and the concept are not. It is not actually a statement on Christianity or a definition of Christianity. It is always "A Jewish Statement..." or "Christianity in Jewish Terms," which does not mean Christianity itself. Christians have in Jewish-Christian relations always been trying to present Judaism in Jewish terms, to correct the misrepresentation of Judaism by their forebears, and it is therefore interesting, if ironic, that the position has been reversed, and Jews are now doing what Christians have been trying not to do. But this may be uncharitable. Given the long history of hostility, the intention in Christianity in Jewish terms is to allow Jews to appreciate Christianity by the way that seems easiest and that is through Jewish eyes. A particular theme is presented in Jewish tradition, which is then shown to have a corresponding value in Christian beliefs. Seeing the theme in Jewish theological tradition first allows for appreciation of it in Christian tradition.[39]

There is, however, one tenet that has been largely ignored by commentators on the statement so far, but that is in its way the most important. It is the recognition of "the humanly irreconcilable difference between Jews and Christians." Our dialogue should probably begin on this basis, even if some of the similarities can be used as a spur to dialogue. The differences between the religions in the modern context are the real problems between the two communities and the reasons why we must have dialogue. The attempts mentioned earlier to portray Jesus the Jew, and to understand Christianity by that historical means, circumvented the problem of this irreconcilable difference, and therefore never faced up to real Christianity and the real problem. It is still true that *Dabru Emet* does not follow its own principle all the time on this, by suggesting that Christians seek authority from the Old Testament without acknowledging the far greater importance of the New Testament, or by saying that Christians know and serve God through Jesus Christ rather than saying that Jesus is actually God for Christians. Such misrepresentations are probably intended to make Christianity intelligible to Jews, but in so doing it fails truly to present Christianity. An honest appreciation of Christianity would have been preferred, one in which the Trinity, one of the elements of Christianity that Jews often express as being the hardest to accept or to recognize as monotheistic, should be given full weight. The need is for Jews to say that they may not understand Christianity, they may not be able to accept the divinity of Jesus, but that they understand that Christians believe in it, and that the Christian belief in the Trinity is a wrestling with the complexity of revelation, while holding onto a monotheistic belief. That would be to accept the "irreconcilable difference," and that would be to accept that Christians are different theologically, but that their desire for justice and peace is the same.

The Challenge of Christianity in Jewish Terms

The timing of *Dabru Emet* and *Christianity in Jewish Terms* could not have been foreseen, but it could not have been better for its publicity. It came only a month after the declaration of the Congregation for the Doctrine of the Faith's *Dominus Iesus*, which referred to Jesus as the sole road to salvation and spoke of the need for mission *ad gentes*. Jewish critics saw this, probably correctly, as an attack on Jewish-Christian relations and interfaith work, even though it reflects more inner tensions within the Catholic Church rather than a definite change in Catholic thinking. It is not a revocation of *Nostra Aetate*. The result of such timing, nevertheless, has been the utter generosity of the reception of *Dabru Emet* and of the concept of Christianity in Jewish terms. And the intentions of the authors are indeed openhearted and honest, and based on their own religious convictions. This should not obscure the misleading presentation of Christianity, especially of the function of Christ.

We opened with the question: Do Christians not expect anything from Jews? It is vital that they should. We should expect such expressions of understanding from Jews, even given the centuries of persecution that Christians have executed on Jews. The reason is that hope for the future rests in every generation's hands, and despite the burden of history, every generation has the potential for good. It is not for Jews to blame the past as a reason for not reaching out into the wider community and for attempting to heal the wounds of the past. These scholars behind the project see it as their duty, as should every Jew and Christian. And they see it as their duty that they should repair the world, a joint task of Jews and Christians in cooperation. It is an ethical mission that the late Lord Donald Coggan preached should be the basis of future relations between Jews and Christians. This is the challenge that the concept of Christianity in Jewish terms sets before us. It is to be hoped that Christians as well as Jews will take up the challenge. For this there still remains one challenge for Jews, and that is to understand Christianity yet more. To do this is to understand the complexity of every religion, that no religion can be reduced to either historical explanation or simple propositions, and no belief is ever simple. That way Jews may understand why Christianity has been a source of enmity in the past, and yet remains a vital source to be appreciated to this day.

NOTES

1. *New York Times,* September 10, 2000.

2. Examples include the 1988 *Emet ve-Emunah* statement on behalf of American Conservative Jews and the 2000 Statement on Catholic-Jewish Relations by the Central Conference of American Rabbis (Reform) and the Rabbinical Assembly (Conservative).

3. E.g., H. Küng, Judaism (London: SCM Press, 1992); A. Eckardt and R. Eckardt, *Long Night's Journey into Day* (Oxford: Pergamon Press, 1988); R. Eckardt, *Jews and Christians: The Contemporary Meeting* (Bloomington:

Indiana University Press, 1986). For institutional statements see www. jcrelations.net/statemt.

4. D. Novak, *Jewish-Christian Dialogue: A Jewish Justification* (Oxford/New York: Oxford University Press, 1992); E. Borowitz, *Contemporary Christologies: A Jewish Response* (New York: Paulist Press, 1980).

5. C. G. Montefiore, *The Old Testament and After* (London: Macmillan, 1923), 561.

6. There were significant exceptions to the rule, such as Rabbis Leo Baeck and Samuel Sandmel, who called for a positive Jewish response to Christianity.

7. For further details, see J. Parkes, *The Conflict of the Church and the Synagogue* (London/New York: Soncino Press, 1934); E. Flannery, *The Anguish of the Jews* (New York: Macmillan, 1965).

8. For further details, see J. Katz, *Exclusiveness and Tolerance* (London: Oxford University Press, 1961); J. Cohen, ed., *Essential Papers on Judaism and Christianity in Conflict* (New York: New York University Press, 1991).

9. See J. Isaac, *The Teaching of Contempt* (New York: Holt, Rinehart and Winston, 1964).

10. See A. Brockway, ed., *The Theology of the Churches and the Jewish People* (Geneva: WCC, 1988); E. Fisher, *Catholic-Jewish Relations: Documents from the Holy See* (London: Catholic Truth Society, 1999).

11. It is interesting that some Christian theologians have also begun to reconsider the role of land in Christian thought. See, e.g., W. Brueggemann, *The Land: Place as Gift, Promise and Challenge in Biblical Faith* (Philadelphia: Fortress Press, 1977).

12. Rabbi James Rudin of the American Jewish committee has been one of the more outspoken critics of the paragraph on Nazism. His comments are recorded on http://www.beliefnet.com, and discussed by J. K. Aitken, "Jews and Christians Take Counsel," *Church Times* (London) October 20, 2000, p. 15; M. Czajkowski, "Let Us Speak Truth," *Dialogue and Universalism* 11 (2000): 16; and Stanislaw Krajewski, "Respect Christians as Christians (Rabbis and Jewish Theologians on Christianity)," *Dialogue and Universalism* 11 (2000): 27–28.

13. A. Doetzel, writing on behalf of "Relation and Encounter," the Christian-Jewish office of the Sisters of Our Lady of Sion in North America. Recorded on http://www.icjs.org.

14. Czajkowski, "Let Us Speak Truth," 15.

15. Aitken, "Jews and Christians Take Counsel," 17.

16. Statement adopted by the Consultative Panel on Lutheran-Jewish Relations of the Department for Ecumenical Affairs, Evangelical Lutheran

Church in America, at its meeting in Chicago on October 18, 2000. Recorded on http://www.icjs.org.

17. "The Power of Words: A Catholic Response to *Dabru Emet*," issued by the National Conference of Catholic Bishops/United States Catholic Conference. Recorded on http://www.jcrelations.net.

18. "An Ecumenical Response to *Dabru Emet:* A Jewish Statement on Christians and Christianity," issued by the Interfaith Relations Commission of the National Council of Churches of Christ in the United States, February 24, 2001. Recorded on http://www.jcrelations.net.

19. The text has been republished in Tikva Frymer-Kensky, David Novak, Peter Ochs, David Fox Sandmel, and Michael A. Signer, eds., *Christianity in Jewish Terms,* Radical Traditions (Boulder, CO/Oxford: Westview, 2000), xvii–xx.

20. Tikva Frymer-Kensky et al., *Christianity in Jewish Terms.*

21. Tikva Frymer-Kensky is a professor at the University of Chicago; David Novak, at the University of Toronto; Peter Ochs, at the University of Virginia; and Michael Signer, at the University of Notre Dame.

22. Frymer-Kensky et al., *Christianity in Jewish Terms,* xii.

23. Samuel Sandmel, *We Jews and You Christians* (Philadelphia/New York: J. B. Lippincott, 1967), 144–46.

24. Jerusalem, 1922; English translation: *Jesus of Nazareth: His Life, Times, and Teaching,* trans. H. Danby (London: George Allen, 1929). On Klausner see G. Abramson, "Klausner, Joseph Gedaliah," in *The Blackwell Companion to Jewish Culture: From the Eighteenth Century to the Present,* ed. G. Abramson (Oxford: Basil Blackwell, 1989), 415–16.

25. 2 vols. (Tel Aviv, 1939). English translation: *From Jesus to Paul* (London: George Allen, 1942).

26. See the helpful survey by W. Klassen, *The Contribution of Jewish Scholars to the Quest for the Historical Jesus,* Themes in Jewish-Christian Relations (Cambridge: Centre for Jewish-Christian Relations, 2000).

27. *Two Types of Faith,* trans. N. P. Goldhawk from the German *Zwei Glaubensweisen* (London: Routledge & Kegan Paul, 1951).

28. On the problems of distinguishing Jewish from "Hellenistic," see now the collection of essays edited by D. Stern in issues 1 and 2 of *Poetics Today* 19 (1998). On its use in anti-Jewish arguments, see Tessa Rajak, "Jews and Greeks: The Invention and Exploitation of Polarities in the Nineteenth Century," in *The Uses and Abuses of Antiquity,* ed. M. Bidiss and M. Wyke (Bern: Peter Lang, 1999), 57–77. A recent Christian attempt to restore Christian creedal formulations in the light of their Jewish roots also falls prey to the Hebrew/Hellenic dichotomy. See the chapter tellingly entitled "Wisdom in Greek Dress" in Fredrick C. Holmgren, *The Old Testament and the Significance of Jesus: Embracing Change—Maintaining Christian*

Identity. The Emerging Center in Biblical Scholarship (Grand Rapids, MI: Eerdmans, 1999).

29. Jesus is only mentioned in *Dabru Emet* in reference to the humanly irreconcilable difference between Jews and Christians. It is noted that "Christians know and serve God through Jesus Christ and the Christian tradition." This is contrasted to Jewish experience through "Torah and the Jewish tradition." Jesus and Torah are not to be paralleled so easily, even if some New Testament passages imply some equivalence. Even though *Dabru Emet* here is trying to contrast Judaism and Christianity, it has been unable to do so accurately, misrepresenting Christian doctrine, and thereby producing a heresy. The attempt to present the similarities of Christianity to Judaism even when discussing "the humanly irreconcilable difference" has led to the presentation of Jesus as some form of channel to enable knowledge and worship of God. Jesus is not a channel, which in patristic terms would imply he is created and therefore not God, but he is the uncreated nature of God. Trinitarian questions have been circumvented.

30. Recent Jewish views of Christianity have been summarized by J. T. Pawlikowski, *What Are They Saying about Christian-Jewish Relations?* (New York: Paulist Press, 1980), 69–92.

31. For a survey of covenantal views in Jewish-Christian dialogue, see J. T. Pawlikowski, "The Search for a New Paradigm for the Christian-Jewish Relationship: A Response to Michael Signer," in *Reinterpreting Revelation and Tradition: Jews and Christians in Conversation,* ed. J. T. Pawlikowski and H. G. Perelmuter (Franklin, WI.: Sheed & Ward, 2000), 25–48.

32. See especially I. Maybaum's *Trialogue between Jew, Christian and Muslim* (London: Routledge & Kegan Paul, 1973).

33. Novak discusses Rosenzweig in *Jewish-Christian Dialogue: A Jewish Justification* (New York/Oxford: Oxford University Press, 1989), 93ff. The role of Christians, especially in relation to the keeping of the Noahide laws, in Jewish thought is explored by Novak in *The Image of the Non-Jew in Judaism: An Historical and Constructive Study of the Noahide Laws,* Toronto Studies in Theology, vol. 14 (New York: E. Mellen Press, 1983). He has returned to the topic as a stated theological background to Christianity in Jewish terms in "Avoiding Charges of Legalism and Antinomianism in Jewish-Christian Dialogue," *Modern Theology* 16 (2000): 275–91.

34. Frymer-Kensky et al., *Christianity in Jewish Terms,* xi.

35. Ibid., xi–xii.

36. In this sense post-Christian, like postcolonialism but unlike postmodernism, does not merely indicate the end of Christianity, but its surpassing and yet leaving enduring consequences. S. Hauerwas, "Christian Ethics in Jewish Terms: A Response to David Novak," *Modern Theology* 16 (2000): 293, suggests that the Jewish engagement with Christianity is an indication of

the world no longer being Christian, even if many Christians still hold to the idea of a "Christian society."

37. Krajewski, "Respect Christians as Christians," 28.

38. *Scripture* is itself an ambiguous term, and it could be used to refer to all religious texts, including classical texts that are noncanonical but important in the tradition. It is possible that this is meant, but the capital letter suggests it is more likely denoting the Bible, and perhaps the ambiguity is intentional — not wishing to restrict themselves to the Bible, but at the same time implying that the Bible is of prime importance.

39. See, for example, the essays by P. Ochs and D. Ellenson in Frymer-Kensky et al., *Christianity in Jewish Terms,* 49–69, 69–76.

14
Jewish-Christian Relations in the Interfaith Encounter

Martin Forward

This chapter proposes that Jewish-Christian dialogue has much to offer other forms of bilateral and multilateral dialogue. It also suggests that Jewish-Christian relations might benefit from being mapped on a wider map of interfaith encounter. To justify this contention, we examine four important issues raised by this particular dialogue. Since most of my experience has been within the British scene, I propose to concentrate on this region, to indicate why and how such a dialogue began and has been sustained.

We begin with what may fancifully be regarded as a parable of interreligious relationships. In the eighteenth century, French Protestant Huguenots, escaping from persecution in their homeland, built a church in Brick Lane in London's East End. They made good in their new situation, moved to other localities, and sold their church to a Methodist group. They too, by dint of hard work, improved their economic situation, and moved to less deprived areas. They sold the church to Jews, fleeing persecution in mainland Europe, who turned it into a synagogue. In their turn, they flourished and moved to Hampstead in North London. Now that building is in the hands of Muslims from a poor, rural area of Bangladesh. Thus far, this place of worship has heard prayers offered in French, English, Hebrew, and Arabic. It is fascinating to speculate: What next for this remarkable building? One hopes that, if its Bengali worshipers make good and move on, it will remain a holy place, a parable of religious diversity in our contemporary world.[1]

If this is a parable, it is one that has a difficult as well as a positive message. It is gratifying, even heart-warming, to note that different religious groups have felt comfortable about selling a treasured and hallowed property to other religious groups. Maybe each leaving congregation has preferred to sell its sacred property to those who pray differently, but at least pray, rather than to a purchaser who would use it for purely material purposes. Still, this form of goodwill for members of other faith groups, if such it be, is of limited significance. What interaction did Huguenots, Methodists, Jews, and Muslims actually have? One assumes not much. One can commend a generalized and mild form of generosity by one religious group toward another, without thinking that such benevolence is enough for our increasingly interlinked world. The appalling fate of Jews in mainland Europe in the twentieth century illustrates that the apparent tolerance of religious groups toward others cannot withstand the machinations of evil people working to convince otherwise well-meaning people of the truth of age-old, often deep-seated and unconscious prejudices that justify the marginalization and even persecution and murder of the outsider.

Jewish-Christian relations have had a particular urgency since the dark years of the Second World War. In the United Kingdom, the Council of Christians and Jews was founded in 1942, as news came of the death camps in mainland Europe. A decision of March 20, 1942, brought the CCJ into being. A resolution proposed:

> That since the Nazi attack on Jewry has revealed that antisemitism is part of a general and comprehensive attack on Christianity and Judaism and on the ethical principles common to both religions which form the basis of the free national life of Great Britain, the Council adopts the following aims:
>
> (a) To check and combat religious and racial intolerance.
> (b) To promote mutual understanding and goodwill between Christians and Jews in all sections of the community, especially in connection with problems arising from conditions created by the war.

(c) To promote fellowship between Christian and
     Jewish youth organizations in educational and cul-
     tural activities.
(d) To foster co-operation of Christians and Jews in
     study and service directed to post-war reconstruc-
     tion.[2]

Of the important themes that emerge from this resolution, two have
become very significant in Jewish-Christian relations: the emphases on
education and on antisemitism. The council was nearly sunk before it
floated by Dr. Hertz, the chief rabbi, largely because of its educative
strategy. In fact, he objected to two things. First, he insisted that Jews
and Christians should not interfere in the other's teaching and he reck-
oned that part of CCJ's educational work breached that insistence. He
also claimed that Orthodox Jews were inadequately represented on the
executive.[3] Matters were patched up but the issues raised by CCJ's
foundation have cast long shadows on Jewish-Christian relations.

     One could put the deepest issues this fourfold way: Does a civi-
lized land such as the United Kingdom really need to deal with antisemitism? Are institutional Jewish-Christian relations at the mercy of
internal religious angst and self-definition? What form of education is
necessary and acceptable in order to improve Jewish-Christian relations? As wicked as antisemitism was and remains, is it still an adequate basis for Jewish-Christian relations? In the rest of this paper, we
shall deal with these issues.

     Despite the United Kingdom's sometimes self-serving reputation
for sheltering refugees from foreign oppression, such liberality of
action has only recently been matched, at least to some extent, by a
generosity of spirit and its enshrinement in legislation. The work of the
Council of Christians and Jews not only needed to draw attention to
dark bigotry and foul acts in other countries but also has needed to
challenge British xenophobia and antisemitism.

     That chauvinism and hatred of Jews goes back centuries. They
were expelled in 1290 by the Plantagenet king Edward I, the first expulsion of all Jews from any country in the medieval period. They were permitted back during Oliver Cromwell's protectorate in 1656—grudgingly,
not for reasons of natural justice but because Cromwell believed Jews
could renew England's trade as, in his opinion, they had helped the
economic growth of Amsterdam and other mainland European cities,

especially ports. Full emancipation did not occur until the second half of the nineteenth century. Baron de Rothschild took his seat in the House of Commons on July 26, 1858. It was the fourth time he had been elected as the representative of the City of London, but he was forbidden from taking his place as an MP because he would not take the oath of allegiance in the time-honored Christian way. He was not a particularly active member of Parliament; he is not recorded as ever having made a speech in the House of Commons. A more important marking post in the integration of Jews into national life was probably when Gladstone made Sir George Jessel solicitor general in 1871; he was the first Jew to become a Minister of the Crown. Three years earlier, Benjamin Disraeli, a Christian of Jewish origin, had briefly become prime minister; he served as premier for a second, longer period from 1874–80.[4]

The CCJ had its precursors in England, who sought to improve Jewish-Christian relations. The London Society for the Study of Religions was founded in 1904. It has been a forum for scholarly debate, and included Jews from its foundation. The London Society of Jews and Christians (LSJC) was formed in 1927. It organizes regular discussions and debates between Jews and Christians of different persuasions. It has an annual garden party in Westminster Abbey's grounds, and a lecture in Church House, the Church of England's administrative headquarters. It seeks to understand how both religions are practiced as well as what they believe. There have been joint celebrations of Hanukkah and Christmas. Every other year there is a model Seder, to which Christians are invited.[5] The LSJC has aimed to increase religious understanding and mutual respect for differences of faith, and practice and has sought to combat religious intolerance.[6]

The work of dedicated individuals is also noteworthy. In particular, James Parkes (1896–1981), an Anglican clergyman, became aware of antisemitism when he went to work in Geneva in 1928. He was one of the first Christians to recognize that the origins of antisemitism were partly in the teaching of the churches, from the early church fathers onward. He argued this in his doctoral thesis of 1934. He was put on Hitler's list of people to be eliminated. When he retired in 1966, he gave his library to Southampton University. We also have the benefit of his autobiography.[7]

Subterranean and implicit antisemitism is often as shocking and as revealing as its straightforward forms. Some of English literature's most influential descriptions of Jews have arisen out of ignorance and prejudice: Shakespeare's depiction of Shylock was written when any Jew in England was illegally present and could hope only for exposure and death; Charles Dickens's distressing caricature of Fagin can be seen against a background of continuing mid-Victorian antisemitism.

Many authors of popular British twentieth-century literature exemplify a reflex antisemitism. A particularly noteworthy example of such unthinking prejudice is Agatha Christie, the so-called Queen of Crime, whose publishers declare that she is the world's best-selling novelist, writing works that have been translated into every major language. In her *Three Act Tragedy,* first published in 1935, Mr. Satterthwaite, an elderly snob yet acute observer of the human condition, contemplates a young man named Oliver Manders:

> A handsome young fellow, twenty-five at a guess. Something, perhaps, a little sleek about his good looks. Something else—something—was it foreign? Something unEnglish about him...
>> Egg Lytton Gore's voice rang out:
>> "Oliver, you slippery Shylock-"
>> "Of course," thought Mr. Satterthwaite, "that's it— not foreign—Jew!"[8]

Actually, the great Belgian detective Hercules Poirot is benevolently disposed toward the young man, who gets his girl in the end. Appallingly, that book was published the same year as the Nazis enacted the Nuremberg Laws to deprive German Jews of the ordinary rights of citizens. It is not only in *Three Act Tragedy* that Christie used barbed language about Jews, but also in many more of her works. The point is not that she was a particularly virulent exponent of anti-Jewishness or even consciously anti-Jewish. Worse in a way, her casual comments illustrate the stereotypes and caricatures widespread in British society of her day. To be fair, while at an archeological dig in Iraq with her distinguished husband, Max Mallowen, she encountered the German director of antiquities in Baghdad, one Dr. Jordan, whom she thought at first to be gentle and considerate. She recorded:

> Then there was a mention by someone, quite casually, of Jews. His face changed; changed in an extraordinary way that I had never noticed on anyone's face before.

He said: "You do not understand. Our Jews are perhaps different from yours. They are a danger. They should be exterminated. Nothing else will really do but that."

I stared at him unbelievingly. He meant it. It was the first time I had come across any hint of what was to come later from Germany. People who travelled there were, I suppose, already realizing it at that time, but for ordinary people, in 1932 and 1933, there was a complete lack of fore-knowledge.[9]

At about the same time as she wrote *Three Act Tragedy,* a little after the above event, Dame Agatha could write that, "He's a Jew, of course, but a frightfully decent one." One of her most perceptive reviewers notes that, despite this remark, her offensive remarks against Jews cease from this time. In later books, her reference to Jews and their critics are part of one of her most nimble sleights of hand: to use a reader's bigotry against him so as to mislead him.[10]

Still, there is no evidence that Dame Agatha ever expressed embarrassment at her unthinking acceptance of antisemitism. Nor did she question the appropriateness of using her readers' intolerance as a part of her strategy to bamboozle and misdirect them. In a world of Holocaust and genocide, she missed the point of her own deception by deep-rooted societal antipathies, nurtured by her deep Christian faith. Christie was a creature of her time and location; others saw the point more clearly than did she, but some never observed it even as naively as she did. So we need an educative process that seeks to help religious people not simply to tolerate but also to rejoice in the otherness of the other, a process that regards diversity as of transcendent value rather than the result of human sin or ignorance.

We turn now to the issue: are institutional Jewish-Christian relations at the mercy of internal religious angst and self-definition? We have seen how the chief rabbi nearly withdrew Orthodox Jewish support from CCJ just after it was founded. In November 1954, Cardinal Griffin withdrew as a president on orders from Rome, arguing that "in the educational field...the promotion of mutual understanding is being conducted in a way likely to produce religious indifferentism." Several articles in *Common Ground,* the CCJ journal, were accused of promoting this point of view. In particular, one by Arnold Toynbee was mentioned, in which he argued, rather movingly but perhaps not convincingly, that:

In reality mankind has never been divided into an elect minority monopolizing the light of God's countenance and a gentile majority sitting in outer darkness. There has never been any supernaturally privileged inner circle within the human family. The only treatment of history that is objective is one that treats all communities as equals; and this objective view of history is the only view that we can afford to present to our children in our now rapidly shrinking world.[11]

Other Roman Catholics than the cardinal also withdrew until the *aggiornamento* (updating) of Pope John XXIII's pontificate (1958-1963) permitted a return of Roman Catholic voices to the inner circles of the CCJ.

Such institutional brinkmanship is always a problem for organizations that promote Jewish-Christian relations. The unwise words of the chief rabbi Jonathan Sacks in the wake of the death of the much-loved and non-Orthodox Jewish rabbi Hugo Gryn, when he seemed to imply that Gryn was not a Jew and had caused others to stumble, led to calls in the British Jewish community for non-Orthodox Jewish presidents of CCJ. Up until then, the chief rabbi had been the only Jewish president, though the Archbishops of Canterbury and Westminster, and the moderator of the Free Church Federal Council represented Christians. In 1999, a Progressive Jewish leader, Rabbi Albert Friedlander, became a vice president. Also, despite Pope John Paul II's remarkable advocacy of positive Jewish-Christians relations, toward the end of his papacy he was dogged by seemingly disjointed and equivocal actions that caused outsiders to ponder the consistency of Roman Catholic teaching about other ways of faith. Had the Pope's position been most clearly seen in his Universal Prayer of March 12, 2000, asking for forgiveness for sins against the Jewish people and other groups? Or was it seen in his attempt in the Vatican document *Dominus Iesus,* published on August 6 2000, to resurrect traditional teaching that the Roman church alone embodies the truth, noting, as it does, that other religions result from a purely human quest for God?[12] No doubt, to some extent this bewildering ambivalence is illustrative of how factions fight for the victory of their point of view in the twilight years of stricken leaders. Still, it does little to improve Jewish–Roman Catholic relations.

Institutional dialogue is fraught with perils, at the mercy of internal rifts and maneuverings for power and influence. Still, the recent history of Jewish-Christian relations has shown how important it is. There has been very little if any attempt by the ancient Orthodox churches of the East to reformulate teaching about Jews. As a result, antisemitism not only flourishes in Russia and other countries where this form of Christianity is present but is condoned or even justified by the church hierarchy, whereas the Protestant churches and especially the Roman Catholic Church have been transformed by institutional statements.

The seminal postwar document was *Nostra Aetate,* issued on October 28, 1965, in the pontificate of Paul VI, though it had its origins in his predecessor, John XXIII's, deepest concerns and his summoning of a council to update the church's teaching on a wide range of issues. It marked a great leap forward in Jewish–Roman Catholic relations. It declared that the church had her origins in ancient Israel, upon which she is dependent for her teaching, life, and worship. So Catholics must not teach that God has rejected the Jews, nor that God and Christians should teach contempt for or hatred of them.[13] Hitherto, the official teaching of the church had portrayed the Jews as a deicide people, killers of God, who were therefore abandoned and rejected by him. Note, for example, the bowed, broken, and humiliated images of Jews on cathedrals of medieval Europe, like Notre Dame in Paris, begun in 1163, and Strasbourg, mostly dating from the end of the twelfth century onward, which had encouraged illiterate worshippers, who would have learned church teaching from such artifacts to shun and loathe Jews.[14] It has taken many more years since 1965 for the Roman Catholic Church to face up to some of the worst aspects of its history. *Nostra Aetate* makes no mention of the church's grave complicity in the history of Christian contempt for Jews. The Vatican recognized the State of Israel only in 1994. A series of further statements has continued to update attitudes toward Jews, for example, in dealing with antisemitism in the liturgy, the catechism, and other teaching. Despite certain hiccups in the progress, and the understandable desire of many Jews that the church should move more quickly and radically in updating its teaching, Jewish–Roman Catholic relations have improved immeasurably since the pontificate of the wartime Pius XII. Recent attempts to beatify him have caused renewed anger among Jews, not least in the light of a severely critical biography of him by a Catholic author.[15] But the point is that, by and large, Jewish and Roman Catholic officials now trust one another enough to cope with the anger surrounding such inept and even provocative actions. Recent years have not so much diminished the capacity of Jews and Roman Catholics to misunderstand and irritate one another, but have provided a context of mutual respect that allows for discussion and amelioration of fraught issues.

Protestant relations also have improved immeasurably with the Jewish people.[16] The World Council of Churches was under the baleful influence of a Barthian theology from its beginnings in 1948 until the New Delhi assembly in 1961.[17] Since then, this umbrella organization of Protestant and some Orthodox churches has issued a number of significant statements. Member churches have also issued their own statements about their church and the Jewish people. The statements by individual churches have had more teeth, since they are binding on their members, whereas the WCC documents have, at best, a moral force only.

I can illustrate the importance of individual churches making their own statements in a personal way. From 1983 to 1995, I was the director of interfaith relations for the British Methodist Church. In 1994, the annual governing body of the Methodist Church passed a resolution about interfaith relations. It included a section that ran as follows:

> A particular relationship that all churches need to get right is that with the Jewish people. Methodists have no special involvement in the shameful Christian history of anti-semitism. Nevertheless, sweeping statements about "the Pharisees" or "the Jews" are frequently made from our pulpits as though there were an easy leap from the first century Jews to those at the end of the twentieth century. Recent research has shown the Pharisees in a far more sympathetic light than Christians have hitherto seen them, and this changing perception may mark a watershed in Jewish-Christian relations. The 1940s holocaust largely resulted from, and was justified by, centuries of Christian "teaching of contempt about Jews." We, who stand in the shadow of that appalling episode in modern history, cannot perpetuate such attitudes.[18]

It is possible to criticize a number of judgments in that single paragraph, and forcefully to regret its rather evasive second sentence. Still, the point is that it forbade British Methodists from uttering and acting on antisemitic statements as though they were the continuing teaching of the church. I was accustomed, in that post, to travel in Britain and abroad, talking to church and other groups about Christian relations with people from other religions. I took some pleasure, in the final year of my work, in telling the occasional bigot that, not only were his views offensive and dangerous, but also that they flew in the face of the teaching of the church, so he could not justify them by reference to an outdated and shameful teaching.

The British Methodist Church's statement is a very minor and tentative one. Other churches have been much more forward looking and bold in their positive comments about Jewish-Christian relations. For example, the Evangelical Church of the Rhineland resolved in January 1980 that, "We believe the permanent election of the Jewish people as the people of God and realize that through Jesus Christ the church is taken into the covenant of God with his people."[19]

It is of course true that it takes time for reformed views to be accepted by the rank and file of Christian believers, especially after so many centuries when Jews have been accused of killing the Christ or even murdering God. Still, the effect has been remarkable in transforming attitudes. It has been met on the Jewish side by a willingness to meet and trust Christians after years when many Jews had felt unable to do either.

This sustained reflection in the form of rabbinical and church documents by Jews and particularly by Christians on the meaning of Jewish-Christian relations is not paralleled in seriousness and urgency in the wider world of interfaith relations. Of course, many branches of Christianity are set up, even more than Judaism is, with clear or relatively obvious structures of authority. This is not quite matched by many other religions. Even so, there are, in most religious groups, people or institutions that have religious authority. The wider world of dialogue could learn from the recent history of Jewish-Christian relations, the importance of reforming institutional evils that demonize and even seek to destroy the other. It is not enough to leave the resolution of prejudice to people of goodwill. Structures have to change, as well as individuals. Although many religions do not have the equivalent of a pope and a curia, most have some form of conferring and all of them, even when some of their members claim otherwise, have the capacity to develop beliefs and practices to speak to each new context.

The third issue we raised was: What form of education is necessary and acceptable in order to improve Jewish-Christian relations?

One area that has been tackled with great bravery by post-Holocaust Christian scholars, joined by Jewish ones, has been that of Christian origins; in particular, there has been a new look at the New Testament. This has been assisted by the official permission of the churches, so that Catholic and Protestant scholars have been encouraged to recover the Jewishness of both Jesus and Paul.

For all the brilliance of many German biblical scholars of the recent past (which has greatly influenced scholars from other countries), the scholarship about Jesus that emerged from the pages of their works was often strongly anti-Jewish. They depicted Judaism at the time of Jesus as "late Judaism" *(Spätjudentum),* as if Jewish religion had ended after 70 CE or should have. This position was based on the conviction that post-exilic Judaism had ossified and betrayed the prophetic faith of Israel. Jesus stands outside such a hardened, legalistic religion, a stranger to it, condemning the scribes and the Pharisees who were the fathers of rabbinic Judaism and who have thus misled modern Judaism into perpetuating this sterile, legalistic religion. It is somewhat disquieting that German biblical scholars as important, interesting, and (in many other ways) perceptive as, for example, Martin Noth, Rudolph Bultmann, Martin Dibelius, Gunther Bornkamm, and Joachim Jeremias should have depicted Judaism by the time of Jesus in this way.[20] This is particularly so, since most lived through the Holocaust years but still seemed oblivious to the Christian teaching of contempt about Jews that watered the roots of antisemitism and that persists, even if only as an unconscious and instinctive habit, in their works.

One of the tools by which some Gospel scholars assess the genuineness of a saying or deed of Jesus is the criterion of dissimilarity, which focuses on those words and works of Jesus that cannot be derived from the Judaism of his day (or, indeed, from the early church). For example, using this criterion, some scholars would claim an authentic word from Jesus when Matthew records his sweeping prohibition of all oaths (5:34, 37; but cf. James 5:12). Yet (among other objections to it), this tool divorces Jesus totally from the Judaism of his day. He was a Jew, deeply influenced by its unusual emphasis on belief in one God and his gift of the Torah to his people. Jesus was not an alien intruder in first-century Palestine. Whatever else he was, he was a reformer of Jewish beliefs, not an indiscriminate faultfinder of them.

Can we take a step further and admit that anti-Jewishness is a feature of the New Testament itself? The Jewish theologian of the Holocaust Eliezer Berkowits disagreed with those who refuse to admit that Christian scripture itself is a cause and a source of the history of the teaching of contempt. In an article entitled "Facing the Truth," published in the summer 1978 edition of *Judaism,* he wrote that,

> Christianity's New Testament has been the most dangerous anti-Semitic tract in history. Its hatred-charged diatribes against the Pharisees and the Jews have poisoned the hearts and minds of millions and millions of Christians for almost two millennia. No matter what the deeper theological meaning of the hate passages against the Jews might be, in the history of the Jewish people the New Testament lends its support to oppression, persecution and mass murder of an intensity and duration that were unparalleled in the entire history of man's degradation. Without Christianity's New Testament, Hitler's *Mein Kampf* could never have been written.

Berkowits challenged Christians about antisemitism thus, "To face this truth is the first condition of meaningful Jewish-Christian dialogue. Is Christianity orally capable of doing it? And what is it able to do about it?" (pp. 323–24).

The work that persuaded some Christian scholars to face up to the fact that the New Testament itself is seriously flawed in its anti-Jewishness was Rosemary Ruether's *Faith and Fratricide,* first published in 1974, before Berkowits's impassioned plea. James Parkes and his successors had argued that antisemitism goes back to the church fathers of the second century and later. Ruether, a Roman Catholic theologian, went further and argued that parts of the New Testament were intended to turn Christians against Jews. She described anti-Judaism as "the left hand of Christology." In her opinion, the New Testament's proclamation of Jesus as the messiah implies the rejection of the Jews, who must suffer for not recognizing him as such. Moreover, the Church's beliefs about Jesus led to its self-understanding as the "New Israel," which renders Judaism obsolete. She inquired: "Is it possible to say that 'Jesus is the Messiah' without, implicitly or explicitly, saying at the same time 'and the Jews be damned'?"[21]

This question is sharply put, and we shall return to it later. Certainly, scholarship about Jesus (and also Paul) has been transformed in the last quarter century. We can briefly illustrate this from the works of the Christian Ed Sanders and the Jew Geza Vermes, who were, at one time, colleagues at Oxford University.

Ed Sanders is one of a number of recent scholars who have contributed to the recovery of the Jewishness of Jesus. His great achievement has been to paint the story of Jesus against a wider background of Jewish belief and practice. His *Judaism: Practice and Belief 63BCE–66CE* is an unusual treatment from a New Testament specialist, rather telling in that it is a book that is not dominated by Jesus as Christians falsely assume that Jewish faith in that period must have been. In an epilogue to that work, Sanders confesses that,

> I rather like the Pharisees. They loved detail and precision. They wanted to get everything just right. I like that. They loved God, they thought that he had blessed them, and they thought that he *wanted* them to get everything just right. I do not doubt that some of them were priggish. This is a common fault of the pious, one that is amply demonstrated in modern criticizm of the Pharisees. The Pharisees, we know, intended to be humble before God, and they thought that intention mattered more than outward show. These are worthy ideals.[22]

One of the ongoing issues in Jesus studies is to distinguish whether it is possible to locate a substratum of relatively accurate factual information about him from later interpretation. In *Jesus and Judaism,* Sanders offers his view on this issue. There, he classifies Gospel readings under six heads as: certain, highly probable, probable, possible, conceivable, and incredible. To give two examples from the extreme points of his rainbow arch: under *certain,* Jesus certainly proclaimed the kingdom of God to all, including the wicked; but, under *incredible,* he definitely was not one of the rare Jews of his day who believed in love, mercy, grace, repentance, and the forgiveness of sins, and Judaism was not destroyed as a result of his work. Sanders believes that Jesus offended his Jewish contemporaries in three ways. First, he included the "wicked," who were outside the law, within the scope of God's kingly rule, even though they remained outside rather than repenting and becoming observant; this,

Sanders believes to have been a very trivial difference. The second offense was the commandment to the prospective disciple to leave his dead father (Matt 8:21f. and par.), which conflicted with the law to honor one's parents; this, again, was relatively insignificant, probably a one-off occasion rather than an indication that Jesus intended to oppose, root and branch, the Deuteronomic legislation (21:18–21). Third, Jesus' prohibition of divorce (Matt 19:3–9; Mark 10:2–9) was a radical indication that the Mosaic Law was not strict enough. However, it was the conflict over the Temple, which must have struck numerous people as particularly impious, that probably led to his execution. According to Sanders, the threat of destroying and the promise of rebuilding the Temple are embedded in the early tradition and, however interpreted, were for most Jews deeply offensive. Yet the Romans executed Jesus, and if the Jews had anything to do with it, it must have been those with access to Pilate: the leaders of the priesthood.[23]

Geza Vermes stands in the line of earlier twentieth-century Jewish scholars of Jesus, such as Joseph Klausner and Martin Buber, who approved the man's ethical teaching but not the divine status accorded to him by Christians. His *Jesus the Jew,* first published in 1973, opened the eyes of many to the Jewishness of Jesus, whom Vermes depicted as a Galilean *Hasid,* holy man. He was that kind of Jew rather than a Pharisee, Essene, Zealot, or Gnostic. More problematic for Christians was the careful examination of titles claimed for him: prophet, lord, Messiah, Son of Man, and son of God. Vermes concluded, controversially, that none of the claims and aspirations of Jesus link him with the Messiah, that no titular use of *Son of Man* is attested in Jewish literature, and that *prophet, lord,* or even, figuratively, *son of God* could be easily applied to holy men in the Judaism of Jesus' day. In works since, Vermes has developed his picture of Jesus: he was a charismatic teacher, healer, and prophet.

What then of the Christian church or churches, of the phenomenon of Christianity itself? According to Vermes, this owes more to the hellenizing theologies of John and Paul than to Jesus the Jew, to its migration to the Graeco-Roman, Gentile world than to its Jewish origins. But he observes that, through the three ancient witnesses of Matthew, Mark, and Luke, Jesus the Jew emerges to challenge traditional Christianity of the Pauline-Johannine variety. In Vermes's opinion, the decline in the numbers of Torah-observing Jews who followed the teaching of Jesus, without believing the virgin birth or the deification of Christ, allowed

the dominant hellenized Christianity a free run. Indeed, by the beginning of the fifth century, important figures in the church had ruled that it
was heretical for Christians of Jewish origin to keep the law. Vermes
observes that,

> Despite all this, in fairness, it must be emphasized that
> notwithstanding all its alien dogmatic and ecclesiastical fea-
> tures, Christianity still possesses fundamental elements of the
> piety of Jesus, such as his emphasis on the purity of intention
> and generosity of heart, exemplified in a Francis of Assisi who
> relinquished wealth to serve the poor, and even in our century,
> an Albert Schweitzer, who abandoned fame to heal the sick in
> God-forsaken Lambaréné, and a Mother Teresa who, age-old,
> cares for the dying in the filthy streets of Calcutta.[24]

Much of this thesis is old and somewhat discredited currency.
Muslims at the turn of the nineteenth and twentieth centuries who were
anxious to portray their religion as progressive and tolerant did so by
drawing on early nineteenth-century biblical scholarship that depicted
Paul as the founder of a Christianity that betrayed or at least deviated
from the ideals of Jesus of Nazareth.[25] This was not particularly con-
vincing then and has become even less so.

   Still, Vermes's representation of the meaning of Jesus is insight-
ful. His work can also be interpreted, to some extent, as a brilliant piece
of polemics: he himself converted to Christianity and was a Roman
Catholic priest and then eventually reverted to Judaism.[26] His works are
an implicit response and answer to the traditional Christian claim that it
knows what Jewish faith should be and that Jews have got it wrong, by
insinuating that Jews know what Jesus' faith would have been and that
Christians have got it wrong. Despite its confrontational nuances,
Vermes's work on the Jewishness of Jesus has profoundly influenced
Christian writers such as his former colleague at Oxford E. P. Sanders,
whose work we have noticed and will no doubt long endure. Christians
as well as others who would locate Jesus against his historical background have reason to be grateful for Vermes's books on Jesus.

   This willingness by Christian and Jewish scholars to treat the New
Testament to historical criticism so as redeem the past is an unusually
bold one. This could profitably though not easily be extended by other
faith groups to their scriptures. The treatment of Jesus in the Qur'an is

not in accord with that of Christian understandings of his meaning or even of things that he did and said. Muslims accord the Qur'an the status of God's word, mediated to the prophet Muhammad through the angel Gabriel. It is therefore difficult for many Muslims to hear Christian criticisms of its accounts about Jesus. A start could be made by more imaginative Muslim commentaries on the meaning of Qur'anic verses, such as that attempted in nineteenth-century India by Sir Sayyid Ahmad Khan (1817–98). Although, at present, it is hard to see that the willingness of some Christians to evaluate the Bible as a human document would appeal to many Muslims, some have already begun the process.[27] Religions have transformed themselves so much in the modern world that it is not beyond the bounds of possibilities that Islam and other religions may soon have to reassess certain central beliefs, a reassessment that many now believe will never happen. Indeed, you have only to compare the debate between Jews and Christians about Jesus the Jew with that between Christians and Muslims over the meaning of Muhammad and Jesus to realize how the painful honesty of the Jewish-Christian debate, though it is present to some extent in Christian-Muslim dialogue, could helpfully be extended there.

At the end of Jesus' life, the Qur'an records two events that are difficult to interpret: the death of Jesus and his return to herald the last day. Most Muslims believe that Jesus did not die, but was taken up by God and will return as a sign of the last day. However, that is probably not the meaning of the Qur'an but rather how many Muslims have interpreted it.

It can be argued that the weight of the Qur'an, as opposed to many interpretations of it, is in favor of a real death. For example, Q19.33 "Peace is upon me [Jesus], the day of my birth and the day of my death," indicates that Jesus died and that his raising up is at the general resurrection of all people when the world ends. Jesus' return to God is mentioned in Q3.55 and Q5.117, which are most naturally interpreted to refer to his death. The first of these passages runs,

> So God said: "Jesus, I shall take you up and draw you to me, and make you pure from those who disbelieve, and place those who follow you ahead of those who disbelieve until the day when all are raised. Then your return will be to me, and I shall arbitrate among you all about the disagreements between you."

The Arabic word *mutawaffika,* employed in these passages of Jesus, is used of people dying in Q2.240; and, in Q6:60, of believers being called to God in the night, raised up to complete a stated term and returning to him. The most contentious passage between Muslims and Christians about Jesus is Q4.157, which most Muslims see as a denial of the crucifixion. This in turn has led them to interpret Q3.55 against its natural sense, to mean that Jesus did not die. Q4.157 comes in a section (Q4.155-159) that runs,

> So for their breaking their [the Jews'] covenant, and disbelieving the signs of God, and killing the prophets without right,...and for their unbelief, and their speaking against Mary a great slander; and for their saying: "We killed the Messiah, Jesus the Son of Mary, the messenger of God", — though they did not kill him, and did not crucify him, but only a likeness of it was shown to them. Truly, those who have gone in different ways about him are in doubt about him; they have no knowledge of him and only follow speculation; though they certainly did not kill him. No, to be sure, God raised him to himself. God is almighty and wise. And there is no People of the Book but will surely believe in him before his death, and on the day of resurrection he will be a witness against them.

The most widely held view among Muslims about this passage is that the Jews tried to kill Jesus but were unable to do so. Many believe that there was a substitute who suffered in his place. The canonical Gospels affirm that Jesus truly died and have no suggestion of a replacement figure. Against them, Muslims have slender support in the teaching of the second century CE Egyptian Gnostic and Christian Basilides whose views only survive in rather diverse interpretations by his opponents. Some notable Muslim commentators of the Qur'an have accepted the idea of a substitute, perhaps Judas Iscariot or Simon of Cyrene. For example, Tabari (d. 923) believed that a Jewish chief called Joshua, whom God gave the form and appearance of Jesus, died in his place. However the passage hardly demands this interpretation, which does not seem its obvious import. I have rendered the Arabic *shubbiha la-hum* as "only a likeness of it was shown to them." It is possible that the Arabic words mentioned should be attached to the crucifixion and not to Jesus.

Then the meaning of a very difficult passage could be that the Jews did not kill Jesus rather than that he did not die. Such an interpretation could lead to interesting dialogue between Muslims and Christians.

The Muslim Egyptian surgeon and educationalist Kamel Hussein has argued that:

> No cultured Muslim believes...nowadays [that someone sub-stituted for Jesus on the cross]. The text is taken to mean that the Jews thought they killed Christ but God raised him unto Him in a way we can leave unexplained among the several mysteries which we have taken for granted on faith alone.[28]

Christians, of course, would not feel able to leave this simply as a mystery. Along with Paul, most believe that "in Christ God was recon-ciling the world to himself, not counting their trespasses against them, and entrusting the ministry of reconciliation to us" (2 Cor 5:19). Naturally, Christian scholars such as Kenneth Cragg and Geoffrey Parrinder who have examined the Qur'anic accounts of the death of Jesus offer their own estimates of how this event might be fruitful for conversation between Christians and Muslims.

Cragg in particular offers much food for thought. He would affirm that Muhammad is a prophet, but that the deepest needs of humanity cannot be met by a prophet but only by a suffering messiah. His affirmation shows how an assessment of Jesus between the two faiths cannot be done independently from a Christian interpretation of Muhammad, often hitherto lacking, partly because Muhammad has no place in Christian scriptures, as Jesus does in Islam's. This lack is not just for that reason. The difficult history between Christianity and Islam has not led the former to be generous toward the latter. Further, as Cragg himself has ventured to suggest: "How is the Christian to con-template positive acknowledgement of Muhammad when his prophetic significance [for Muslims] involves such crucial disavowal of truths Christian [not least that Jesus is the suffering Messiah]."[29]

Muslims are reluctant to be drawn into such a discourse. Though an important figure, Jesus himself is not central to their faith. Muhammad is, and both he and the Qur'anic Jesus emphasized rather different attitudes to faith and practice than did the Jesus of the New Testament and Orthodox Christian doctrine.

This debate between Muslims and Christians could do with a dose of greater realism and close attention to historical as well as theological issues that are better mapped out in Jewish-Christian dialogue.

The last of the issues we deduced from the creation of the Council of Christians and Jews is: As wicked as antisemitism was and remains, is it still an adequate basis for Jewish-Christian relations?

In the post-Holocaust world, it has seemed to be axiomatic to many Jews and Christians that the Shoah should dominate their discussions. Christians have begun to disentangle the threads of antisemitism from the tapestry of their faith and practice. Some Jews have seen Hitler's "Final Solution" as a defining moment in Jewish history and belief: for example, Emil Fackenheim proposed a 614th commandment to the traditional 613, forbidding Jews to grant Hitler a posthumous victory.[30] Yet it is difficult to accept any suggestion that the Holocaust can be compared to Sinai as a seminal revelatory experience. As Jews work out where exactly it does fit in what it says about God and humans, both Jews and Christians should ponder whether the Holocaust is of as much moment for their relationship as is the sense of being communities bound in a covenant with each other and with God. The answer is surely no.

One result of making the Holocaust the center of Jewish-Christian relations is that it forbids a truly adult relationship, in which one can respectfully differ from the other. The Holocaust is too bound up with guilt, pain, manipulation, and other negative factors to be able to function as the basis for mature reflection. In the past, disagreements have led to anger, alienation, and even murder. So it has been natural to seek common ground. The task of Jews and Christians in the future is to recognize, respect, and cope with difference. Muslims in dialogue with others will often present a point of view forcefully and then, with a smile and a shrug of the shoulders say, in Arabic: "But God knows best." Quite so.

Here is one illustration of recognizing difference in the area of biblical studies. The earliest Gospel, that of Mark, calls Jesus "Messiah" in its first verse. This depiction goes back to Christianity's early moments and may even be part of Jesus' own self-understanding: the Gospel accounts of the entry into Jerusalem would seem to confirm this (Mark 11:1–11 and parallels). No mainstream Jew believes this. It is much more candid and fruitful for Jews and Christians to recognize this than to avoid the issue altogether or for Christians to play down

Christology and its importance to their identity as religious people. On this matter, Ruether is to be resisted.

Other issues in biblical studies also raise uncomfortable questions. Regina Schwartz, a Jewish professor of English at Northwestern University, Illinois, has argued that monotheism has left a violent legacy in history because it defines the other as being "not-it": so Egypt is "not Israel." Diana Eck, a Christian scholar of Hinduism, has made a similar point,

> In monotheistic consciousness, the singular is the proper number for questions of Truth: There is one God, one Only-Begotten Son of the Father, one seal of the Prophets, one Holy Book, one Holy and Apostolic Church. It might be called "the myth of monotheism"; that there is one and only one holy story to be told, to be reflected upon by theologians, and to be participated in by the faithful....It is a myth in the sense that it is the powerful story we tell about reality, so powerful we do not recognize it as our story. It is not the world-shaping myth of religious people alone, but it is a particular way of seeing and evaluating that has shaped equally the world-views of Marxists, secularists and atheists in the West.[31]

So, opponents of this myth can be seen as in deep error. Schwartz perceptively notes that "Conquering the Canaanites was a fantasy of an exiled people; it could only carry force when it was adopted by groups who held the reins of power in Christendom."[32] Still, the roots of violence are present in the Hebrew Bible. The command of Samuel to Saul to exterminate utterly the Amalekites (1 Sam 15:3) may have little relevance to a contemporary world without Amalekites, but it locates teaching found in the Hebrew Bible as part of the seedbed whence, with appalling irony, Christian violence toward Jews grew and flourished. A generation ago, such an observation would have seemed insensitive and tactless to many Christians, and freighted with implicit or actual antisemitism to many Jews. An adult relationship should encourage us to reflect together on hard sayings not just of the New Testament but also from the Hebrew Bible so as to mend the world; we must not bypass them for the sake of tact or some other secondary virtue.[33] The religion of Islam shares the same monotheistic tradition. Although medieval Christian depictions of Islam and the prophet Muhammad were shamefully biased and libelous,[34] one reason for this was Christendom's sense of insecurity. Islam made spectacular conquests in the early days of that religion, which sorely wounded the Byzantine Empire and squeezed Christianity in a pincer movement between east and west over many centuries. This debate about monotheism's violent tendencies is one that, if Jews and Christians were to begin, could profitably be joined by other voices.

Just as the Holocaust may not be an adequate basis for developing Jewish-Christian relations, one might also say that the wider debate about Orientalism is also an insufficient basis for adult interreligious relationships. The proponents of Orientalism have argued that Western Christians, Jews, and secularists have seen the Eastern religions, particularly Islam but also Hinduism and Buddhism, through the inappropriate and uncomprehending lenses of an all-powerful outsider.[35] Such a well-founded but overstated discourse is understandable in a postcolonial world, but it has proved to generate as much heat as light. So-called Orientalists have retorted that Muslims and other supposed victims are themselves guilty of failing to figure out the real meaning of the other.[36] At issue is not so much a question of who understands, for few seem to do so on either side of the debate; the real issue is which uncomprehending group or groups has more power to do damage to whom. There are ironic echoes here with Jewish-Christian relations. Still, current Jewish-Christian relations could teach participants in the debate about Orientalism a thing or two about honesty and realism. There is, frankly, an element of whining among proponents of Orientalism and of angry defensiveness on the part of Occidentalists. Past relations do not permit us to affirm that only the oppressor misunderstands. Nor can they justify the dumping of guilt upon contemporary people who wish to undo the past. The course of Jewish-Christian dialogue has underlined these points in recent years, and others should take note.

Adult Jewish-Christian relationships must surely deal in an honest way with theological issues, not least with disagreements about God. Marcus Braybrooke has noted that, unlike the Council of Christians and Jews, the London Society of Jews and Christians "has not been constrained to avoid theological discussion."[37] Nowadays, the LSCJ's position may make better sense in promoting grown-up interaction between Jews and Christians. To some extent, the British CCJ's longstanding doubt about raising theological matters is at odds with the International Council of Christians and Jews. In a meeting in Berlin in

October 1999, the ICCJ built on preliminary work to contemplate the involvement, in some form, of Muslims within an Abrahamic forum. The British CCJ has been more cautious, so a Three Faiths Forum has recently been founded as an organization to bring together all three monotheistic religions.

This disagreement raises an important issue in contemporary concerns about interreligious dialogue. Doubtless, there are reasons for continuing bilateral relations between Jews and Christians as well as extending those associations to other groups. Quite how to resolve this dilemma is difficult to see, and people of goodwill disagree rather strongly about it. Still, an important point is that Jewish-Christian relations could certainly benefit from, as well as contribute to, involvement in the wider world on interfaith dialogue. I offer the example of Israel.

CCJ has long brought the importance of Israel for Jews to the attention of Christians. Although it has been criticized for failing to condemn some of Israel's actions toward its own citizens and neighbors, it has run annual tours there for young adults and for church leaders. Both groups meet Jews and Arabs who present a wide range of different views about Israel; I went on a CCJ tour myself in 1993 and was impressed by the content of the itinerary and its fairness. Israel willy-nilly raises the issue of Muslim participation in interreligious debates. For many years, people of the three faiths have been at the forefront of working for peace in one another's shared holy land.[38] Jews are not the only religious group to locate a particular sacred place as supremely important. Still, it is special in a way that the Vatican is not quite for Roman Catholics; it is more like Amritsar and the wider province of the Punjab functions for Sikhs. The Punjab, however, is split between largely Hindu India and largely Muslim Pakistan, and recent violent calls for Khalistan, a homeland for Sikhs, have split the community and caused grave problems in India. The attempt of Zvi Werblowsky and others to argue that Jerusalem is special for Jews in ways that it is not for Christians (who have Rome and the heavenly Jerusalem) and Muslims (who have Mecca and Medina) has its interesting points but is not quite free from the charge of special pleading.[39] There would be much to learn from interreligious ruminations on the meaning of sacred space. An attempt has already been made to locate the question of Israel within a Jewish-Christian conversation in Asia.[40] Interesting though that was, there is scope for a greater imaginative vision. If the importance of Israel, including the particular issue of

Jerusalem, were to be discussed in the context of multilateral religious discussions about other uniquely important sacred spaces, that might prove to be an intriguing, stimulating, and fruitful enterprise.

Any reflection on Jewish-Christian relations must recognize the enormous strides forward that have taken place since the locust years of Nazi Germany. Thanks to many distinguished scholars and activists, the relationship has been immeasurably transformed for the better. Yet, there needs to be a move into a future less dominated by the Holocaust and, in certain cases, less obsessed by the need to avoid contentious doctrinal or even missiological issues. The last sixty years have produced much that is worth sharing with those involved in other interreligious relationships. It remains to be seen whether Jewish-Christian relations also might learn from mapping itself on the wider world of interfaith dialogue.

NOTES

1. D. Cohn-Sherbok, ed., *Many Mansions* (London: Bellew, 1992), 104.

2. M. Braybrooke, *Children of One God: A History of the Council of Christians and Jews* (London: Vallentine Mitchell, 1991), 14.

3. Braybrooke, *Children of One God,* 15–16.

4. C. Roth, *A History of the Jews in England* (Oxford: Clarendon Press, 1978), 85–88, 164–66, 259–70.

5. G. Parrinder, *Encountering World Religions* (Edinburgh: T&T Clark, 1987), 120ff.

6. Braybrooke, *Children of One God,* 3.

7. J. Parkes [Hadham], *Voyages of Discovery* (London: Victor Gollancz, 1969), passim.

8. A. Christie, *Three Act Tragedy* (London: Fontana, 1935), 19, 21.

9. A. Christie, *An Autobiography* (London: Collins, 1977), 465–66.

10. R. Barnard, *A Talent to Deceive: An Appreciation of Agatha Christie* (London: Collins, 1980), 24.

11. Braybrooke, *Children of One God,* 34.

12. The text can be found on the website http://www.vatican.va, in the section "The Roman Curia."

13. An enthusiastic, though rather unself-critical, account of the making of *Nostra Aetate* is that of J. M. Oesterreicher, *The New Encounter between Christians and Jews* (New York: Philosophical Library, 1986).

14. This Christian depiction of Jews is brilliantly illustrated in H. Schreckenberg, *The Jews in Christian Art* (London: SCM Press, 1996).

15. J. Cornwell, *Hitler's Pope* (New York/London: Viking, 1999).

16. The best source of up-to-date information about Roman Catholic, Protestant, and Jewish documents, which seem to be added to almost on a daily basis, is the website http://www.jcrelations.net.

17. Karl Barth's ambivalent attitude to the Jews and his appraisal of them wholly from a certain naïve and negative Christian theological stance, are well illustrated by S. R. Haynes, *Jews and the Christian Imagination* (London: Macmillan, 1995), ch. 4.

18. British Methodist Church, "The Methodist Conference 1994 Agenda," 592.

19. http://www.jcrelations.net.

20. C. Klein, *Anti-Judaism in Christian Theology* (London: SPCK, 1978), passim; R. P. Ericksen, *Theologians under Hitler* (New Haven, CT/London: Yale University Press, 1985), passim.

21. R. R. Ruether, *Faith and Fratricide* (Eugene, Oregon: Wipf and Stock, 1997), 246.

22. E. P. Sanders, *Judaism: Practice and Belief 63BCE–66CE* (London: SCM Press, 1992), 494.

23. E. P. Sanders, *Jesus and Judaism* (London: SCM Press, 1985), esp. 321–27.

24. G. Vermes, *The Religion of Jesus the Jew* (London: SCM Press, 1993), 214.

25. M. Forward, *The Failure of Islamic Modernism? Syed Ameer Ali's Interpretation of Islam as a Religion* (Bern: Peter Lang, 1999), 58–59.

26. G. Vermes, *Providential Accidents: An Autobiography* (London: SCM Press, 1998), passim.

27. E.g., F. Rahman, *Islam* (Chicago/London: University of Chicago Press, 1979), 32–33.

28. M. K. Hussein, *City of Wrong: A Friday in Jerusalem* (Oxford: Oneworld, 1994), 231.

29. K. Cragg, *Muhammad and the Christian* (London: Darton Longman and Todd, 1984), 11.

30. E. Fackenheim, *God's Presence in History* (New York: New York University, 1970), 67–98. Idem., *To Mend the World* (Bloomington: Indiana University Press, 1994), xix–xx.

31. D. Eck, *Encountering God* (Boston: Beacon Press, 1993), 59.

32. R. M. Schwartz, *The Curse of Cain* (Chicago/London: University of Chicago Press, 1997), x.

33. Such work already has promising beginnings. See, for example, M. Hilton with G. Marshall, *The Gospels and Rabbinic Judaism: A Study*

Guide (London: SCM Press, 1988), passim; and M. Forward in *Christianity and the Wider Ecumenism,* ed. P. Phan (New York: Paragon House, 1990), 103–15.

34. R. W. Southern, *Western Views of Islam in the Middle Ages* (Cambridge, MA: Harvard University Press, 1962), passim; N. Daniel, *Islam and the West* (Oxford: Oneworld, 1993), passim.

35. E. Said, *Orientalism* (London: Routledge & Kegan Paul, 1978), passim.

36. J. G. Carrier, ed., *Occidentalism* (Oxford: Oxford University Press, 1995), passim.

37. Braybrooke, *Children of One God,* 30.

38. C. J. Birkland, ed., *Unified in Hope: Arabs and Jews Talk about Peace* (Geneva: WCC, 1987), passim.

39. E.g., R. J. Z. Werblowsky, *The Meaning of Jerusalem to Jews, Christians and Muslims,* rev. ed. (Jerusalem: Israel Universities' Study Group for Middle Eastern Affairs, 1978), passim.

40. H. Ucko, ed., *People of God, Peoples of God* (Geneva: WCC, 1996), passim.

Combined Bibliography

Abbott, W. M., ed. *The Documents of Vatican II, with Notes and Comments by Catholic, Protestant and Orthodox Authorities*. New York: America Press, 1966.

Abramson, G. "Klausner, Joseph Gedaliah." In *The Blackwell Companion to Jewish Culture: From the Eighteenth Century to the Present,* edited by G. Abramson, 415–16. Oxford: Basil Blackwell, 1989.

Abravanel, Isaac. *Perush 'al Nevi'im Rishonim*. Jerusalem: Torah ve-Da'at, 1955.

ADL Interfaith Relations, Interfaith Focus. *A Dialogue: The Anti-Defamation League and the National Council of Churches* 1, no. 1. New York: Anti-Defamation League, 1994.

Adorno, Theodor W. *Negative Dialectics*. London: Routledge & Kegan Paul, 1990.

Aitken, James K. "Jews and Christians Take Counsel." *Church Times*. October 20, 2000, pp. 15, 17.

Alami, Solomon. *"Iggeret Musar."* St. Petersburg, 1912. Reprint edition, Jerusalem, 1965.

Alter, R. *The Art of Biblical Narrative*. London: Allen & Unwin, 1981.

Altmann, Alexander. *Moses Mendelssohn: A Biographical Study*. University: University of Alabama Press, 1973.

Ankori, Zvi. "Encounter in History: Jews and Christian Greeks in their Relation through the Ages" [in Hebrew]. *Yehude Yawan le-dorotam* 1. Tel Aviv: University of Tel Aviv, 1984.

243

Archer, Léonie. *Her Price Is Beyond Rubies: The Jewish Woman in Greco-Roman Palestine*. JSOTSS 60. Sheffield: Sheffield Academic Press, 1990.

Aronsfeld, C. C. "Jews and Christians in England." *Midstream* 39, no. 8 (November 1993): 16–18.

———. *The Text of the Holocaust: A Study of the Nazi's Extermination Propaganda 1919–1945*. Marblehead, MA: Micah Publications, 1985.

Assis, Yom Tov. "Sexual Behavior in Mediaeval Hispano-Jewish Society." In *Jewish History: Essays in Honour of Chimen Abramsky*, edited by Ada Rapoport-Albert and Steven Zipperstein, 25–59. London: Peter Halben, 1988.

———. *The Golden Age of Aragonese Jewry: Community and Society in the Crown of Aragon*, 1213–1327. London: Littman Library, 1997.

Ateek, Naim. *Justice and Only Justice: A Palestinian Theology of Liberation*. Maryknoll, NY: Orbis Books, 1989.

Bach, Alice, ed. *The Pleasure of Her Text: Feminist Readings of Biblical and Historical Texts*. Philadelphia: Trinity Press International, 1990.

Baker-Fletcher, Karen. *Sisters of Dust, Sisters of Spirit: Womanist Wordings on God and Creation*. Minneapolis: Fortress Press, 1998.

Barnard, R. *A Talent to Deceive: An Appreciation of Agatha Christie*. London: Collins, 1980.

Baron, Salo Wittmayer. *A Social and Religious History of the Jews*. 2nd ed. 18 vols. Philadelphia: Jewish Publication Society; New York: Columbia University Press, 1952–1983.

Barton, J., ed. *The Cambridge Companion to Biblical Interpretation*. Cambridge: Cambridge University Press, 1998.

Baskin, Judith R., ed. *Jewish Women in Historical Perspective*. Detroit: Wayne State University Press, 1991.

Bazak, Jacob. *Jewish Law and Jewish Life*. New York: Union of American Hebrew Congregations, 1979.

Beer, Moshe. "Acts of Atonement by Penitents in Rabbinic Literature" [in Hebrew]. *Zion* 46 (1981): 161–76.

Bemporad, Jack. "Jesus for Jews." *Church* (spring 1997): 11–12.

Bemporad, J., and M. Shevack. *Our Age: The Historic New Era of Christian-Jewish Understanding.* Hyde Park, NY: New City Press, 1996.

Benevich, Grigori. "Judaism and the Future of Orthodoxy." In *Theology after Auschwitz and Its Correlation with Theology after the Gulag,* edited by Natalia Pecherskaya. Saint Petersburg: School of Religion and Philosophy, 1998.

Berkovits, E. *Faith after the Holocaust.* New York: Ktav, 1973.

Biblical Encyclopedia [in Hebrew]. 9 vols. Jerusalem: Mosad Bialik, 1955–1988.

Bideleux, Robert, and Richard Taylor, eds. *European Integration and Disintegration: East and West.* London: Routledge & Kegan Paul, 1996.

Birkland, C. J., ed. *Unified in Hope: Arabs and Jews Talk about Peace.* Geneva: WCC, 1987.

Bleich, J. David. "Teaching Torah to Non-Jews." *Tradition* 18 (1980): 192–211.

Borelli, John. "The Catechism and Interreligious Dialogue: The Jews and World Religions." In *Introducing the Catechism of the Catholic Church: Traditional Themes and Contemporary Issues,* edited by Berard L. Marthaler, 72–86. London: SPCK, 1994.

Borowitz, E. *Contemporary Christologies: A Jewish Response.* New York: Paulist Press, 1980.

Borts, Barbara. "On Trespassing the Boundaries: A Reflection on Men, Women and Jewish Space." In *Hear Our Voice: Women Rabbis Tell Their Stories,* edited by Sibyl Sheridan, 169–79. London: SCM Press, 1994.

Boswell, John. *The Royal Treasure: Muslim Communities under the Crown of Aragon in the Fourteenth Century.* New Haven, CT: Yale University Press, 1977.

Braude, William, ed. and trans. *Pesikta Rabbati.* 2 vols. New Haven, CT: Yale University Press, 1968.

Braybrooke, Marcus. *Children of One God: A History of the Council of Christians and Jews.* London: Vallentine Mitchell, 1991.

————. *Time to Meet: Towards a Deeper Relationship between Jews and Christians.* London/Philadelphia: SCM Press, 1990.

Brenner, A., and C. Fontaine, eds. *A Feminist Companion to the Bible* (first series). 10 vols. Sheffield: Sheffield University Press, 1993–1998.

Briggs, Sheila. "A History of Our Own: What Would a Feminist History of Theology Look Like?" In *Horizons in Feminist Theology: Identity, Tradition, and Norms,* edited by Rebecca S. Chopp and Sheila Greeve Davaney, 165–78. Minneapolis: Fortress Press, 1997.

Brockway, A., ed. *The Theology of the Churches and the Jewish People.* Geneva, WCC, 1988.

Brooten, Bernadette J. *Women Leaders of the Ancient Synagogue.* Chico, CA: Scholars Press, 1982.

Brown, R. A. *Unexpected News: Reading the Bible with Third World Eyes.* Philadelphia: Westminster Press, 1984.

Brubaker, Roger. *Nationalism Reframed: Nationhood and the National Question in the New Europe.* Cambridge: Cambridge University Press, 1996.

Brueggemann, Walter. *The Land: Place as Gift, Promise and Challenge in Biblical Faith.* Philadelphia: Fortress Press, 1977.

Buber, Martin. *Two Types of Faith,* translated by N. P. Goldhawk from the German *Zwei Glaubensweisen.* London: Routledge & Kegan Paul, 1951.

Burns, R. J. *Has the Lord Indeed Spoken Only through Moses? A Study of the Biblical Portrait of Miriam.* SBLDS 84. Atlanta: Scholars Press, 1987.

Camp, C., and C. R. Fontaine. *Women, War and Metaphor: Language and Society in the Study of the Hebrew Bible.* Atlanta: Fortress Press, 1993.

Carrier, J. G., ed. *Occidentalism.* Oxford: Oxford University Press, 1995.

Castelli, E., S. D. Moore, G. A. Phillips, and R. M. Schwartz, eds. *The Postmodern Bible.* The Bible and Culture Collective. New Haven, CT: Yale University Press, 1995.

Catholics Remember the Holocaust. Published by the Secretariat for Ecumenical and Interreligious Affairs of the National Conference of Catholic Bishops. Washington, DC, 1998.

Chaves, Mark. *Ordaining Women: Culture and Conflict in Religious Organisations.* Cambridge, MA/London: Harvard University Press, 1997.

Chazan, Robert. *Church, State and Jew in the Middle Ages.* New York: Behrman House, 1980.

——. *European Jewry and the First Crusade.* Berkeley: University of California Press, 1987.

Chopp, Rebecca S., and Sheila Greeve Davaney, eds. *Horizons in Feminist Theology: Identity, Tradition and Norms.* Minneapolis: Fortress Press, 1997.

Christ, Carol M. *Rebirth of the Goddess: Finding Meaning in Feminist Spirituality.* London: Routledge & Kegan Paul, 1997.

Christie, Agatha. *An Autobiography.* London: Collins, 1977.

——. *Three Act Tragedy.* London: Fontana, 1935.

Chrysostom, John. *Discourses against Judaizing Christians,* translated by Paul W. Harkins. Washington, DC: The Catholic University of America Press, 1979.

Clines, D. J. A., ed. *Interested Parties: The Ideology of Writers and Readers of the Hebrew Bible.* Sheffield: Sheffield Academic Press, 1996.

Cohen, Gerson. "The Blessing of Assimilation." In *Jewish History and Jewish Destiny,* 145–56. New York: Jewish Theological Seminary of America, 1997.

Cohen, J. *"Be Fertile and Increase; Fill the Earth and Master It" (Genesis 1:28): The Ancient and Medieval Career of a Biblical Text.* Ithaca, NY: Cornell University Press, 1989.

——, ed. *Essential Papers on Judaism and Christianity in Conflict: From Late Antiquity to the Reformation.* New York: New York University Press, 1991.

Cohen, Mark R., ed. *The Autobiography of a Seventeenth-Century Venetian Rabbi: Leon Modena's Life of Judah.* Princeton, NJ: Princeton University Press, 1988.

Cohn-Sherbok, Dan. *The Crucified Jew: Twenty Centuries of Christian Anti-Semitism.* London: HarperCollins, 1992.

————, ed. *Many Mansions.* London: Bellew, 1992.

————, ed. *Using the Bible Today.* Canterbury Papers III. London: Bellow, 1991.

Conybeare, F. "Antonius Strategos' Account of the Sack of Jerusalem (614)." *English Historical Review* 25 (1910): 506–8.

Cooey, Paula M. "The Redemption of the Body: Post-Patriarchal Reconstruction of Inherited Christian Doctrine." In *After Patriarchy: Feminist Transformations of the World Religions,* edited by Paula M. Cooey et al., 106–30 Maryknoll, NY: Orbis Books, 1992.

Cornwell, J. *Hitler's Pope.* New York/London: Viking, 1999.

Cragg, K. *Muhammad and the Christian.* London: Darton Longman and Todd, 1984.

Czajkowski, Michal. "Let Us Speak Truth." *Dialogue and Universalism* 11 (2000): 13–17.

Dan, Joseph. "Demonological Stories of R. Judah the Hasid" [in Hebrew]. *Tarbiz* 30 (1961): 273–89.

Dandelion, B. P. *A Sociological Analysis of the Theology of Quakers: The Silent Revolution.* Lampeter, Wales: Edwin Mellen, 1993.

D'Angelo, Mary Rose. "Remembering Women: Prophecy and Resistance in the Memory of the Early Churches." *Horizons* 19 (1992): 199–218.

Daniel, N. *Islam and the West.* Oxford: Oneworld, 1993.

Davaney, Sheila Greeve. "Continuing the Story, but Departing the Text: A Historicist Interpretation of Feminist Norms in Theology." In *Horizons in Feminist Theology: Identity, Tradition and Norms,* edited by Rebecca S. Chopp and Sheila Greeve Davaney, 198–214. Minneapolis: Fortress Press, 1997.

Davies, A. T., ed. *Anti-semitism and the Christian Mind: The Crisis of Conscience after Auschwitz.* New York: Herder and Herder, 1969.

Dawson, Christopher. *Understanding Europe.* London: Sheed and Ward, 1952.

Eck, Diana. *Encountering God.* Boston: Beacon Press, 1993.

Eckhardt, A. L., and A. R. Eckhardt. *Long Night's Journey into Day: A Revised Retrospective on the Holocaust.* Oxford: Pergamon Press; Detroit: Wayne State University Press, 1982.

Eckardt, R. *Jews and Christians: The Contemporary Meeting.* Bloomington: Indiana University Press, 1986.

Ellis, Jane. *The Russian Orthodox Church: A Contemporary History.* London: Routledge & Kegan Paul, 1986.

Epstein, Simon. *Extreme Right Electoral Upsurges in Western Europe: The 1984–1995 Wave as Compared with the Previous Ones.* ACTA, no. 8. Jerusalem: Vidal Sassoon International Centre for the Study of Antisemitism, 1996.

Ericksen, R. P. *Theologians under Hitler.* New Haven, CT/London: Yale University Press, 1985.

The Evanston Report: The Second Assembly of the World Council of Churches 1954. London: SCM Press, 1955.

Exum, Cheryl. *Fragmented Women: Feminist (Sub)versions of Biblical Narratives.* JSOTSS 163. Sheffield: Sheffield Academic Press, 1993.

———. *Plotted, Shot and Painted: Cultural Representations of Biblical Women.* JSOTSS 215. Sheffield: Sheffield Academic Press, 1996.

Exum, Cheryl, and Stephen D. Moore. *Biblical Studies/Cultural Studies.* Sheffield: Sheffield Academic Press, 1998.

Fackenheim, Emil. *God's Presence in History.* New York: New York University, 1970.

———. *To Mend the World,* Bloomington: Indiana University Press, 1994.

Falk, Marcia. "Notes on Composing New Blessings: Toward a Feminist-Jewish Reconstruction of Prayer." *Journal of Feminist Studies in Religion* 3 (1987): 39–56.

Farmer, W. R., ed. *Anti-Judaism and the Gospels*. Harrisburg, PA: Trinity Press International, 1999.

Fishbane, M. A. *Biblical Text and Texture: A Literary Reading of Selected Texts*. Oxford: One World, 1998.

Fisher, Eugene J., *Catholic-Jewish Relations: Documents from the Holy See*. London: Catholic Truth Society, 1999.

———. "Judaism and Christianity: Their Respective Roles in the Strategy of Redemption." In *Visions of the Other: Jewish and Christian Theologians Assess the Dialogue*, edited by Eugene J. Fisher with Frank DeSiano. Studies in Judaism and Christianity. Mahwah, NJ: Paulist Press 1994.

———. "Theological Education and Christian-Jewish Relations." In *Academic Approaches to Teaching Jewish Studies*, edited by Z. Garber, 213–32. Lanham, MD/New York/London: University Press of America, 2000.

Fishman, Talia. "The Penitential System of *Hasidei Ashkenaz* and the Problem of Cultural Boundaries." *Journal of Jewish Thought and Philosophy* 9 (1999): 1–29.

Flannery, A., ed. *Vatican Council II: The Conciliar and Post-Conciliar Documents*. Leominster, Hereford: Fowler Wright, 1981.

Flannery, E. *The Anguish of the Jews*. New York: Macmillan, 1965.

Fleischner, E. *Judaism in German Christian Theology since 1945: Christianity and Israel Considered in Terms of Mission*. Metuchen, NJ: Scarecrow Press, 1975.

Ford, David. "A Messiah for the Third Millennium." *Modern Theology* 16, no. 1 (2000): 75–90.

———. *Self and Salvation, Being Transformed*. Cambridge: Cambridge University Press, 1999.

Forward, Martin. *The Failure of Islamic Modernism? Syed Ameer Ali's Interpretation of Islam as a Religion*. Bern: Peter Lang, 1999.

Frankiel, T. *The Voice of Sarah: Feminine Spirituality and Traditional Judaism*. San Francisco: Harper, 1991.

Friedlander, M., ed. and trans. *The Commentary of Ibn Ezra on Isaiah.* London: Trubner, 1873–1877.

From the Martin Buber House 27: Destruction and Renewal—The Role of Religion in Changing Society. Heppenheim: ICCJ, 2000.

From the Martin Buber House 28: The Concept of Monotheism in the Abrahamic Traditions. Heppenheim: ICCJ, 2001.

Fry, H. P. *Christian-Jewish Dialogue: A Reader.* Exeter: University of Exeter Press, 1996.

Frymer-Kensky, Tikva, David Novak, Peter Ochs, David Fox Sandmel, and Michael A. Signer, eds. *Christianity in Jewish Terms.* Radical Traditions. Boulder, CO/Oxford: Westview, 2000.

Fulton, John, and Peter Gee. *Religion in Contemporary Europe.* Lampeter, Wales: Edwin Mellen Press, 1994.

Fussell, Paul. *The Great War and Modern Memory.* London: Oxford University Press, 1979.

Gill, D., ed. *Gathered for Life: Official Report. Sixth Assembly World Council of Churches, Vancouver, Canada.* Geneva: WCC, 1983.

Ginzberg, L. *Legends of the Jews,* vol. 4. Philadelphia: Jewish Publication Society, 1947.

Glubokovsky, Nicholai. *The Good News according to St Paul and Jewish Rabbinical Theology.* St. Petersburg: Svetoslov, 1998.

Goldenberg, Naomi. *Changing of the Gods: Feminism and the End of Traditional Religions.* Boston: Beacon Press, 1979.

Goodkin, J., and J. Citron, eds. *Women in the Jewish Community: Review and Recommendations.* London: Office of the Chief Rabbi, 1994.

Gottlieb, Lynn. *She Who Dwells Within: A Feminist Vision of a Renewed Judaism.* San Francisco: Harper, 1995.

Green, Arthur, ed. *Menahem Nahum of Chernobyl.* New York: Paulist Press, 1982.

Greenberg, Blu. "Confrontation and Change: Women and the Jewish Tradition." In *Women of Faith in Dialogue,* edited by Virginia Ramey Mollenkott, 17–25. New York: Crossroad, 1987.

————. "Judaism and Feminism." In *The Jewish Woman: New Perspectives,* edited by E. Koltun, 179–92. New York: Schocken, 1976.

————. *On Women and Judaism: A View from Tradition.* Philadelphia: Jewish Publication Society, 1981.

Greenberg, I. "Cloud of Smoke, Pillar of Fire: Judaism, Christianity and Modernity after the Holocaust." In *Auschwitz: Beginning of a New Era? Reflections on the Holocaust,* edited by E. Fleischner, 7–55. New York: Ktav, 1977.

Greenberg, Moshe. *Ezekiel 1–20: A New Translation with Introduction and Commentary.* Anchor Bible Series 22. New York: Doubleday, 1983.

————. "You Are Called 'Man'" [in Hebrew]. *Shedemot* (1980): 67–76.

Gregg, Joan Young. *Devils, Women, and Jews: Reflection of the Other in Medieval Sermon Stories.* Albany: State University of New York Press, 1997.

Gross, David. *1001 Questions and Answers about Judaism.* New York: Hippocrene, 1987.

Grünenfelder, Regula, et al. "Roundtable Discussion: From Generation to Generation." *Journal of Feminist Studies in Religion* 15 (1999): 102–38.

Hackel, Sergij. "The Relevance of Western Post-Holocaust Theology to the Thought and Practise of the Russian Orthodox Church." In *Theology after Auschwitz and Its Correlation with Theology after the GULag,* edited by Natalia Pecherskaya. Saint Petersburg: School of Religion and Philosophy, 1998.

Hampson, Daphne. *After Christianity.* London: SCM Press, 1996.

————. *Theology and Feminism.* Oxford: Blackwell, 1990.

Handelman, S. A. *Slayers of Moses: The Emergence of Rabbinic Interpretation in Modern Literary Theory.* Albany: State University of New York Press, 1982.

Hauerwas, Stanley. "Christian Ethics in Jewish Terms: A Response to David Novak." *Modern Theology* 16 (2000): 293–98.

Hayes, J. H., ed. *A Dictionary of Biblical Interpretation.* 2 vols. Nashville: Abingdon, 1999.

Haynes, S. R. *Jews and the Christian Imagination.* London: Macmillan, 1995.

Heldt, Petra, and Malcolm Lowe. "Theological Significance of the State of Israel." *Immanuel* 22/23 (1989).

Herlihy, David, and Christiane Klapisch-Zuber. *Tuscans and Their Families: A Study of the Florentine Catasto of 1427.* New Haven, CT: Yale University Press, 1985.

Heschel, Susannah. "Jesus as Theological Transvestite." In *Judaism since Gender,* edited by Miriam Peskowitz and Laura Levitt. New York: Routledge & Kegan Paul, 1997.

Hilton, Michael. *The Christian Effect on Jewish Life.* London: SCM Press 1994.

Hilton, M., with G. Marshall. *The Gospels and Rabbinic Judaism: A Study Guide.* London: SCM Press, 1988.

Hoeckman, R. "The Teaching On Jews and Judaism In Catholic Education." *Seminarium* 2 (1992): 346–59.

Hogan, Linda. *From Women's Experience to Feminist Theology.* Sheffield: Sheffield Academic Press, 1995.

Holladay, W. *The Psalms through 3000 Years.* Minneapolis: Fortress Press, 1993.

Holmgren, Fredrick C. *The Old Testament and the Significance of Jesus: Embracing Change—Maintaining Christian Identity. The Emerging Center in Biblical Scholarship.* (Grand Rapids, MI: Eerdmans, 1999.

Horowitz, Elliott. "'The Vengeance of the Jews Was Stronger Than Their Avarice': Modern Historians and the Persian Conquest of Jerusalem in 614." *Jewish Social Studies* 4, no. 2 (1998): 1–39.

Houlden, J. L. "Christian Interpretation of the Old Testament." In *A Dictionary of Biblical Interpretation,* edited by R. J. Coggins and J. L. Houlden, 108–12. London: SCM Press, 1990.

Hussein, M. K. *City of Wrong: A Friday in Jerusalem.* Oxford: Oneworld, 1994.

Hyman, Paula. "The Other Half: Women in the Jewish Tradition." In *The Jewish Woman: New Perspectives,* edited by E. Koltun, 105–13. New York: Schocken, 1976.

Idel, Moshe. *Messianic Mystics*. New Haven, CT: Yale University Press, 1998.

———. "The Attitude toward Christianity in *Sefer ha-Meshiv*." *Immanuel* 12 (1981): 77–95.

Ilan, Tal. *Jewish Women in Greco-Roman Palestine*. Peabody, MA: Hendrickson, 1996.

Isaac, J. *The Teaching of Contempt*. New York: Holt, Rinehart and Winston, 1964.

Jackson, Glenna. "Jesus as a First-Century Feminist: Christian Anti-Judaism?" *Feminist Theology* 19 (1998): 85–98.

Jay, Nancy. "Sacrifice as Remedy for Having Been Born a Woman." In *Immaculate and Powerful: The Female in Sacred Image and Social Reality,* edited by C. W. Atkinson et al., 283–310. Boston: Crucible, 1985.

Jeffrey, D. L., ed. *A Dictionary of Biblical Tradition in English Literature*. Grand Rapids, MI: Eerdmans, 1992.

Jensen, Anne. *God's Self-Confident Daughters: Early Christianity and the Liberation of Women*. Kampen, The Netherlands: Kok Pharos, 1992.

Jones, Sian, Tony Kushner, and Sarah Pearce, eds. *Cultures of Ambivalence and Contempt*. London: Vallentine Mitchell, 1998.

Katz, Jacob, *Exclusiveness and Tolerance: Jewish-Gentile Relations in Medieval and Modern Times*. London: Oxford University Press, 1961; New York: Schocken Books, 1962.

———. *A Time for Inquiry, a Time for Reflection: A Historical Essay on Israel through the Ages* [in Hebrew]. Jerusalem: Merkaz Zalman Shazar, 1999.

Kepel, Gilles. *La revanche de Dieu: Chrétiens, juifs et musulmans à la reconquête du monde*. Paris: Seuil, 1991.

Kienzle, Beverly Mayne, and Pamela J. Walker, eds. *Women Preachers and Prophets through Two Millennia of Christianity*. Berkeley: University of California Press, 1998.

Klassen, W. *The Contribution of Jewish Scholars to the Quest for the Historical Jesus*. Themes in Jewish-Christian Relations. Cambridge: Centre for Jewish-Christian Relations, 2000.

Klausner, Joseph. *From Jesus to Paul,* translated by W. F. Stinespring. London: Allen & Unwin, 1942.

———. *Jesus of Nazareth: His Life, Times, and Teaching,* translated by H. Danby. London: George Allen, 1929.

Klein, C. *Anti-Judaism in Christian Theology,* translated by E. Quinn. London: SPCK; Philadelphia: Fortress Press, 1978.

Klinghoffer, David. "Anti-Semitism without Anti-Semites." *First Things* 82 (April 1998): 10–13.

Koltun, E., ed. *The Jewish Woman: New Perspectives.* New York: Schocken, 1976.

Kraemer, Ross Shepard. *Her Share of the Blessings: Women's Religions among Pagans, Jews and Christians in the Greco-Roman World.* Oxford: Oxford University Press, 1992.

———, ed. *Maenads, Martyrs, Matrons, Monastics: A Sourcebook on Women's Religions in the Greco-Roman World.* Philadelphia: Fortress Press, 1988.

Kraemer, Ross S., and Mary Rose D'Angelo, eds. *Women and Christian Origins.* Oxford: Oxford University Press, 1999.

Krajewski, Stanislaw. "Respect Christians as Christians (Rabbis and Jewish Theologians on Christianity)." *Dialogue and Universalism* 11 (2000): 23–28.

Kratzert, Thomas. *Wir sind wie die Juden: Der griechisch-orthodoxe Beitrag zu einem ökumenischen jüdisch-christlichen Dialog.* Berlin: Inst. Kirche und Judentum, 1994.

Küng, Hans. *Judaism.* London: SCM Press, 1992.

Kunze, Bonnelyn Young. *Margaret Fell and the Rise of Quakerism.* London: Macmillan, 1994.

Kuraev, Andrej. *How They Make Anti-Semites.* Moscow: Odigitria, 1998.

Kysar, R. "Anti-Semitism and the Gospel of John." In *Anti-Semitism and Early Christianity: Issues of Polemic and Faith,* edited by C. A. Evans and D. A. Hagner, 113–27. Minneapolis: Fortress Press, 1993.

LaCocque, A. *The Feminine Unconventional: Four Subversive Figures in Israel's Tradition.* Minneapolis: Fortress Press, 1990.

Langmuir, Gavin. *Toward a Definition of Antisemitism.* Berkeley: University of California Press, 1990.

Larsson, G. *Bound for Freedom: The Book of Exodus in Jewish and Christian Traditions.* Peabody, MA: Hendrickson, 1999.

Levine, Amy-Jill, ed. *"Women Like This": New Perspectives on Jewish Women in the Greco-Roman World.* SBL Early Judaism and Its Literature. Atlanta: Scholars Press, 1991.

Levinskaya, I. "Ranny Gitler, Pozdny Stalin, niezlobivy Ivan Grozniy i drugiye." *Barier* (St. Petersburg 1994): 11–13.

Levy, Richard S., ed. *Antisemitism in the Modern World: An Anthology of Texts.* Lexington, MA: D. C. Heath, 1991.

Lewis, Bernard. *Semites and Anti-Semites.* New York: W.W. Norton, 1986.

Liebes, Yehuda. "The Messiah of the Zohar" [in Hebrew]. In *The Messianic Idea in Jewish Thought* [in Hebrew], 87–236. Jerusalem: Israel Academy of Sciences and Humanities, 1982.

Linafelt, T. "Biblical Interpretation and the Holocaust." In *Dictionary of Biblical Interpretation.* 2 vols., edited by J. H. Hayes, 514–15. Nashville: Abingdon Press 1999.

———, ed. *Strange Fire: Reading the Bible after the Holocaust.* Sheffield: Sheffield Academic Press, 2000.

Lipton, Sara. *Images of Intolerance: The Representation of Jews and Judaism in the Bible moralisée.* Berkeley: University of California Press, 1999.

Littell, F. H. *The Crucifixion of the Jews.* Macon, GA: University of Mercer Press, 1986.

Lloyd-Jones, Gareth. *Hard Sayings: Difficult New Testament Texts for Jewish-Christian Dialogue.* London: CCJ, 1993.

Lochhead, David. *The Dialogical Imperative: A Christian Reflection on Interfaith Encounter.* London: SCM Press, 1988.

Loewe, R. "Jewish Exegesis." In *Dictionary of Biblical Interpretation,* edited by R. J. Coggins and J. L. Houlden, 346–54. London: SCM Press, 1990.

Long, Asphodel. "The Goddess Movement in Britain Today." *Feminist Theology* 5 (1994): 11–39.

The Longer Commentary of David Kimhi on the First Book of Psalms, translated by R. G. Finch with an introduction by G. H. Box. London: SPCK, 1919.

Lowe, Malcolm, ed. *Orthodox Christians and Jews on Continuity and Renewal.* Immanuel 26/27. Jerusalem, 1994.

Lunn, Pamm. "Do Women Need the Goddess: Some Phenomenological and Sociological Reflections." *Feminist Theology* 4 (1993): 17–38.

Luther, Martin. *On the Jews and Their Lies.* Vol. 47, *Luther's Works.* 55 vols. St. Louis: Concordia, 1955–86; Philadelphia: Fortress Press, 1955–.

Luxmoore, Jonathan, and Jolanta Babiuch. *The Vatican and the Red Flag: The Struggle for the Soul of Eastern Europe.* London: Geoffrey Chapman, 1999.

Maccoby, Hyam. *Judaism on Trial: Jewish-Christian Disputations in the Middle Ages.* 2nd ed. London: Valentine Mitchell, 1993.

———. *Paul and Hellenism.* London: SCM Press, 1991.

Mack, Phyllis. *Visionary Women: Ecstatic Prophecy in Seventeenth Century England.* Berkeley/Oxford: University of California Press, 1992.

Man's Disorder and God's Design: World Council of Churches (1st Assembly: 1948: Amsterdam). New York: Harper, 1948.

Mapu, Avraham. *Ahavat tziyyon* (Love of Zion). Vilna, 1853. English translation: A. M. Schapiro, trans. *In the Days of Isaiah.* New York: Translator, 1902; and *The Shepherd Prince.* New York: Translator, 1922, 1930.

Marcus, David. *Jephthah and His Vow.* Lubbock: Texas Tech Press, 1986.

Marcus, Ivan. *Piety and Society: The Jewish Pietists of Medieval Germany.* Leiden, The Netherlands: Brill, 1981.

———. *Rituals of Childhood: Jewish Acculturation in Medieval Europe.* New Haven, CT: Yale University Press, 1996.

Marcus, Jacob. *The Jew in the Medieval World.* Revised ed. Cincinnati: Hebrew Union College Press, 1999.

Maybaum, Ignaz. *Trialogue between Jew, Christian and Muslim*. London: Routledge & Kegan Paul, 1973.

Mazower, Mark. *The Dark Continent: Europe's Twentieth Century*. London: Allen Lane, 1998.

McBrien, Richard. "Papal Apology." *The News Hour with Jim Lehrer.* Transcript: http://www.pbs.org/newshour/bb/religion/jan-jun98/vatican_4-8.html.

McEwan, Dorothea. "Joan on Joan: 'Clearly Confrontational and Boldly Orthodox.' An Interview with Joan Chittester OSB." *Feminist Theology* 16 (1997): 100–117.

McKane, W. *Selected Christian Hebraists*. Cambridge: Cambridge University Press, 1989.

Meirovich, Harvey Warren. *A Vindication of Judaism: The Polemics of the Hertz Pentateuch*. New York: Jewish Theological Seminary of America, 1998.

Metz, Johann B. "Facing the Jews: Christian Theology after Auschwitz." In *The Holocaust as Interruption,* edited by Elisabeth Schüssler Fiorenza and David Tracy, 26–33. *Concilium* 175. Edinburgh: T&T Clark, 1984.

———. *Faith in History and Society: Toward a Practical Fundamental Theology,* translated by David Smith. London: Burns and Oates, 1980.

Meyerson, Mark. *The Muslims of Valencia in the Age of Fernando and Isabel: Between Coexistence and Crusade*. Berkeley: University of California Press, 1991.

Midrash Rabbah. 2nd ed. 10 vols. New York/London: Soncino, 1951.

Mihaita, Nifon, ed. *The Christian Orthodox–Jewish Consultation II (Bucharest, October 29–31, 1979)*. Bucharest, 1979.

Milano, A. "Un sottile tormento nella vita del ghetto di Roma: La predica coatta." *Rassegna Mensile di Israel* 18 (1952): 517–32.

Milgrom, J. *Numbers: The Traditional Hebrew Text with the New JPS Translation and Commentary*. Philadelphia: Jewish Publication Society, 1989.

Miller, S., et al., eds. *Women in the Jewish Community: Survey Report*. London: Office of the Chief Rabbi, 1994.

Mollenkott, V. R., ed. *Women of Faith in Dialogue*. New York: Crossroad, 1987.

Moltmann, Jürgen. *Church and Israel: A Common Way of Hope?* London: SCM Press, 1989.

Montefiore, C. G. *The Old Testament and After.* London: Macmillan, 1923.

Moore, R. I. *The Formation of a Persecuting Society: Power and Deviance in Western Europe, 950–1250.* Oxford: Basil Blackwell, 1987.

Moore, Zoe Bennett. "A Midrash." *Feminist Theology* 18 (1998): 29–30.

Morteira, Saul Levi. *Giv'at Sha'ul.* Vilna, 1912.

Mulchahey, M. Michèle. *"First the Bow is Bent in Study...": Dominican Education before 1350.* Toronto: Pontifical Institute, 1998.

Myers, Jody, and Rachel Litman. "The Secret of Jewish Femininity: Hiddenness, Power and Physicality in the Theology of Orthodox Women in the Contemporary World." In *Gender and Judaism: The Transformation of Tradition,* edited by T. M. Rudavsky, 51–77. New York: New York University Press, 1995.

Nanos, M. D., *The Mystery of Romans: The Jewish Context of Paul's Letter.* Minneapolis: Fortress Press, 1996.

Nirenberg, David. *Communities of Violence: Persecution of Minorities in the Middle Ages.* Princeton, NJ: Princeton University Press, 1996.

Novak, David. "Avoiding Charges of Legalism and Antinomianism in Jewish-Christian Dialogue." *Modern Theology* 16 (2000): 275–91.

———. *The Image of the Non-Jew in Judaism: An Historical and Constructive Study of the Noahide Laws.* Toronto Studies in Theology 14. New York: E. Mellen Press, 1983.

———. *Jewish-Christian Dialogue: A Jewish Justification.* New York/Oxford: Oxford University Press, 1989.

———. "Jews and Catholics: Beyond Apologies." *First Things* 89 (January 1999): 20–25.

Ochs, Peter. *Peirce, Pragmatism and the Logic of Scripture.* Cambridge: Cambridge University Press, 1998.

Oesterreicher, J. M. *The New Encounter between Christians and Jews*. New York: Philosophical Library, 1986.

Origen. *Against Celus*. In *Ante-Nicene Christian Library*. Vol. 24, edited by A. Roberts and J. Donaldson. Edinburgh: T&T Clark, 1867–72.

Papademetriou, George C. *Essays on Orthodox Christian-Jewish Relations*. Lima, OH: Wyndham Hall Press, 1991.

Pardes, Ilana. *Countertraditions in the Bible: A Feminist Approach*. Cambridge, MA: Harvard University Press, 1992.

Parkes, James. *The Conflict of the Church and the Synagogue*. London/New York: Soncino Press, 1934.

———. *The Foundations of Judaism and Christianity*. London: Vallentine Mitchell, 1960.

———. *Prelude to Dialogue: Jewish-Christian Relationships*. London: Valentine Mitchell, 1969.

———. *Voyages of Discovery*. London: Victor Gollancz, 1969.

Parrinder, G. *Encountering World Religions*. Edinburgh: T&T Clark, 1987.

Pawlikowski, John T. "Christian-Jewish Bonding and the Liturgy of Holy Week." *New Theological Review* (February 1997): 104.

———. "The Search for a New Paradigm for the Christian-Jewish Relationship: A Response to Michael Signer." In *Reinterpreting Revelation and Tradition: Jews and Christians in Conversation,* edited by J. T. Pawlikowski and H. G. Perelmuter, 25–48. Franklin, WI: Sheed and Ward, 2000.

———. *What Are They Saying about Christian-Jewish Relations?* New York: Paulist Press, 1980.

Pecherskaya, Natalia, ed. *Theology after Auschwitz and Its Correlation with Theology after the GULag: Proceedings of the Second International Conference, St. Petersburg School of Religion and Philosophy*. St. Petersburg: School of Religion and Philosophy, 1998.

Phan, P., ed. *Christianity and the Wider Ecumenism*. New York: Paragon House, 1990.

Pirani, A., ed. *The Absent Mother: Restoring the Goddess to Judaism and Christianity*. London: Mandala, 1991.

Plaskow, Judith. "Anti-Judaism in Feminist Christian Interpretation." In *Searching the Scriptures*. Vol. 1, *A Feminist Introduction*, edited by Elisabeth Schüssler Fiorenza, 117–29. London: SCM Press 1993.

―――. "The Jewish Feminist: Conflict in Identities." In *The Jewish Woman: New Perspectives*, edited by E. Koltun, 3–10. New York: Schocken, 1976.

―――. *Standing Again at Sinai: Judaism from a Feminist Perspective*. New York: HarperCollins, 1991.

―――. "Transforming the Nature of Community: Toward a Feminist People of Israel." In *After Patriarchy: Feminist Transformations of the World Religions*, edited by Paula M. Cooey, 87–105. Maryknoll, NY: Orbis Books, 1992.

―――. "We Are Also Your Sisters: The Development of Women's Studies in Religion." *Women's Studies Quarterly* 21 (1993): 9–21.

Plaskow, Judith, and Carol Christ, eds. *Womanspirit Rising: A Feminist Reader in Religion*. San Francisco: Harper, 1979.

Primavesi, Anne. *From Apocalypse to Genesis: Ecology, Feminism and Christianity*. Tunbridge Wells: Burns and Oates, 1991.

Prior, M. *The Bible and Colonialism: A Moral Critique*. Sheffield: Sheffield Academic Press, 1997.

―――. *Zionism and the Bible*. London: Routledge & Kegan Paul, 1999.

Pui-lan, Kwok. "Racism and Ethnocentrism in Feminist Biblical Interpretation." In *Searching the Scriptures*. Vol. 1, *A Feminist Introduction*, edited by Elisabeth Schüssler Fiorenza, 101–13. London: SCM Press, 1993.

Rahman, F. *Islam*. Chicago/London: University of Chicago Press, 1979.

Rajak, Tessa. "Jews and Greeks: The Invention and Exploitation of Polarities in the Nineteenth Century." In *The Uses and Abuses of Antiquity*, edited by M. Bidiss and M. Wyke, 57–77. Bern: Peter Lang, 1999.

Ramet, Sabrina Petra. *Whose Democracy?: Nationalism, Religion and the Doctrine of Collective Rights in Post-1989 Eastern Europe*. Oxford: Rowman and Littlefield Publishers, 1997.

Raphael, Melissa. "Cover Not Our Blood with Thy Silence: Sadism, Eschatological Justice and Female Images of the Divine." *Feminist Theology* 8 (1995): 85–105.

Rapoport-Albert, Ada. "Confession in the Circle of R. Nahman of Braslav." *Bulletin of the Institute of Jewish Studies* 1 (1973–1975): 65–96.

Richmond, C. *"Parkes and I." The Parkes Lectures 1994*. University of Southampton.

Rivkin, E. *What Crucified Jesus? Messianism, Pharisaism, and the Development of Christianity*. New York: UAHC Press, 1997. Originally published: Nashville: Abingdon Press, 1984.

Roemer, Nils. "Turning Defeat into Victory: *Wissenschaft des Judentums* and the Martyrs of 1096." *Jewish History* 13, no. 2 (1999): 65–80.

Rofé, A. *Prophetical Stories*. Jerusalem: Magnes Press, 1989.

Romaine, Suzanne. *Bilingualism*. Oxford: Blackwell, 1989.

Rosenbaum, M., and A. M. Silbermann, eds. and trans. *The Pentateuch with Targum Onkelos, Haphtaroth and Rashi's Commentary*. Jerusalem: Silbermann, 1973.

Rosenzweig, Franz. *The Star of Redemption,* translated from the second edition of 1930 by William W. Hallo. Notre Dame, IN: University of Notre Dame Press, 1971.

Roth, C. *A History of the Jews in England*. Oxford: Clarendon Press, 1978.

———. *The History of the Jews in Italy*. Philadelphia: Jewish Publication Society, 1946.

Rubenstein, R. L. *After Auschwitz: History, Theology, and Contemporary Judaism*. 2nd ed. Baltimore, MD/London: John Hopkins University Press, 1992.

Rudavsky, T. M., ed. *Gender and Judaism: The Transformation of Tradition*. New York: New York University Press, 1995.

Ruether, Rosemary Radford. *Faith and Fratricide: The Theological Roots of Anti-Semitism.* New York: Seabury Press, 1979.

————. *Gaia and God: An Eco-Feminist Theology of Earth-Healing.* London: SCM Press, 1993.

Sacks, Jonathan. *"The Other—Jews and Christians."* In *The Other as Mystery and Challenge. From The Martin Buber House 25,* 31–41. Heppenheim: ICCJ, 1998.

Sacks, Maurie. "An Anthropological and Post-Modern Critique of Jewish Feminist Theory." In *Gender and Judaism: The Transformation of Tradition,* edited by T. M. Rudavsky, 295–305. New York: New York University Press, 1995.

Said, E. *Orientalism.* London: Routledge & Kegan Paul, 1978.

Sanders, E. P. *Jesus and Judaism.* London: SCM Press, 1985.

————. *Judaism Practice and Belief 63BCE–66CE.* London: SCM Press, 1992.

Sanders, Jack T. *Schismatics, Sectarians, Dissidents, Deviants: The First One Hundred Years of Jewish-Christian Relations.* London: SCM Press, 1993.

Sandmel, Samuel. *We Jews and You Christians.* Philadelphia/New York: J. B. Lippincott, 1967.

Saperstein, Marc. *Decoding the Rabbis: A Thirteenth-Century Commentary on the Aggadah.* Cambridge, MA: Harvard University Press, 1980.

————. *Jewish Preaching 1200–1800.* New Haven, CT: Yale University Press, 1989.

————. *"Your Voice Like a Ram's Horn": Themes and Texts in Traditional Jewish Preaching.* Cincinnati: Hebrew Union College Press, 1996.

Sawyer, Deborah R. *Women and Religion in the First Christian Centuries.* London: Routledge & Kegan Paul, 1996.

Sawyer, J. F. A., "Combating Prejudices about the Bible and Judaism." *Theology* 94 (1991): 269–78.

————. *The Fifth Gospel: Isaiah in the History of Christianity.* Cambridge: Cambridge University Press, 1996.

Sawyer, J. F. A., J. L. Kovacs, and C. C. Rowland, eds. Blackwell Bible Commentary Series. Oxford: Blackwell, 2001–.

Scholem, Gershom. "The Beginnings of the Christian Kabbalah." In *The Christian Kabbalah,* edited by Joseph Dan, 17–51. Cambridge, MA: Harvard College Library, 1997.

———. *On the Kabbalah and Its Symbolism.* New York: Schocken Books, 1965.

Schorsch, Ismar. *From Text to Context: The Turn to History in Modern Judaism.* Hanover, NH/London: University Press of New England for Brandeis University Press, 1994.

Schreckenberg, H. *The Jews in Christian Art.* London: SCM Press, 1996.

Schüssler Fiorenza, Elisabeth. *In Memory of Her: A Feminist Theological Reconstruction of Christian Origins.* 2nd ed. London: SCM Press, 1994.

———, ed. *Searching the Scriptures.* Vol. 1, *A Feminist Introduction.* London: SCM Press, 1993.

Schwartz, H. *Reimagining the Bible: The Story-Telling of the Rabbis.* Oxford: Oxford University Press, 1998.

Schwartz, R. M. *The Curse of Cain.* Chicago/London: University of Chicago Press, 1997.

Shatzmiller, Joseph. *Shylock Reconsidered: Jews, Moneylending, and Medieval Society.* Berkeley: University of California Press, 1990.

Sheridan, S., ed. *Hear Our Voice; Women Rabbis Tell Their Stories.* London: SCM Press, 1994.

Sherwin, Byron L. "'Who Do You Say That I Am?' (Mark 8:29): A New Jewish View of Jesus." *Journal of Ecumenical Studies* 31, nos. 3–4 (summer–fall 1994): 255–67.

Sherwood, Y. *The Prostitute and the Prophet: Hosea's Marriage in Literary Theoretical Perspective.* Sheffield: Sheffield Academic Press, 1996.

Shipler, David. *Arab and Jew: Wounded Spirits in the Promised Land.* New York: Penguin Books, 1986.

Shulman, Sheila. "Some Thoughts on Biblical Prophecy and Feminist Vision." In *Hear Our Voice: Women Rabbis Tell Their Stories,* edited by Sibyl Sheridan, 55–63. London: SCM Press, 1994.

Siegman, H. *Fifteen Years of Catholic-Jewish Dialogue 1970–1985*. Rome: ILC, 1988.

Simonsohn, Shlomo. *The Apostolic See and the Jews*. 8 vols. Toronto: Pontifical Institute of Mediaeval Studies, 1988.

Smalley, B. *The Study of the Bible in the Middle Ages*. 3rd ed. Oxford: Basil Blackwell, 1983.

Snaith, N. H., ed. *Torah, Nebi'im u-Ketubim* (1961, 1967) with *Berit Hadashah,* translated by F. Delitzsch (1891). Published in one volume. London: British and Foreign Bible Society, 1968.

Sölle, Dorothée, Joe H. Kirchberger, and Herbert Haag. *Great Women of the Bible in Art and Literature*. Grand Rapids, MI: Eerdmans, 1993.

Southern, R. W. *Western Views of Islam in the Middle Ages*. Cambridge, MA: Harvard University Press, 1962.

Stemberger, Günter. *Jews and Christians in the Holy Land: Palestine in the Fourth Century,* translated by Ruth Tuschling. Edinburgh: T&T Clark, 1999.

Stendahl, Krister. *Paul among Jews and Gentiles, and Other Essays*. London: SCM Press, 1977.

———. *Rhetoric and Reality in the Late 4th Century*. Berkeley: University of California Press, 1983.

Stocker, M. *Judith, Sexual Warrior: Women and Power in Western Culture*. New Haven, CT: Yale University Press, 1998.

Storkey, Elaine. *What's Right with Feminism*. London: SPCK, 1985.

Sugirtharajah, R. S., ed. *The Postcolonial Bible*. Sheffield: Sheffield Academic Press, 1998.

Swatos, William H., Jr., ed. *Politics and Religion in Central and Eastern Europe: Transition and Traditions*. Westport, CT: Praeger, 1994.

Synan, Edward. *The Popes and the Jews in the Middle Ages*. New York: Macmillan, 1965.

Tabak, Yuri. "Relations between the Russian Orthodox Church and Judaism: Past and Present." Online: www.jcrelations.net/en/?id=787 (posted 2000).

Taitz, Emily. "Jewish-Christian Relations in the Middle Ages: The Underside of a Shared Culture." In *Yakar Le'Mordecai: Jubilee Volume in Honor of Rabbi Mordecai Waxman,* edited by Zvia Ginor, 189–201. Hoboken, NJ: Ktav, 1998.

Talmage, Frank. "Apples of Gold: The Inner Meaning of Sacred Texts in Medieval Judaism." In *Jewish Spirituality: From the Bible Through the Middle Ages,* edited by Arthur Green, 313–55. New York: Crossroad, 1989.

Tismaneanu, Vladimir. *Fantasies of Salvation: Democracy, Nationalism and Myth in Post-Communist Europe.* Princeton, NJ: Princeton University Press, 1998.

Toaff, Ariel. *Love, Work and Death: Jewish Life in Medieval Umbria.* London: Littman Library, 1998.

Torjeson, Karen-Jo. *When Women Were Priests: Women's Leadership in the Early Church and the Scandal of Their Subordination in the Rise of Christianity.* San Francisco: HarperCollins, 1993.

Trevett, Christine. *Montanism: Gender, Authority and the New Prophecy.* Cambridge: Cambridge University Press, 1996.

―――. *Previous Convictions and End of the Millennium Quakerism.* London: Quaker Home Service, 1997.

―――. *Quaker Women Prophets in England and Wales,* 1650–1700. Lampeter, Wales: Edwin Mellen, 2000.

―――. *Women and Quakerism in the Seventeenth Century.* York: Sessions, 1991.

Trible, Phyllis. *Texts of Terror: Literary Feminist Readings of Biblical Narratives.* Philadelphia: Fortress Press, 1984.

Troper, Harold, and Morton Weinfeld. *Old Wounds.* London: Penguin Books, 1989.

Ucko, H., ed. *People of God, Peoples of God.* Geneva: WCC, 1996.

Umansky, E. M. "Women in Judaism: From the Reform Movement to Contemporary Jewish Religious Feminism." In *Women of Spirit: Female Leadership in the Jewish and Christian Traditions,* edited by Rosemary R. Ruether and Eleanor McLaughlin, 334–54. New York: Simon and Schuster, 1979.

Valliere, P. *Modern Russian Theology—Bukharev, Soloviev, Bulgakov: Orthodox Theology in a New Key.* Edinburgh: T&T Clark, 2000.

Vermes, Geza, *Jesus the Jew: A Historian's Reading of the Gospels.* London: Collins, 1973.

———. *Providential Accidents. An Autobiography.* London: SCM Press, 1998.

———. *The Religion of Jesus the Jew.* London: SCM Press, 1993.

Villani, Stefano. "I primi Quaccheri e gli Ebrei." *Archivio italiano per la storia della pietà.* Vol. 10, 43–113. Rome: Edizioni di storia e letteratura, 1997.

Volovici, Leon. *Antisemitism in Post-Communist Eastern Europe: A Marginal or Central Issue?* ACTA, no. 5. Jerusalem: Vidal Sassoon International Centre for the Study of Antisemitism, 1994.

Webber, Jonathan, ed. *Jewish Identities in the New Europe.* London: Littman Library of Jewish Civilisation, 1994.

Wei-Hsun, Charles, and Gerhard E. Spiegler, eds. *Religious Issues and Interreligious Dialogue: An Analysis in Developments since 1945.* Westport, CT: Greenwood Press, 1989.

Werblowsky, R. J. Z. *The Meaning of Jerusalem to Jews, Christians and Muslims.* Rev. ed. Jerusalem: Israel Universities' Study Group for Middle Eastern Affairs, 1978.

We Remember: A Reflection on the Shoah. Vatican City: Commission for Religious Relations with the Jews, March 16, 1998.

Whitelam, K. *The Invention of Ancient Israel: The Silencing of Palestinian History.* London: Routledge & Kegan Paul, 1996.

Wiesel, E., and A. H. Friedlander, eds. *The Six Days of Destruction.* New York: Paulist Press, 1988.

Wiesenthal, Simon. *Every Day Remembrance Day: A Chronicle of Jewish Martyrdom*. New York: Henry Holt, 1986.

Wigoder, Geoffrey. *Jewish-Christian Interfaith Relations: Agendas for Tomorrow*. Policy Forum no. 14 of the Institute of the World Jewish Congress. Jerusalem: Institute of the World Jewish Congress, 1998.

———. *Jewish-Christian Relations since the Second World War*. Manchester: Manchester University Press, 1988.

Wilken, Robert L. *John Chrysostom and the Jews: Rhetoric and Reality in the Late Fourth Century*. Berkeley: University of California Press, 1999.

Wilkinson, John. *Israel My Glory*. London: Mildmay Mission, 1889.

Wirszubski, Chaim. *Pico della Mirandola's Encounter with Jewish Mysticism*. Cambridge, MA: Harvard University Press, 1989.

Wistrich, Robert. *Terms of Survival*. London: Routledge & Kegan Paul, 1995.

Wood, Diana. *Clement VI: The Pontificate and Ideas of an Avignon Pope*. Cambridge: Cambridge University Press, 1989.

Wright, Alexandra. "An Approach to Jewish Feminist Theology." In *Hear Our Voice: Women Rabbis Tell Their Stories,* edited by Sibyl Sheridan, 152–61. London: SCM Press, 1994.

Yadin, Yigael. *Bar Kokhba*. New York: Random House, 1971.

Yerushalmi, Yosef. "Response to Rosemary Ruether." In *Auschwitz: Beginning of a New Era?* edited by Eva Fleischner, 98–101. New York: Ktav, 1977.

Young, F. "Origen." In *A Dictionary of Biblical Interpretation,* edited by R. J. Coggins and J. L. Houlden, 501–3. London: SCM Press, 1990.

Yuval, Israel. "Vengeance and Damnation, Blood and Defamation: From Jewish Martyrdom to Blood Libel Accusations" [in Hebrew]. *Zion* 58 (1993): 33–90.

Zernov, N., in collaboration with M. Zernov. *The Fellowship of St. Alban and St. Sergius: A Historical Memoir*. Oxford: Fellowship of St. Alban & St. Sergius, 1979.

OTHER SOURCES

Feuerherd, Peter. *National Catholic Register.* December 17, 1995, p. 10.

Information Service. The official bulletin of the Pontifical Council for Promoting Christian Unity, 82 (1993); 98 (1998); 75 (1990).

Web site: http://www.jcrelations.net.

Web site: http://www.vatican.va.

World Jewish Congress. *Policy Dispatches* 23 (November 1997).

———. *Policy Dispatches* 36 (November 1998).

List of Contributors

James K. Aitken (co-editor) is research fellow in the Department of Classics, University of Reading, a member of the AHRC Parkes Centre for the Study of Jewish/non-Jewish Relations, University of Southampton, and honorary fellow of the Centre for the Study of Jewish-Christian Relations, Cambridge. His publications include *The Semantics of Blessing and Cursing in Ancient Hebrew* (2006).

Edward Kessler (co-editor) is the founder and executive director of the Centre for the Study of Jewish-Christian Relations, Cambridge. His recent publications include *Bound by the Bible: Jews, Christians and the Sacrifice of Isaac* (2005), and he is editor of *A Dictionary of Jewish-Christian Relations* (2005). His academic interests include Jewish-Christian relations in the first five centuries and contemporary relations.

Nicholas de Lange is professor of Hebrew and Jewish studies at the University of Cambridge. His recent publications include *An Introduction to Judaism* (2000) and the edited volume *Ignaz Maybaum: A Reader* (2001).

David F. Ford is Regius Professor of Divinity at the University of Cambridge and a founding member of the Society for Scriptural Reasoning, where Jews, Christians, and Muslims engage together in the interpretation of their scriptures. His books include *Self and Salvation: Being Transformed* (1999); *Theology: A Very Short Introduction* (1999, 2000); *The Shape of Living* (2nd ed., 2002); and the edited volume *The Modern Theologians: An Introduction to Christian Theology in the Twentieth Century* (3rd ed., 2005).

Martin Forward is the Helena Wackerlin Professor of Religious Studies at Aurora University, Illinois, and executive director of its Center for Faith and Action. His two most recent books are *Inter-religious Dialogue: An Introduction* and *Religion: A Beginner's Guide,* both published in 2001.

Remi Hoeckman, OP, was professor of ecumenical studies at the Pontifical University in Rome, and between 1993 and 2001 served as secretary of the Vatican Commission for Religious Relations with the Jews. He held a doctorate in sacred theology from the University of Fribourg and was involved in Catholic education for many years, serving as an official of the Holy See's Congregation for Catholic Education, University Department.

Irina Levinskaya is senior research fellow at the St. Petersburg Institute of History of the Russian Academy of Arts and Sciences. She is an editor of the antifascist journal *Bar'er.* Significant recent publications include *The Book of Acts in Its Diaspora Setting* (English version: 1996; Russian version, revised: 2000), *A Historico-Philological Commentary on the Acts of the Apostles 1–8* [in Russian] (1999); *Adam's Road* (autobiographical prose in Russian: 2001; English: 2003).

Peter Ochs is the Edgar Bronfman Professor of Modern Judaic Studies. His publications include *Peirce, Pragmatism, and the Logic of Scripture* (1998), and the co-authored books *Reasoning after Revelation: Dialogues in Postmodern Jewish Philosophy* (1998), *Reviewing the Covenant: Eugene Borowitz and the Postmodern Renewal of Jewish Theology* (2000). He is one of the editors of *Christianity in Jewish Terms* (2000) and of *Textual Reasonings* (2002).

Friedhelm Pieper was the general secretary of the International Council of Christians and Jews (ICCJ), Martin Buber House, Heppenheim, Germany. He served as chief editor of the Web site www.jcrelations.net and has published "Christlich-Jüdischer Dialog im internationalen Kontext," in *Der Dialog zwischen Juden und Christen, Versuche des Gesprächs nach Auschwitz* (1999).

Marc Saperstein is Charles E. Smith Professor of Jewish History and director of the program in Judaic studies at George Washington University. Among his books are *Moments of Crisis in Jewish-Christian Relations* (1989) and *"Your Voice Like a Ram's Horn": Themes and Texts in Traditional Jewish Preaching* (1996). He is currently on leave to serve as principal of Leo Baeck College-Centre for Jewish Education in London.

John F. A. Sawyer is visiting professor in the Department of Linguistics at the University of Florence. His writings include *The Fifth Gospel: Isaiah in the History of Christianity* (1996), and he co-edited the *Concise Encyclopedia of Language and Religion* (2001).

Stephen D. Smith is the founder and director of the Beth Shalom Holocaust Centre in the United Kingdom. He is one of the editors of *The Holocaust and the Christian World: Reflections on the Past, Challenges for the Future* (2000).

Christine Trevett is a Quaker, teaching mostly biblical and language studies at the University of Wales, Cardiff. Her writings focus on second-century Christianity and seventeenth-century sectarianism. Recent works include *Quaker Women Prophets in England and Wales: 1650-1700* (2000) and *Not Little Women? Not Good Wives? Women in Christian Communities 80–160 CE* (2004).

David Weigall was principal lecturer in history and international relations at Anglia Polytechnic University, Cambridge. His publications include *The Origins and Development of European Integration* (1999) and *International Relations* (2002).

Andrew P. B. White was the director of the International Centre for Reconciliation at Coventry Cathedral and the archbishop of Canterbury's special representative to the Middle East. White coordinated the Alexandria Declaration for Peace in the Holy Land and chaired the implementation committee. He is currently serving as a chaplain in Baghdad, and is the author of *Iraq: Hope through Chaos* (2005).

Index

Other Volumes in This Series

Helga Croner, compiler, *Stepping Stones to Further Jewish-Christian Relations: An Unabridged Collection of Christian Documents* (A Stimulus Book, 1977).

Helga Croner and Leon Klenicki, editors, *Issues in the Jewish-Christian Dialogue: Jewish Perspectives on Covenant, Mission and Witness* (A Stimulus Book, 1979).

Helga Croner, Leon Klenicki, and Lawrence Boadt, CSP, editors, *Biblical Studies: Meeting Ground of Jews and Christians* (A Stimulus Book, 1980).

Clemens Thoma, *A Christian Theology of Judaism* (A Stimulus Book, 1980).

Helga Croner and Martin A. Cohen, editors, *Christian Mission/Jewish Mission* (A Stimulus Book, 1982).

John T. Pawlikowski, OSM, *Christ in the Light of the Christian-Jewish Dialogue* (A Stimulus Book, 1982).

Leon Klenicki and Gabe Huck, editors, *Spirituality and Prayer: Jewish and Christian Understandings* (A Stimulus Book, 1983).

Helga Croner, compiler, *More Stepping Stones to Jewish-Christian Relations: An Unabridged Collection of Christian Documents 1975–1983* (A Stimulus Book, 1985).

Edward Flannery, *The Anguish of the Jews* (A Stimulus Book, 1985).

Clemens Thoma and Michael Wyschogrod, editors, *Understanding Scripture: Explorations of Jewish and Christian Traditions of Interpretation* (A Stimulus Book, 1987).

Bernard J. Lee, SM, *The Galilean Jewishness of Jesus: Retrieving the Jewish Origins of Christianity,* Conversation on the Road Not Taken, Vol. 1 (A Stimulus Book, 1988).

Clemens Thoma and Michael Wyschogrod, editors, *Parable and Story in Judaism and Christianity* (A Stimulus Book, 1989).

Eugene J. Fisher and Leon Klenicki, editors, *In Our Time. The Flowering of Jewish-Catholic Dialogue* (A Stimulus Book, 1990).

David Burrell and Yehezkel Landau, editors, *Voices from Jerusalem* (A Stimulus Book, 1991).

Leon Klenicki, editor, *Toward A Theological Encounter* (A Stimulus Book, 1991).

John Rousmaniere, *A Bridge to Dialogue: The Story of Jewish-Christian Relations,* edited by James A. Carpenter and Leon Klenicki (A Stimulus Book, 1991).

Michael E. Lodahl, *Shekhinah/Spirit* (A Stimulus Book, 1992).

George M. Smiga, *Pain and Polemic: Anti-Judaism in the Gospels* (A Stimulus Book, 1992).

Eugene J. Fisher, editor, *Interwoven Destinies: Jews and Christians Through the Ages* (A Stimulus Book, 1993).

Anthony Kenny, *Catholics, Jews and the State of Israel* (A Stimulus Book, 1993).

Bernard J. Lee, SM, *Jesus and the Metaphors of God: The Christs of the New Testament,* Conversation on the Road Not Taken, Vol. 2 (A Stimulus Book, 1993).

Eugene J. Fisher, editor, *Visions of the Other: Jewish and Christian Theologians Assess the Dialogue* (A Stimulus Book, 1995).

Leon Klenicki and Geoffrey Wigoder, editors, *A Dictionary of the Jewish-Christian Dialogue,* Expanded Edition (A Stimulus Book, 1995).

Vincent Martin, *A House Divided: The Parting of the Ways between Synagogue and Church* (A Stimulus Book, 1995).

Philip A. Cunningham and Arthur F. Starr, editors, *Sharing Shalom: A Process for Local Interfaith Dialogue Between Christians and Jews* (A Stimulus Book, 1998).

Frank E. Eakin, Jr., *What Price Prejudice? Christian Antisemitism in America* (A Stimulus Book, 1998).

Ekkehard Schuster and Reinhold Boschert-Kimmig, *Hope Against Hope: Johann Baptist Metz and Elie Wiesel Speak Out on the Holocaust* (A Stimulus Book, 1999).

Mary C. Boys, *Has God Only One Blessing? Judaism as a Source of Christian Understanding* (A Stimulus Book, 2000).

Avery Dulles, SJ, and Leon Klenicki, editors, *The Holocaust, Never to Be Forgotten: Reflections on the Holy See's Document* We Remember (A Stimulus Book, 2000).

Johannes Reuchlin, *Recommendation Whether to Confiscate, Destroy and Burn All Jewish Books: A Classic Treatise against Anti-Semitism,* translated, edited, and with an introduction by Peter Wortsman (A Stimulus Book, 2000).

Philip A. Cunningham, *A Story of Shalom: The Calling of Christians and Jews by a Covenanting God* (A Stimulus Book, 2001).

Philip A. Cunningham, *Sharing the Scriptures,* The Word Set Free, Vol. 1 (A Stimulus Book, 2003).

Dina Wardi, *Auschwitz: Contemporary Jewish and Christian Encounters* (A Stimulus Book, 2003).

Michael Lotker, *A Christian's Guide to Judaism* (A Stimulus Book, 2004).

Lawrence Boadt and Kevin di Camillo, editors, *John Paul II in the Holy Land: In His Own Words: With Christian and Jewish Perspectives by Yehezkel Landau and Michael McGarry, CSP* (A Stimulus Book, 2005).

STIMULUS BOOKS are developed by the Stimulus Foundation, a not-for-profit organization, and are published by Paulist Press. The Foundation wishes to further the publication of scholarly books on Jewish and Christian topics that are of importance to Judaism and Christianity.

The Stimulus Foundation was established by an erstwhile refugee from Nazi Germany who intends to contribute with these publications to the improvement of communication between Jews and Christians.

Books for publication in this Series will be selected by a committee of the Foundation, and offers of manuscripts and works in progress should be addressed to:

The Stimulus Foundation
c/o Paulist Press
997 Macarthur Boulevard
Mahwah, N.J. 07430
www.paulistpress.com